PETR VOREL

THE WAR OF THE PRINCES

THE BOHEMIAN LANDS AND
THE HOLY ROMAN EMPIRE

1546–1555

HHP

Published in the United States by

HHP

Helena History Press LLC
A division of KKL Publications LLC, Reno, NV USA
www.helenahistorypress.com

ISBN: 978-1-943596-03-4

Order from:
Central European University Press
11 Nádor utca
Budapest, Hungary H-1051
Email: *ceupress@ceu.hu*
Website: *www.ceupress.com*

This publication was supported by
the Grant Agency of the Czech Republic (IKP GA P405/12/1000).

Reviewers: Prof. Dr. Jiří Pešek (Charles University, Prague) and
Prof. Dr. Jaroslav Pánek (Academy of Sciences of Czech Republic, Prague).
Translated from the original Czech by http://hero-translating.com.

Cover Design: Sebastian Stachowski

Printed in Hungary by Prime Rate Kft. Budapest
First English Edition

Contents

INTRODUCTION

The issue of the German Reformation and the power-political crisis that accompanied the battle between some of the imperial Protestant princes and Emperor Charles V. belongs to the main themes of 16th century European history. The climax of this crisis was the Schmalkaldic War, between the years 1546 and 1547, and other subsequent military clashes within the empire, finally ending in the so-called religious Peace of Augsburg in 1555.[1]

Even at the time, all of these events were very intensely watched by contemporary "journalists",[2] and drew deserved attention for many more decades due to the religious background of that clash. After all, for centuries, confessional differences were misused within the context of the contemporary Christian world as a pretext for the domination of "one's neighbour", and the battle for declared or forced confessional unity was simply used by the powerful of that world to steal from those who could not defend themselves, whether directly during the frenzy of war, or in the form of nonsensical and forcibly-collected taxes.[3]

---

1   Fritz Hartung, Karl V. und die deutschen Reichsstände von 1546–1555 (Darmstadt, 1971); Gabriele Haugh-Moritz, "Der Schmalkaldische Krieg (1546/47) - ein kaiserlicher Religionskrieg?", in Religionskriege im Alten Reich und in Alteuropa, ed. Franz Brendle and Anton Schindling (Münster, 2006), 93–106.

2   Gil Bollleau de Buillon, Gil, ed. Commentaire dv seigneur Don Loys d'Auila, contenant la guerre d'Allemaigne, faicte par l'Empereur Charles V. es annes 1547 & 1548 (Paris, 1551); The commentaries of Don Lewes de Auela, and Suniga, great Master of Aranter, which treateth of the great wars in Germany made by Charles the fifth, maximo Emperoure of Rome, king of Spain, against John Frederike Duke of Saxon, and Philip the Lantgraue of Hesson (London, 1555).

3   Thomas Menzel, Der Fürst als Feldherr - Militärische Handeln und Selbstdarstellung zwischen 1470 und 1550. Dargestellt an ausgewählten Beispielen (Berlin, 2003), 258–312; James D. Tracy, Emperor Charles V, Impresario of War – Campaign Strategy, International Finance, and Domestic Politics (Cambridge, 2010), 204–248; David Parrott, The Bussiness of War - Military Enterprise and Military Revolution in Early Modern Europe (Cambridge, 2012), 71–80.

The summarized history of 16ᵗʰ century Europe,⁴ just like synthetic works on the history of the Holy Roman Empire⁵ or Germany,⁶ cannot avoid the issue of the confessional-political clash in the contemporary Holy Roman Empire as, from today's perspective, these two political-geographic terms largely coincide.⁷ Naturally, we also have special monographs available, devoted solely to this conflict and to important figures that played a decisive role in it.

In this situation, the reader will understandably ask themselves what the purpose of this book actually is. What is the point of retelling events that have already been written about many times, and which are universally known? Certainly, each interpretation is slightly different, depending in particular on where the author comes from. Traditionally, Spaniards and Austrians swear by the Habsburgs. As much as the author tries to offer an impartial and objective evaluation, the deep-rooted generational conviction about the history-making, and in the end positive, role of their actions is always in the

4   Eduard Fueter, Geschichte des europäischen Staatensystems von 1492–1559, Handbuch der Mitteralterlichen und Neueren Geschichte, Abteilung II: Politische Geschichte (München and Berlin, 1919); Walter Petry, Irrwege Europas 1519–1648 (Göttingen, 1967), 132–142; Benedict Philip, "Religion and Politics in Europe, 1500–1700", in Religion und Gewalt – Konflikte, Rituale, Deutungen (1500–1800), Veröffentlichungen des Max-Planck-Instituts für Geschichte, Band 215, ed. Kaspar von Greyerz and Kim Siebenhüner (Göttingen, 2006), 156–173; Mark Greengrass, Christendom Destroyed. Europe 1517–1648 (London, 2014), 259–389.

5   James Bryce, The Holy Roman Empire (3ʳᵈ ed. New York, 1966), 371–388; Georg Schmidt, Geschichte des Alten Reiches - Staat und Nation in der Frühen Neuzeit 1495–1806 (München, 1999); Friedrich Heer, The Holy Roman Empire (4ᵗʰ ed. London, 2003), 148–176; Heiliges Römisches Reich Deutscher Nation 962 bis 1806, II. 1495–1806 (Berlin, 2006); Evans, Robert J. W., and Wilson Peter H. The Holy Roman Empire 1495–1806. A European Perspective (Leiden, 2012).

6   Leopold von Ranke, Deutsche Geschichte im Zeitalter der Reformation in zwei Teilen, II, (Essen, 1996), 406–623; Gottlob Egelhaas, Deutsche Geschichte im sechzehnten Jahrhundert bis zum Augsburger Religionsfrieden (Zeitalter der Reformation) Zweiter Band 1526–1555 (Stuttgart, 1892), 697–617; Joachim Streisand, ed. Deutsche Geschichte. Band 1 – Von der Anfängen bis 1789 (3ʳᵈ ed. Berlin. 1974), 563–574; Heinrich Lutz, Das Ringen um deutsche Einheit und kirchliche Erneuerung (Von Maximilian I. bis zum Westfälischen Frieden) 1490 bis 1648. Propyläen Geschichte Deutschlands 4 (Frankfurt am Main, Berlin and Wien, 1983), 270–314.

7   Francis Ludwig Carsten, Princes and Parliaments in Germany from the Fifteenth to the Eighteent Century (Oxford 1959); Hermann Conrad, Deutsche Rechtsgeschichte, Bd. 2 - Neuzeit bis 1806 (Karlsruhe, 1966); Horst Rabe, Reich und Glaubensspaltung (Deutschland 1500–1600), Neue Deutsche Geschichte, Band 4 (München, 1989); Helmut Neuhaus, Das Reich in der Frühen Neuzeit, (München, 1997); Michael Kotulla, Deutsche Verfassungsgeschichte – Vom Alten Reich bis Weimar 1495–1934 (Berlin -Heidelberg 2008); Thomas A. Brady Jr., German Histories in the Age of Reformations, 1400–1650 (Cambridge 2009), 207–228; Joachim Whaley, Germany and the Holy Roman Empire, Volume I: Maximilian I to the Peace of Westphalia 1493–1648. (Oxford 2013), 304–338; Brendan Simms, Kampf um Vorherrschaft. Eine deutsche Geschichte Europas 1453 bis Heute (München 2014), 37–80.

background. The Frenchman, the Dutchman or the German from the north is in a similar position, but from the opposite perspective. How good things would be in Europe if that hapless warrior Emperor Charles V. and his Catholic Spanish advisers, did not keep meddling in history!

What can we say about this theme that's new, when the authors of decades and centuries past have already searched all kinds of archival depositories to complete the mosaic of our knowledge?[8] Most of the sources for the history of the wars in the Empire between the years 1546 and 1555 have already been published in printed editions, recently enriched by the completion of a valuable series of editions of Imperial Diets from the mid-16th century.[9]

Nevertheless, in connection with this theme, there is still one "undiscovered continent" (both from the perspective of the power-political context and from the perspective of the source base) which even the most recent authors of specialized works on the history of the Holy Roman Empire in the 16th century or on the history of the German wars in the mid-16th century practically did not take into account, and that's the role of the Kingdom of Bohemia in these Imperial wars.

This situation has to a large extent been caused by a failure to understand certain historical processes that took place in Central Europe. That's why even a look at the power crisis in the Empire in the mid-16th century is logically different from the perspective of the Kingdom of Bohemia, which may have been located in the vicinity of the German lands, but kept a certain distance from them after the historical experiences of the 15th century, irrespective of the fervour with which Lutheran reformers in Germany claimed allegiance to the legacy of Master Jan Hus, Czech priest and rector at Charles University in Prague.[10] While the first generation of the Empire

---

8 Georg Voigt, "Die Geschichtsschreibung über den schmalkaldischen Krieg", *Abhandlungen der philologisch-historischen Classe der Königl. Sächsischen Gesellschaft der Wissenschaften* VI. (Leipzig, 1874), 569–758; Karl Brandi, *Kaiser Karl V. – Werden und Schicksal einer Persönlichkeit und eines Weltreiches. Zweiter Band – Quellen und Erörterungen* (München, 1941); Karl Schottenloher, *Bibliographie zur deutschen Geschichte im Zeitalter der Glaubensspaltung 1517–1585*, IV. Band (2nd ed. Stuttgart, 1957), 557–564; Franz Schnabel, *Deutschlands geschichtliche Quellen und Darstellungen in der Neuzeit. Erster Teil: Das Zeitalter der Reformation 1500–1550* (Darmstadt, 1972).
9 RTA 1545; RTA 1546; RTA 1547/1548; RTA 1550/1551; RTA 1555.
10 Zdeněk V. David, Finding the Middle Way – The Utraquists' Liberal Challenge to Rome and Luther (Washington, 2003), 76–79.

experienced enthusiasm about the victory of the Reformation, in Bohemia, after four generations of forced inter-confessional coexistence, it was well-known that when things really "get tough", the primary decisive factor would be money. After all, this was precisely demonstrated in Germany during the Schmalkaldic War, whose motives, progress and results were responded to by the contemporary Bohemian political elite from a considerable distance, and without major confessional prejudices.[11]

Before the year 1547, all wealthy nobles and large provincial royal towns in Bohemia maintained permanent armed garrisons, or at least large arsenals of weapons, with which it would be possible to operatively arm a large number of troops in a relatively short time. However, this potential was not used to resolve "domestic" contentious issues. On the contrary, contemporary Bohemian Estates society took pride in being able to come to a reasonable agreement or find a solution by legal means, whether these were property disputes or complicated confessional matters. At the start of the early Modern Ages, this was a big difference in comparison with neighbouring countries, which conducted repeated bloody civil wars during that period, whether we consider the so-called German Peasants' War, the peasant uprising in Hungary, or local wars between Imperial princes conducted in various parts of Germany during the first half of the 16th century.

Inhabitants of the Bohemian lands often participated in these "neighbouring" wars as hired military commanders or ordinary mercenaries. This form of "military business" was highly profitable at the start of the 16th century, and contemporary Bohemian military entrepreneurs made use of the widespread awareness of the high quality of Bohemian troops, originally spread in Central Europe during the previous 15th century. However, in their own country, the Bohemian political elite managed to maintain a "land peace" thanks to the relatively good functioning of internal political cultural instruments which favoured a compromise agreement before a violent solution. It's highly unlikely that, under these circumstances, the Kingdom of Bohemia would have reached the brink of a

---

11 Petr Vorel, "The Importance of the Bohemian Reformation for the Political Culture of Central Europe from the 15th to the 17th century." Comenius – Journal of Euro-American Civilization 2 (2015), No. 2.

domestic war between the Estates and the King in the late 1540s if it wasn't for a strong impetus from the neighbouring Roman-German Empire.

Circumstances forced the Bohemian Estates to react to the requests of their king, Ferdinand I. of Habsburg, who tried to utilize Bohemian military potential to support Habsburg interests in the war in the neighbouring Roman-German Empire. The Bohemian Estates refused these requests. However, they were not willing to join the opposition German Estates in the war against their own king, either. They tried to avoid direct military conflict, and maintain the dispute between the Estates and the monarch at a diplomatic talks level. They demonstrated their military power and temporary unity of opinion as a form of political pressure on the monarch, but they did not have a serious reason to wage war against their king, much less spread the military conflict in the Empire to their own country's territory. They did not lack a broader view, but they did not regard the causes due to which some German princes and Imperial towns waged war with the King as fundamental enough for them to risk their own lives and property, and that of their subjects, for them. Furthermore, in a situation where the opposition itself in the Empire was divided and unstable, a number of important Lutheran princes leaned towards the Habsburgs' side, and Ferdinand I. announced neutrality for his own Austrian hereditary lands in the dispute in the Empire.

In the end, in terms of military results, the Bohemian Estates army's resultant participation in the Schmalkaldic war was insignificant. Nevertheless, the year 1547 represents a fundamental historical milestone in Bohemian history. King Ferdinand I. used the temporary military victory over the Imperial opposition to significantly change the internal political equilibrium in Bohemia, which also enabled a fundamental change in the country's economic structure. In the end, it's not even possible to say that King Ferdinand defeated the Bohemian Estates opposition, as an actual "gauging of powers" (comparable to the Bohemian Estates uprising from the years 1618–1620) had not taken place at all. The dispute was resolved by political agreement, advantageous not only for the King but also for most of the aristocratic segment of the former opposition camp, which the King had managed to win over to his side with the appropriate promises.

In every period it applies that the context of all events reaches deep into the past, and generational historical experiences cannot be quickly replaced or eradicated by political propaganda. This is what King Ferdinand attempted in Bohemia in 1547 when, at the time of his political superiority, he created and mass-distributed his own printed interpretation of what had actually happened in Bohemia in the year 1547.[12] Most of the original written documentation was intentionally destroyed by the very participants in the revolt shortly after its collapse, or later, on the monarch's orders. The King attempted to prevent the spreading of other information by establishing the centralized censorship of all printed matter. For political reasons, the King's "official" description of the Estates Revolt's progress could not be publicly called into question in Bohemia for the remainder of his reign (until the year 1564). With the Monarchal Court's support, it gained such publicity that it became the main source used as a starting point for the interpretation of the Bohemian state's role in the Schmalkaldic War, not only for subsequent Habsburg historiography (which is understandable), but even for historians from the Protestant camp.[13]

Nevertheless, other authentic sources, made partly available in modern editions, were preserved in the Bohemian environment.[14] However, the problem lies in the fact that they mostly came into existence only after the end of the revolt, when everyone already knew how everything had turned out. Additionally, these other ("unofficial") information sources come from the opposite pole of the opinion spectrum: they are interpretations formed in the environment of the two sides most affected by royal sanctions. One of these environments defined itself from an estate perspective (the Bohemian royal towns),[15] and the other confessionally (the Unity of the

---

12 Akta všech těch věcí, které sou se mezi nejjasnějším knížetem a pánem, panem Ferdinandem, římským, uherským, českým etc. králem etc., a některými osobami z stavu panského, rytířského a městského království českého léta tohoto etc. XLVII zběhly, (Praha, 1547).

13 Hortleder, Friedrich, ed. Der Römischen Keyser- Vnd Königlichen Maiestete, Auch des Heiligen Römischen Reichs Geistlicher vnnd Weltlicher Stände, Churfürsten, Fürsten, Graffen, Reichs- vnd andeder Stätte, zusampt der heiligen Schrifft, geistlicher und weltlicher Rechte Gelehrten, Handlungen und Außschreiben, Rathschäge, Bedencken, Send- und andere Brieffe, Bericht, Supplicationsschriften, Befehl, Entschuldigungen, Protestationes, Recusationes, Außführungen, Verantwortungen, Ableinungen, Absagungen, Achtserklärungen, Hülfsbrieffe, Verträge, Historische Beschreibungen und andere viel herrliche Schriften und Kunden, mehr: Von Rechtmässigkeit, Anfang, Fort- und endlichen Ausgang deß Teutschen Kriegs, Keyser Karls deß Fünfften, wider die Schmalkaldische Bundsoberste, Chur- und Fürsten, Sachsen und Hessen, und. I. Chur- und Fürstl. G. G. Mitwerwandte, Vom Jahr 1546. biß auf das Jahr 1558. (Frankfurt am Main, 1618).

14 Sněmy české od léta 1526 až po naši dobu, sv. II, 1546–1547 (Praha, 1880).

15 Teige Josef, ed. Sixt z Ottersdorfu - Knihy památné o nepokojných letech 1546–1547. I-II. (Praha, 1919).

Brethren).[16] These contemporary authentic sources differ in their interpretation of the Estates Revolt's progress and background from King Ferdinand's "official" version so fundamentally that the actual historical reality apparently lies somewhere in the centre of these two opinion poles. That is why even the specific level of involvement of individual persons in the revolt's organizational preparation and progress, and the motives for their behaviour, are still not completely clear today. In terms of language, this source base has been preserved in Czech, which is why it was used outside the circle of domestic Bohemian historiography only in exceptional cases in the past. This is also one of the reasons why, in more comprehensive modern works devoted to mid-16th century Central European history, the Bohemian context is not adequately taken into account.[17]

The first modern work devoted to the history of the Estates Revolt in Bohemia in the years 1546–1547 became Karl Tieftrunk's extensive monograph from the year 1872.[18] The author factographically summarized the main information relating to this issue, from the sources that were available to him at the time. Tieftrunk's work remained a basic source of information for an entire century; a starting point for all authors dealing with this event in the context of 16th century Bohemian history.[19]

New source research on the given topic was only performed in the 1960s and 1970s by Czech historian Josef Janáček, who summarized a newer interpretation of this event in the second volume of his historical monograph devoted to Bohemian history in the years 1526–1547.[20] In later years, the issue of the relationship between the Bohemian Estates and the mon-

---

16 Just Jiří, "Acta Unitatis Fratrum," Folia Historica Bohemica 29 (2014): 451–462.

17 Ranke, Deutsche Geschichte, II, 399–401: "Unterwerfung von Böhmen"; Karin J. MacHardy, War, Religion and Court Patronage in Habsburg Austria - The Social and Cultural Dimensions of Political Interaction, 1521–1622 (New York, 2003), 43, 48; J. D. Tracy, Emperor Charles V, 205; M. Greengrass, Christendom Destroyed, 382–383.

18 Karel Tieftrunk, Odpor stavův českých proti Ferdinandovi I. 1547 (Praha 1872). In the late 19th century, Tieftrunk's younger contemporaries, Antonín Rezek and Václav Vladivoj Tomek produced important component contributions regarding Estates politics and the role of the Prague Towns in the revolt, Antonín Rezek, "Statky zkonfiskované r. 1547 a jejich rozprodávání," Památky archeologické a místopisné 10 (1874 -1877), 451–475; Václav Vladivoj Tomek, Dějepis města Prahy, XI. (Praha, 1897).

19 Paula S. Fichtner, "When Brothers Agree, Bohemia, the Habsburg, and the Schmalkandic wars (1546–1547)", Austrian History Yearbook 11 (1975), 67–78; Kenneth J. Dillon, King and Estates in the Bohemian Lands 1526–1564 (Bruxelles 1976).

20 Josef Janáček, České dějiny – Doba předbělohorská 1526–1547, I/II (Praha 1984).

arch in the broader context of Central European history in the mid-16th century was dealt with by Winfried Eberhard on the German side,[21] and Jaroslav Pánek on the Czech side.[22] An important impetus for the research of the above-mentioned theme became the scientific conference held on the occasion of the 450th anniversary of the Estates Revolt in the year 1997 in Pardubice Castle.[23]

Newer Czech works, published at the start of the 21st century,[24] summarize the issue of the Estates Revolt both in the broader context of the Habsburgs' Central European battle against the Estates opposition, and in the broader framework of 16th century Bohemian history. Nevertheless, in my opinion, a number of questions remain unanswered. I think that the view from the Czech perspective of the confessional and political clashes that took place in mid-16th century Central Europe can be interesting and stimulating for every researcher or person interested in this historical period. That was also one of the reasons that led me to write this book, which looks at this complicated period of history in this part of Europe from a slightly different angle than usual.

So what really happened in Bohemia at the time that was so revolutionary, when no actual war was waged in the country (unlike in Germany)? Was it the betrayal of Lutheran co-religionists in the Empire and former political allies on the domestic political scene, or the statesmen's prudence, that prevented the country's military devastation? How is it possible that, for the following several decades of the second half of the 16th century (i.e.

---

21 Kenneth J. Dillon, King and Estates in the Bohemian Lands 1526–1564 (Bruxelles 1976); Winfried Eberhard, Monarchie und Widerstand - Zur ständischen Oppositionsbildung im Herrschaftssystem Ferdinands I. in Böhmen (München 1985).

22 Jaroslav Pánek, "Das Ständewesen und die Gesellschaft in den Böhmischen Ländern in der Zeit vor der Schlacht auf dem Weißen Berg (1526 - 1620)", Historica 25 (1985), 73 – 120.

23 Petr Vorel, ed., Stavovský odboj roku 1547 – První krize habsburské monarchie - Sborník příspěvků z konference konané v Pardubicích ve dnech 29. a 30. září 1997 (Pardubice – Praha 1999).

24 Jaroslav Pánek, "Kaiser, König und Ständerevolte (Die böhmischen Stände und ihre Stellung zur Reichspolitik Karls V. und Ferdinands I. im Zeitalter der Schmalkandischen Krieges)" in Karl V. 1500–1558 (Neue Perspektiven seiner Herrschaft in Europa und Übersee), ed. A. Kohler, B. Haider and Ch. Ottnar Ch. (Wien 2002), 303 – 406; Petr Vorel, Velké dějiny zemí Koruny české - VII. 1526–1618 (Praha 2005), 7–167; Jaroslav Pánek, "Regierungsstrategie und Regierungsformen Ferdinands I. in den böhmischen Ländern" in Kaiser Ferdinand I. – Ein mitteleuropäischen Herrscher, ed. M. Fuchs, T. Oborni and G. Ujváry, 323–338. (Münster 2005), 323–338; Josef Válka, "Konflikt české zemské obce s králem 1546–1547 (Ferdinand I. a počátky absolutismu II)", Časopis Matice moravské 125 (2006), 33–51.

after the Estates opposition was suppressed by King Ferdinand in the year 1547) the Kingdom of Bohemia experienced a long period of peaceful life, unusually extensive religious freedom and extraordinary economic prosperity, even accompanied by the transfer of the Emperor's permanent residence to Prague (in 1583)? Why, for the Bohemian royal towns which were stripped of all their assets and had their political power removed in 1547, does the second half of the 16th century represent a "golden era", i.e. a time of extraordinary internal cultural and structural development? Also, the Unity of the Brethren, whose members were expelled from Bohemia in 1547, represented the most important and well-organized political power in the country just half a century later. In terms of long-term intergenerational development, the monarchal sanctions against part of the Bohemian Estates in 1547 actually brought about a strengthening of independent domestic development, whose basis, since the end of the 15th century, was the principle of power-guaranteed confessional plurality. How is it possible that the Bohemian political elites, weakened by monarchal sanctions in the year 1547, managed to reject the principle of the so-called Religious Peace of Augsburg of 1555 a few years later? Why, instead of politically-enforced confessionalization, commonly applied in the neighbouring Roman-German Empire, did the Kingdom of Bohemia offer the already confessionally-broken Christian Europe its own solution in the form of the so-called Charter on Religious Freedom (1609)?

For now, we cannot precisely answer the questions, and this book does not offer any simple solution. Nevertheless, in my opinion, it can contribute in the future to the understanding of the deeper roots of the complicated situation in Central Europe two generations later (at the start of the 17th century), when the Bohemian Estates and the Prague intellectual political centre became (for the last time in its long existence) a driving force of "great" European history.

The Holy Roman Empire of the German Nation around 1530

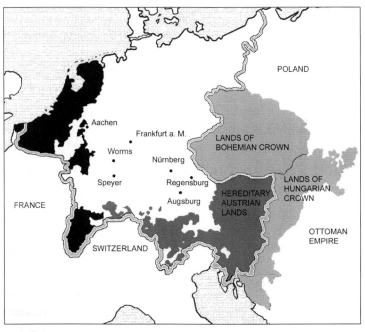

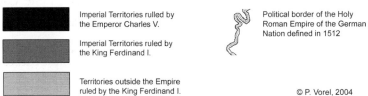

Imperial Territories rulled by the Emperor Charles V.

Imperial Territories ruled by the King Ferdinand I.

Territories outside the Empire ruled by the King Ferdinand I.

Political border of the Holy Roman Empire of the German Nation defined in 1512

© P. Vorel, 2004

CHAPTER 1

THE INTERNAL CRISIS IN THE HOLY ROMAN EMPIRE OF THE GERMAN NATION, AND THE EFFORT TO RESOLVE IT (1530–1546)

The overall results of the first ten years of the Imperial government of young Charles V., who was elected King of Rome when he was 19 years old (in 1519), did not seem very successful.[1] Repeated wars with France on the Burgundy and north Italian front and with the Ottoman Empire in the Mediterranean and the hereditary Austrian lands exhausted the financial resources of both the Habsburgs and the Empire as a whole. The surge of social tension, which culminated in the so-called German Peasants' War (1525), showed the weakness of the system as a whole, regardless of the confessional affiliation of individual Imperial princes. The rapid expansion of the Lutheran Reformation in all parts of the Empire during the 1520s brought a new dynamic to the integration process of the early modern German state. The advantage of this new model was clear – the Catholic Church's assets, amassed over centuries, could resolve the princes' long-term indebtedness at once. The inexpensive Church, finding itself de facto under the control of the ruling princes, burdened the country's future economy significantly less that the medieval Roman Church. The destruction and pillage of Papal Rome by an undisciplined mercenary army, formed in large part of German Lutherans (1527), seemed to be a symbolic turning point in the process of the further shaping of the Holy Roman Empire of the German Nation as a state, whose new internal bond becomes the Lutheran Reformation, whether with the Habsburgs or without them.

---

[1]   Geoffrey Parker, "Die politische Welt Karls V.," in Karl V. 1500–1558 und seine Zeit, ed. Hugo Soly (Köln, 2003), 113–126.

At that time, the Habsburgs found themselves in a difficult position. The elected King of Rome, Charles V., (1500–1558) was bound by the Electoral Capitulation of 1519, which guaranteed Imperial princes considerable autonomy. From the time of Charles' predecessor and grandfather Maximilian I. (†1519), the Empire had already formed all of the important common legislative, judicial and tax institutions that could become the foundation of the modern state. At the start of the 16th century, none of the creators of this system could have anticipated the fundamental manner in which confessional problems would complicate Imperial integration. By this I'm not referring the basic issues of Christian doctrine, to which the Lutheran Reformation brought fundamental stimuli, but the political significance which the Reformation brought with it from the 1520s, especially from the perspective of the anti-Habsburg opposition.

Political opposition to Imperial power had always existed within the Empire; however, it could not define itself confessionally, as that was too dangerous. In connection with the Papal Curia, the Emperor (if no other solutions were available to him) could use the authority of the Church against his opponents, including instruments such as an interdict, Church anathema, declaration as a heretic, or even the announcement of a crusade for the purpose of suppressing the anti-Imperial opposition (purposefully declared to be a hereditary movement).[2]

This purposeful combination of Imperial and Papal power, which occurred from time to time during the High or Late Middle Ages, was always an accompanying manifestation of an internal political crisis in the Empire. Only in exceptional cases was such a temporary political alliance between Imperial and Papal power unsuccessful against the political opposition in the Empire. Actually, throughout the whole history of the Empire, only one such exception exists: the Kingdom of Bohemia in the 15th century.[3] I would like to briefly mention this exception in another part of this book, as this is a significant precedent for the theme of this book that still

2   Richard Kieckhefer, Repression of Heresy in Medieval Germany (Philadelphia 1979), 83–98; Norman Houley, The Later Crusades from Lyons to Alcazar 1274–1580 (Oxford 1995), 249–259.
3   Kamil Krofta, "Bohemia in the Fifteenth Century", in The Close of the Middle Ages. Cambridge medieval History, Volume VIII, ed. C. W. Previté-Orton and Z. N. Brooke (Cambridge 1936), 65–155.

played an important role in religious-political talks between the Habsburgs and the Lutheran opposition in the mid-16th century.

As part of the early modern Holy Roman Empire of the German Nation, created by Maximilian I. in the form of an estate monarchy and symbolically established by the foundation of the new Imperial Diet in 1495,[4] the early modern Empire "inherited" a relatively unbalanced power system. This was due to the fact that the structure of the Imperial Diet itself was created in 1495 on the basis of an older medieval system. Thus, the representation of individual territorial parts of the Empire in political life was both unequal (favouring the area of the Rhine, with its traditionally strong influence of direct Imperial assets), and contained potential for disputes in the event that changes occurred in the structure of the Empire.

This became evident shortly after the death of Maximilian I., at the first Imperial Diet, which was formally convened by the newly-elected ruler, the twenty-one-year-old Charles V.. It was at this Diet, held in 1521 in Worms, that the imbalance between the de jure representation of Imperial Estates at the Diet, and the actual distribution of political power, was shown distinctively for the first time.[5] The Imperial Diet, at which representatives of the Catholic side prevailed in terms of the number of votes, also invited Martin Luther to its talks, with the requirement that he retract his critical opinions of the Catholic Church. The Diet also referred to the Papal bull from May 1520, in which Pope Leo X. (1513–1521) condemned Luther's teaching and declared it to be heretical. After Luther refused to retract his opinions, the

---

4   The older medieval Holy Roman Empire was formed as a feudal state, whose parts were either directly subject to Imperial power (Imperial cities and territories, belonging to the Emperor directly), or was dependent on it in some form within the feudal system. Various forms of conferences between the Emperor and the princes (medieval "assemblies") were occasionally convened. It was only as part of Imperial reform, commencing with the election to Maximilian I. as King of Rome in 1486, that the Empire was gradually reshaped into an estate-type state, in which the Emperor had to cede part of his legislative, judicial and fiscal powers to estate institutions that were de facto independent of the Imperial Court, and formed a counterweight to Imperial power in this system. The main institution of this type was the Imperial Diet, established, and sitting for the first time, in the town of Worms in 1495. More precisely, from 1495 (thanks to the establishment of an Imperial Diet with a clear political representation), the political borders of the Empire are newly defined, including only the "German" territories of the former medieval Empire. That's why the new title "Holy Roman Empire of the German Nation" also began to be officially used at this time. This is why the year 1495 is regarded as a key milestone in the Empire's history. See J. Bryce, The Holy Roman Empire, 368–369; M. Kotulla, Deutsche Verfassungsgeschichte, 48–63 (§ 4 / I, Der Reichstag zu Worms 1495).

5   Alfred Kohler, Das Reich im Kampf um die Hegemonie in Europa 1521–1648 (München 1990), 15–21.

Diet decided to impose an Imperial anathema on him in May 1521 (the so-called Edict of Worms) which was then followed by a Papal anathema and Luther's excommunication from the Church in October 1521.

By 1521, however, a number of important Imperial princes had joined Luther's side, starting with Frederick III., Elector of Saxony (1486–1525). In this way, "Causa Luther" became a suitable catalyst for the rapid formation of anti-Habsburg opposition in the Empire, especially as the Saxon Wettins (who could lean on a strong economic base in the form of their silver mines in the Ore Mountains) created a natural second power centre in the Empire as early as the time of Emperor Maximilian I.. After all, Frederick III. Elector of Saxony himself (born in 1463) held the position of Imperial Governor at the start of the 16th century, and in 1519 most of the German princes considered him to be a more suitable candidate for the Imperial throne than the young grandson of the deceased Emperor Maximilian I., Charles of Habsburg, who was only nineteen years old at the time.

During the election of the new ruler of the Empire, Frederick III., Elector himself eventually leaned towards the young Habsburg's side, but he was well aware of the extent of his own political power. This is why he could afford to completely ignore the decision of the Imperial Diet, Charles V., King of Rome, and Pope Leo X., and provide Martin Luther with a safe sanctuary, although for this he was de jure threatened with the same penalty as the Imperial and Papal anathema stipulated for Luther himself.

Frederick III., Elector, was well aware that the King of Rome did not have sufficient power resources to actually implement the decision of the Imperial Diet. The political support that was provided to Luther by the formally second (but really first in terms of influence) most powerful man in the Empire, became an exceptionally strong impulse for spreading Luther's teaching in German territory. The main bearers of the Reformation became the Imperial territorial princes and free Imperial cities. The introduction of the Reformation was also accompanied by the secularization of Church property. Every fundamental social change of this kind understandably leads to an increase in social tension, which in the case of the Empire took the form of many smaller, more or less organized, uprisings by minor rural nobility and serfs, which we collectively refer to as the "German Peasants' War," culminating in 1525.

An interest in the rapid suppression of the social movement which threatened the princes and their property, regardless of their confessional orientation, temporarily brought the Habsburgs and the opposition closer together; Charles V. also urgently needed the support of the Imperial princes and cities in his wars in northern Italy, where the so-called League of Cognac was formed against him in 1526 (France, Pope Clement VII., Milan, Venice and Genoa, with the support of England). Nevertheless, shortly after the fiasco which the ineffective Edict of Worms (1521) meant for the Habsburgs, the Habsburg side began preparations for broader power platforms, which were to become a basis of support for Habsburg policy in the Empire.

As early in 1524, in Bavarian Regensburg, a league of Imperial Catholic Estates was established, aimed at enforcing the resolution of the Imperial Diet in Worms from 1521, directed against Lutheran Reformation. This league of Regensburg mainly protected the interests of the Habsburg power centre. The main members of this group, besides Catholic Church princes (i.e. Church Electors and bishops, represented at the Imperial Diet) were mainly the hereditary Habsburg lands (a significant number of which were ceded by Charles V. to the direct rule of his younger brother Ferdinand I.) and Bavaria. Other Catholic princes founded their own political association in 1525, the so-called League of Dessau, led by George, Duke of Saxony, cousin of Frederick III., Elector. (†1525). In opposition to this, Lutheran princes (led by Philip of Hesse and John, the new Elector of Saxony, brother of the deceased Frederick III.) founded the so-called Torgav association (1526) which was intended to be a common defence against the Edict of Worms.

As a result of the ongoing social unrest (the German Peasants' War), and developments on Habsburg battlefields elsewhere in Europe, this confessionally-defined political grouping may not have been outwardly very active, but it was available as a basis for a political platform for a more suitable time. During the twenties, Charles V. was not yet prepared for any major power intervention in the Empire, and his relations with the Papal Curia was quite complicated by the "regrettable oversight" of 1527, when his badly-paid German and Spanish mercenaries, feeling like lords of Italy after a victory over the League of Cognac army, occupied and pillaged Papal

Rome (Sacco di Roma) without a fight. Pope Clement VII. (1523–1534) himself became a de facto hostage of Charles V., and the new political friendship between the Imperial and Papal Court actually lasted for quite a long time after these experiences.

For Habsburg policy, more opportune conditions only occurred at the actual end of the 1620s and start of the 1630s. In return for minor concessions, Charles V. normalized his relations with Pope Clement VII. in 1529, and commenced talks on the preparation of a peace treaty with Francis I., King of France (1515–1547); these talks were rounded off with a peace treaty in Cambrai. This treaty resolved the older problematic obligations by Francis I. towards Charles V. from the time of France's defeat at the Battle of Pavia (1525), as well as older territorial disputes in Burgundy and in Flanders, and the treaty also anticipated a future link between both dynasties by way of marriage (Francis I. was to marry the sister of Charles V.). Although these peace treaties did not last very long, his temporary arrangement of a "cease-fire" on the main European battleground in 1529 provided Charles V. with room to manoeuvre and allowed him to more strictly enforce his own interests on the Imperial political scene, if only at a diplomatic level for now.

The normalization of relations with Pope Clement VII. was a condition for obtaining the Imperial title, also contingent at that time on the coronation of the elected King of Rome at the hands of the Pope. The Imperial coronation of Charles V., which took place in February 1530 in Bologna, then allowed the Habsburgs to raise the issue of the election of a new King of Rome, who would be both a successor to the Roman throne in the event of the Emperor's death, and his representative in times of absence. It's well known that Charles V. was the ruler of various parts of Europe that did not belong to the Holy Roman Empire of the German Nation, i.e. mainly Spain and Naples. He spent a significant portion of his time outside the territory of the Empire, whether as a result of his direct participation in various military campaigns, or for other reasons. As early as the 1520s, he authorized his younger brother Ferdinand I. to represent him in the Empire, but it was only thanks to the Imperial coronation in Bologna in 1530 that Charles' royal Roman title was "vacated" (Charles V. became Emperor).

The election of the new King of Rome was theoretically possible even while the existing Emperor was alive (a so-called "vivente imperatorem" election), but this was last used in Imperial history in 1376, when such an election was used by Emperor Charles IV. of Luxembourg to ensure that his first-born son Wenceslas succeeded him on the Roman throne. Even this, however, was an inter-generational vote, guaranteeing sovereign succession in the future. There was never a situation in the older history of the Empire when an existing Emperor let their brother – peer be elected as their successor (King of Rome); Ferdinand I. was only three years younger.[6] The announcement of the election of new King of Rome shortly after the Imperial coronation was clearly perceived by the Imperial Estates as both an effort to strengthen the influence of the Habsburgs and a threat to the system of estate freedoms,[7] which in the preceding decades had always been confirmed and possibly even expanded during pre-election talks. This was the case during the previous elections of the King of Rome, in 1486 and 1519.

However, a situation occurred that was very favourable for the Habsburgs, as Ferdinand I. was elected King of Bohemia after the death of Ludwig of Jagiellonia, King of Bohemia, in 1526. At that time, the Kingdom of Bohemia may no longer have been part of the Holy Roman Empire of the German Nation, which was ruled by Charles V., but on the basis of political agreements on the singling out of Bohemian lands from the Empire between 1486 and 1489, the King of Bohemia still had the right to one vote in the election of the King of Rome. The King of Bohemia remained a so-called external Elector, who never became a member of the Electors' collegium at the Imperial Diet, established in 1495, but he had voting rights in the event of an election of a new ruler of the Empire. Therefore, only six members sat in the Electors' collegium in the Imperial Diet (three secular: the Duke of Saxony, the Duke of Palatine and the Margrave of Brandenburg, and three Church: the Archbishops of Mainz, Trier and

---

6   Ernst Laubach, "Karl V., Ferdinand I. und die Nachfolge im Reich", Mitteilungen des österreichisches Staatsarchivs 29 (1976), 1–51; Helmut Neuhaus, "Die Römische Königswahl vivente imperatore in der Neuzeit (Zum Problem der Kontinuität in einer frühneuzeitlichen Wahlmonarchie)" in Neue Studien zur frühneuzeitlichen Reichsgeschichte - Zeitschrift für historische Forschung (Vierteljahreschrift zur Erforschung des Spätmittelalters und der frühen Neuzeit), Beiheft 19, ed. Johannes Kunisch (Berlin 1997), 1–54.

7   Alfred Kohler, "Die innerdeutsche und die außerdeutsche Opposition gegen das politische System Karls V.", in Das römisch-deutsche Reich im politischen System Karls V., Schriften des Historischen Kollegs – Kolloquien 1, ed. Heinrich Lutz (München – Wien 1982), 107–127.

Cologne), but during the election of the King of Rome, a seventh vote was also counted (the King of Bohemia). Therefore, if the Habsburgs added the fourth Bohemian vote to the three Catholic Church Electors' votes (Ferdinand I. could vote for himself), they were guaranteed a majority of votes despite the dissent of all the three remaining secular Electors. In this way, in 1531, Ferdinand I., King of Bohemia, was also elected the King of Rome by a majority vote, and de jure became the co-ruler of his brother Charles V. in the Empire.

This process resulted in dissent both by the secular Electors (who did not agree with the election of a future ruler of the Empire while the existing Emperor was alive), and by many other influential princes and Imperial towns. Disputes on the confessional scene intensified at that time: regardless of the actual political situation, the Habsburg (pro-Catholic) side had numerical superiority in the Imperial Diet,[8] and the Imperial Diet which took place in 1529 in Speyer confirmed the formal validity of the Edict of Worms from 1521.[9] Supporters of the Lutheran Reformation, who already had a power majority on the actual Imperial political scene, protested against this resolution by the Imperial Diet; that's why the religiously-motivated part of the Imperial opposition began to be labelled "Protestants".[10] As a result of this political pressure, adherents of the Reformation managed both to agree on the precise formulation of the actual doctrinal principles (the so-called Augsburg Confession of 1530), and to commence talks on common military defence.

On the basis of older conventions from Torgau (1526), a new defensive alliance was established to protect the interests of the Lutheran portion of the Imperial Estates, which (under the pressure of a threatened military intervention by the Habsburgs) already achieved specific agreements on mutual military assistance. These talks commenced at the end of December

---

8   Winfried Schulze, Majority Decision in the Imperial Diets of the Sixteenth and Seventeenth Centuries." In Politics and Society in the Holy Roman Empire, 1500–1806. The Journal of Modern History, Volume 58 – Supplement, December 1986 (Chicago 1986), 46–63.

9   Heinz Schilling, Aufbruch und Krise - Deutschland 1517–1648 (Berlin 1998), 211; Heide Stratenwerth and Horst Rabe, "Politische Kommunikation und Diplomatie", in Kaiser Karl V. (1500–1558) – Macht und Ohnmacht Europas (Eine Ausstellung des Kunsthistorischen Museums Wien), ed. Wilfried Seipel (Wien 2000), 27–34.

10   Heinrich Bornkamm, Das Jahrhundert der Reformation – Gestalten und Kräfte (2nd ed. Göttingen, 1966), 112–125.

1530 in the Hessen town of Schmalkalden, which is why this new formation on the Imperial Political became known as the Schmalkaldic League.[11]

The first version of the alliance agreement, concluded on the 27th of February 1531, ensured the rapid convention and financing of an army numbering 2,000 cavalry and 10,000 infantry, quite a large military force in contemporary terms, in the event of an attack against one of the signatories by
the Habsburgs. The main advantage of the Schmalkaldic League consisted
of the fact that its members were wealthy Imperial towns that were able to
mobilize and arm soldiers very quickly. Political weight was given to the
Schmalkaldic League mainly by the fact that its founding members
included several wealthy and influential Lutheran princes.

The most important of these was the contemporary doyen of the Imperial political scene, John, Elector of Saxony (born 1468, † 1532), father of
John Frederick, Elector, who later clashed with Emperor Charles V. in the
Schmalkaldic War. In this (so-called Ernestine) branch of Saxon Wettins,
support for the Lutheran Reformation was a long-term political programme, as the primary protector of Luther himself, Frederick III, Elector, was John's older brother. The Saxon Wettins rules a vast territory,
which was formed of several historic lands (the Margraveship of Meissen,
the Margraveship of Thuringia, the Duchy of Saxony and other smaller
ones), but formed a more-or-less compact territorial whole. For the theme
of this book, it's important that the Saxon domains were immediately
adjacent to the lands of the Crown of Bohemia: its southern part pressed
against the north-western border of the Kingdom of Bohemia; in the east,
the Wettin lands bordered Lusetia. Since medieval times, the Saxon Wettins traditionally had very close contact with the Bohemian environment,
not only on a property-legal level (part of the territory held by the Saxon
Wettins was subject to the feudal authority of the King of Bohemia) but
also on a family level. Even these old relations played an important role at
the time of the Schmalkaldic War. The division of assets between the two
branches of the Saxon Wettins took place in 1485, creating two family

---

11   Ekkehard Fabian, Die Entstehung des Schmalkaldischen Bundes und seiner Verfassung 1524/29 -
     1531/35 (Tübingen 1962); Jürgen Reich, "Schmalkalden und der Schmalkaldische Bund", in Grenz-
     gänge (Festgabe für Hans Geißer), ed. Horst Licker (Zürich 2003), 111–119.

branches: the older "Ernestine" branch (bearer of the title of Elector; John Frederick, Elector, was one of its members), and the younger "Albertine" branch (one of its member was the Elector's second cousin, Duke Moritz of Saxony).

The second most important man in the Schmalkaldic League was Landgrave Philip of Hesse (1504–1567), the wealthy and educated ruler of Hesse and founder of the Lutheran University in Marburg (1527). In the first part of the 16th century, Hesse was one of the most important territorial units in the north-west of Germany, comparable in size to the contemporary tenures of individual Saxon Wettin branches. Hesse only lost this significance during the next generation, when its territory was divided among Landgrave Philip's numerous sons in 1568.[12] The compact core of the former unified Hesse spread south-west from the town of Göttingen almost as far as Frankfurt am Main; other smaller territorial units belonged to Hesse to the south and west of Frankfurt. This rich land was inherited by Landgrave Philip, as his father's only son, at five years of age. In order for him to be able to rule, Emperor Maximilian declared him to be an adult in 1518 (under normal circumstances, he could only take over the property at eighteen years of age). Thus, Landgrave Philip entered high Imperial politics at a very young age. At seventeen, he personally participated in the Imperial Diet in Worms, and as a nineteen-year-old ruler (1523), he introduced the Lutheran Reformation to his country. He even belonged to the more politically active part of the leadership in the Schmalkaldic League,[13] although later (after 1540), his position became highly problematic.

Other founding signatories of the Schmalkaldic League from the ranks of the Imperial princes were Margrave George of Brandenburg, Duke Ernest of Brunswick-Luneburg († 1546), prince Wolfgang of Anhalt-Bernburg, and counts Albert and Gebhart of Mansfeld. The alliance agreement was signed by several wealthy and influential Imperial towns, such as Magdeburg, Bremen, Strasbourg, Nuremberg, Ulm and Konstanz, but also by smaller towns

---

12   Walter Heinemeyer, "Das Zeitalter der Reformation", in Das Werden Hessens, ed. Walter Heinemeyer (Marburg 1986), 225–266; here the Map "Die Landgrafschaft Hessen Teilung 1568" (between pp. 256–257).

13   Franz Petri, "Nordwestdeutschland im Wechselspiel der Politik Karls V. und Philipps des Großmütigen von Hessen", Zeitschrift des Vereins für hessische Geschichte und Landeskunde 71 (1960), 37–60.

in Germany (Heilbronn, Reutlingen, Weissenburg, Windsheim, Memmingen, Kempten, Lindau, Biberach a Isny) and in Switzerland (Zurich and Basel).[14]

Membership of the Schmalkaldic League wasn't merely a political declaration. Members undertook not only to finance the common forces in case of an attack against one of them by the Habsburgs, but also agreed on the payment of a relatively high "membership contribution", paid every year into the common budget – i.e. basically a constant tax, collected independently of the decision of the Imperial Diet. Thus, the number of immediate members of the Schmalkaldic League was precisely specified, and acceptance into the alliance or withdrawal from it had not only political, but also economic consequences. That's why the Schmalkaldic League, in addition to its immediate members, also had the political support of other Imperial Lutheran princes and towns, which however were not willing or able to contribute financially.

The establishment of the Schmalkaldic League led to the creation of a completely autonomous political platform within the Empire, which gathered for regular parliamentary talks independently of Imperial Diet sessions.[15] In this way, the Lutheran opposition resolved a paradoxical situation in which a minority of Catholic Estates that, however, had a majority representation at the Imperial Diet, could accept Diet resolutions (even relating to religious issues), with which the majority of the Lutheran Estates did not agree.

Thus, at the start of the thirties, this situation very quickly led to the political polarization of the Empire into two relatively precisely defined camps. Opposition Estates may have had to accept the fact that the Habsburgs would be the long-term formal rulers of the Empire (Charles V., Emperor of Rome, and his brother Ferdinand I., King of Rome, were still young), but they created their own parallel power system, which guaranteed them independence from central Imperial power and also de facto immunity from prosecution if they did not observe Imperial Diet resolutions.

The first major conflict which tested the power ratio between both sides was the dispute over the Duchy of Württemberg in 1534. This Duchy, located

---

14 Paul Burckhardt, "Basel zur Zeit des Schmalkaldischen Krieges", Basler Zetschrift für Geschichte und Altertumskunde 38 (1939), 5–103.

15 Thomas A. Brady, "Phases and Strategies of the Schmalkaldic League, A Perspektive after 450 Years", Archiv für Reformationsgeschichte 74 (1983), 162–181.

in south-west Germany, was confiscated in 1519 from its feudal ruler Ulrich of Württemberg after a military intervention by the so-called Swabian League (which was a Late Middle Ages union of south German towns and princes), for completely logical and understandable reasons.[16] In his youth, prince Ulrich was a very argumentative and extravagant person, in both his family and social life. In exchange for compensation of 220,000 Rhenish guilders, King Charles V. took over reign of Württemberg in 1519, and he ceded this territory (as Emperor) to his brother Ferdinand of Habsburg after his election as King of Rome (1531). The former holder of this land, Ulrich of Württemberg, found himself in long-term exile in Switzerland and in France. He entered the military service of Francis I., King of France, and continued trying to win back his land. After earlier unsuccessful efforts in the 1520s, he gained the support of Landgrave Philip of Hesse who, as one of the leaders of the Schmalkaldic League, supported Ulrich of Württemberg's claims.[17]

In April 1534, the forces of the Schmalkaldic League and Ulrich of Württemberg (supported by France) commenced the occupation of Württemberg, which the Habsburgs were not able to prevent. In this military conflict, the Schmalkaldic League had significant military superiority. It had a military force of 4,000 cavalry and 20,000 infantry at its disposal, while Ferdinand of Habsburg had less than half of that (only 400 cavalry and 9,000 infantry).[18] After a brief military conflict, which Ferdinand of Habsburg lost in the Battle of Lauffen on the 13th of May 1534, King Ferdinand was forced to resign his tenure of Württemberg.[19] Peace treaties, which granted Ulrich of Württemberg tenure of his princedom (but with a restriction on his possible participation in Imperial Diet talks), were concluded between both parties in June 1534 in Bohemia, in the west Bohemia town of Kadaň (Kaaden).[20]

---

16 Franz Brendle, Dynastie, Reich und Reformation (Die württembergischen Herzöge Ulrich und Christoph, die Habsburger und Frakreich). Veröffentlichungen der Kommission für geschichtliche Landeskunde in Baden-Württemberg, Reihe B – Forschungen, 141. Band. (Stuttgart 1998), 57–71.

17 Jakob Wille, Philipp der Grossmuthige von Hessen und die Restitution Ulrichs von Wirtemberg (Tübingen 1882); Franz Brendle, "Um Erhalt und Ausbreitung des Evangeliums: Die Reformationskriege der deutschen Protestanten", in Religionskriege im Alten Reich und in Alteuropa, ed. Franz Brendle and Anton Schindling (Münster, 2006), 71–92.

18 Joachim Whaley, Germany and the Holy Roman Empire, Volume I, Maximilian I to the Peace of Westphalia 1493–1648 (Oxford 2013), 308–309.

19 F. Brendle, "Um Erhalt und Ausbreitung", 73–79.

20 F. Brendle, Dynastie, Reich und Reformation, 172–184.

The short and successful war for Württemberg became a significant incentive for the internal re-organization of the Schmalkaldic League. After lengthy talks, the League Assembly resolution was accepted in December 1535, relating mainly to the practical issues of commanding the army in the event that League members had to be defended against the Habsburgs. The young John Frederick, Elector of Saxony (who inherited the rule of the land, the title of Elector and the leading role in the Schmalkaldic League after his deceased father, John, in 1532), and his peer, Landgrave Philip of Hesse, were appointed the main military commanders of the League. The agreement of the 23rd of December 1535 specified not only the issues of the financing of the army, but also the strategic procedure for various variants of possible attacks by the Habsburgs. If a pan-Imperial military conflict took place, a main League army commander was to be appointed (the choice was to be between John Frederick of Saxony, Philip of Hesse, or Ernest of Brunswick-Luneburg). A nine-member League Council was to decide on the activities of the Schmalkaldic League, in which, apart from the two main representatives of the Schmalkaldic League (John Frederick of Saxony and Philip of Hesse), towns were also to be strongly represented, having four votes in total.[21] During the year 1536, after the expansion of the Schmalkaldic League, the number of votes in the Council was increased to thirteen.[22]

During the second half of the thirties, other Lutheran princes and Imperial towns joined the Schmalkaldic League. The afore-mentioned Ulrich of Württemberg joined in 1536, followed a year later by the rulers of Anhalt, Pomerania and the wealthy Imperial towns of Augsburg[23] and Frankfurt am Main,[24] as well as other smaller ones (e.g. Kempten). Thus, by 1537, the number of contractually-bound members increased to 18 princes and 28 Imperial and Hanseatic towns, resulting in the Schmalkaldic

---

21 Ekkehard Fabian, Die schmalkaldischen Bundesabschiede 1533–1536 (Mit Ausschreiben der Bundestage und anderen archivalischen Beilagen), Schriften zur Kirchen- und Rechtsgeschichte (Darstellungen und Quellen), 8. Heft (Tübingen 1958).

22 Thomas A. Brady, German Histories in the Age of Reformations 1400–1650 (Cambridge 2009), 220–221.

23 Heinrich Lutz, "Augsburg und seine politiche Umwelt 1490–1555", in Geschichte der Stadt Augsburg - 2000 Jahre von der Römerzeit bis zur Gegenwart (Stuttgart 1984), 413–433, especially p. 425.

24 Paul Collischon, Frankfurt a. M. im Schmalkaldische Kriege (Strassburg 1890); Irene Haas, Reformation - Konfesion - Tradition, Frankfurt am Main im Schmalkandischen Bund 1536–1547 (Frankfurt am Main 1991).

League having territorial influence in all parts of the Empire.[25] It was then divided internally, according to territorial affiliation, into a lower German (north-eastern) part, whose main representative was John Frederick, Elector of Saxony, and an upper German (south-western) part, which was led by Landgrave Philip of Hesse. This division of the Schmalkaldic League (but, in a way, also the whole Empire) reflected, to a large extent, the Empire's old language duality. The two contemporary basic forms of the German language were mutually difficult to understand, never mind the numerous provincial and local dialects whose existence led to communication problems even during Imperial Diet talks.

The main instrument for internal communication within the Schmalkaldic League became the League Assemblies, which were convened at least once a year (regardless of Imperial Diet sessions), but usually twice a year, in one of the member towns.[26] From a practical perspective, the number of members of the Schmalkaldic League was not as important as its economic potential; i.e. the members' ability to finance the army. And it was from this very perspective that the Schmalkaldic League was particularly dangerous for the Habsburgs, as it not only brought together the wealthiest of the Imperial Estates, but constantly expanded the circle of its members: in 1539, Joachim II. Hector, Elector of Brandenburg (1535–1571) joined, followed in 1545 by the newly-succeeding Frederick II, Elector of Palatine (1544–1556). Thus, not only all three secular Electors, but also many wealthy princes and Imperial towns, became members of the Schmalkaldic League, making the economic potential of the Schmalkaldic League significantly greater than that of the "Habsburg-Catholic" part of the Empire. This led to the rapid formation of the foundations of a new federal-type state, formed independently of the traditions of the medieval Empire and the Emperor.

However, the Schmalkaldic League became not only the de facto second power centre within the Empire. It also acted as a legal entity that concluded alliance contracts with foreign allies, independently of the will of Emperor Charles V. In 1535, the Schmalkaldic League even concluded an alliance agreement with Francis I., King of France, and in 1538 with the

---

25 J. D. Tracy, Emperor Charles V, 211.
26 J. Reich, "Schmalkalden", 111–119.

Kingdom of Denmark, which had adopted the Reformation at that time.[27] Habsburg foreign policy may have managed to stifle the political significance of such agreements later, but at the end of the 1530s it was obvious that Charles V. did not really rule the Empire. His influence was limited to a relatively small area of direct rule by the Habsburgs and some of their allies. In 1538, most of these formed the so-called League of Nuremberg, which was to form a political counterweight to the Schmalkaldic League in the Empire.[28]

As a result of unequal representation in parliamentary curias, Imperial Diets were still dominated by the Habsburg side. Members of the Schmalkaldic League may have participated in Imperial Diet talks, but no political power existed that would force them to submit to Diet resolutions with which they did not agree. That is why, in matters relating to Schmalkaldic League members and their territory, they accepted the decisions of the League Assembly, independently of the will of Emperor Charles V. and the Imperial Diets. This approach reflected the basic principle that guided Lutheran opposition in relation to Imperial power, and which formed part of the basis for the establishment of the Schmalkaldic League: i.e. the right to a defence against erroneous Imperial power decisions.

Members of the Schmalkaldic League did not have any doubts about this right that they had; their passionate discussions were merely conducted about the extent to which such a defence could be active.[29] The basic standpoints of Lutheran theologians (starting with Martin Luther himself) differed in this respect; they maintained that all religious or legal disputes within the Empire must be resolved only in the form of discussions, and mutual persuasion using arguments. On the contrary, the princes, who after all were familiar with the practical side of the political environment, preferred active resistance, and preparation for a military conflict with the Emperor.[30]

At the end of the 1530s, the influence of the Schmalkaldic League was at its peak. This was also helped by the fact that the Habsburgs, under the pressure of an external threat from France and the Ottoman Empire, were

---

27 Rudolf Häpke, Die Regierung Karls V. und der europäische Norden (Lübeck 1914).
28 Martti Salomies, Die Pläne Kaiser Karls V. für eine Reichsreform mit Hilfe eines allgemeinen Bundes. (Helsinki 1953), 73–91.
29 T. A. Brady, "Phases and Strategies", 162–181.
30 T. A. Brady, German Histories, 221; J. Whaley, Germany and the Holy Roman Empire, 304–316.

willing to grant small concessions and pledges, relating mainly to religious issues and the normalization of relations between the Catholic Church and the Lutheran Reformation, which was to be resolved by the long-prepared general Church Council. So, on a political level, potential religious disputes were moved aside, and a temporary so-called Religious Peace of Nuremberg was concluded at the Imperial Diet in Nuremberg in 1541. This agreement guaranteed Lutherans (but not supporters of other reformatory directions) that they could not be legally persecuted in any way due to a different interpretation of the faith. This eliminated the possible legal consequences of the so-called Edict of Worms from 1521.

The reaching of this agreement was perceived by contemporary leading Lutheran opposition intellectuals as a partial victory, because it entailed the expectation that an agreement with the Catholic Church was still possible, and that imminent political conflicts could be resolved by discussions among intellectuals. This was also the opinion of Martin Luther († 1546) himself, who was highly respected among Lutheran princes. That is why the consent to the conclusion of the Religious Peace of Nuremberg was welcomed by part of the political representation of the Lutheran side as a helpful step by the Emperor, and it was willing to meet the Habsburg side halfway in the financing of military activities directed outside the Empire. Nevertheless, it was the very start of the forties that saw two military operations taking place within the Empire, during which the forces of the Schmalkaldic League and the Habsburgs did not clash directly, but which were still perceived as a form of measurement of actual power, and which showed who really ruled in the Empire.

On the outside, the victor in these two minor internal Imperial "wars" between 1541 and 1543 seemed to be the Schmalkaldic League, but in reality it was a "Pyrrhic victory". For the Habsburg side, these conflicts brought an important experience: a suitable "diplomatic preparation", leading to the collapse of the unity of the opposition camp, can be significantly more effective (and ultimately also cheaper) than military superiority in a direct conflict. This experience was later extensively used during the clash with the Imperial opposition in the Schmalkaldic War (1546–1547), as well as in the concurrently-running confrontation with the Estates opposition in the Kingdom of Bohemia.

What it was about:

The most important case in which the Schmalkaldic League assumed the executive powers of Imperial institutions to a certain extent was the dispute between Duke Henry V. Junior of Brunswick-Wolfenbüttel[31] with the neighbouring Imperial town of Goslar. The main subject of the dispute were the profitable silver mines. Duke Henry attacked the town of Goslar in 1540, and overran it with military force. The Imperial Diet condemned his actions as a breach of Imperial peace and imposed an Imperial anathema on him; however, Emperor Charles V., later decided to revoke it.

In this situation, the Empire as a whole was not able to enforce a legal procedure, as the Emperor had intervened in favour of his ally. This was due to the fact that Duke Henry V. was a founding member of the Catholic League of Nuremberg (1538)[32] and his Duchy of Brunswick-Wolfenbüttel belonged among the last important areas in north-west Germany where the ruling prince still formally maintained Catholicism as the main provincial religion.[33]

However, the town of Goslar was a member of the Schmalkaldic League, and asked the League for military protection.[34] This was provided to the town to the full extent. The town was freed in 1542, practically without a fight. Afterwards, the Schmalkaldic League also used military force to occupy the Duchy of Brunswick-Wolfenbüttel, and its ruler Henry V. Junior had to retire into exile in Bavaria, where his allies from the League of Nuremberg provided him with shelter but not with military assistance.

The pretexts for the occupation of the Duchy of Brunswick-Wolfenbüttel by the Schmalkaldic League army were the older disputes between Duke Henry V., and the town of Brunswick (Braunschweig) itself. Brunswick was an old Hanseatic town, and the economic centre of a wide area of northwest Germany; however, the town formally belonged to said Duchy. The citizens of Brunswick pledged allegiance to the Lutheran Reformation and, despite their Duke's opposition, reformed the town monasteries of St.

---

31 L. Ranke, Deutsche Geschichte, II, 266–280; Günther Kieslich, Das "Historische Volkslied" als publizistische Erscheinung (Untersuchungen zur Wesenbestimmung und Typologie der gereimten Publizistik zur Zeit des Regensburger Reichstages und des Krieges der Schmalkaldener gegen Herzog Heinrich den Jüngeren von Braunschweig 1540–1542), Studien zur Publizistik, Band 1 (Münster 1958), 53–58.

32 Walter Ziegler, "Braunschweig – Lüneburg, Hildesheim", in Die Territorien des Reichs, Bd. 3, edd. A. Schindling and W. Ziegler (Münster 1995), 25.

33 H. Schilling, Aufbruch und Krise, 227.

34 Gundmar Blume, Goslar und der Schmalkaldische Bund 1527/31–1547 (Goslar 1969).

Blaise and St. Cyriac (1538). The town of Brunswick itself became a member of the Schmalkaldic League, and one of the regular League Assemblies took place there in March 1538.

After 1542, the Schmalkaldic League obtained the majority support of both the urban and the rural population in the occupied Duchy of Brunswick-Wolfenbüttel (the Brunswick cathedral has been in the Lutheran Church's administration since 1543), but from a diplomatic perspective this issue remained unresolved. Henry V., Duke of Brunswick-Wolfenbüttel, understandably continued attempting to obtain diplomatic and military support so that he could regain the rule of his land, and for the Habsburg side this cause represented a suitable pretext for military intervention, which just had to be "timed" properly. [35]

This military intervention by the Schmalkaldic League was later actually used by Emperor Charles V. as a pretext for launching the Schmalkaldic War (1546) but in reality, from a military perspective, the Schmalkaldic League had assumed a defensive stance, and even the actual intervention in Goslar and in Brunswick was not aimed directly at the Habsburgs. However, it had an exceptionally strong diplomatic meaning, as it showed that the Schmalkaldic League was willing and able to provide it members with effective help in cases of need (unlike the Empire as a whole).

That is why, from the start of the 1540s, the Habsburg diplomacy began to expend a great effort aimed at disrupting the unity of the Lutheran opposition. The Emperor made suitable use of the options he had available in the given matter in his own dispute, which he conducted over the Dutch county of Geldern[36] with William of Cleves between 1541 and 1543. This was the second of the afore-mentioned "minor wars" within the Empire at the start of the 1540s.

Although neither the afore-mentioned Dutch county nor William of Cleves were members of the Schmalkaldic League, the stance that the

---

35 F. Brendle, "Um Erhalt und Ausbreitung", 79–84.

36 At the time, the county of Geldern was made up of four parts; the coastal area of Arhhem and its immediate neighbours, Nijmegen to the south and Zutphen to the south-west; the fourth part (Roermond, also known as the "Ower-kwartier"; i.e. the "outer quarter") was separated from the main core of the county by the territories of Cleves and Brabant. In this way, the county of Geldern as a whole significantly rounded off and connected the Habsburg territories in the Netherlands (it formed a "territorial bridge" between the counties of Overijssel, Utrecht and Brabant). See Gerben Graddesz Hellinga, Karel V – Bondgenoten en tegenstanders (Zutphen 2010), 44, 55.

League would take in relation to the given matter was important. This was a highly sensitive matter in terms of international diplomacy. Not only was William of Cleves' sister, Anna, the formal wife of English King Henry VIII. From January to July of 1540, but Duke Henry himself married Johanna, daughter of deceased French king Henry II. (i.e. the niece of ruling King Francis I.) in 1541.[37] In addition, Henry's other sister Sybil was the wife and mother of the children of John Frederick, Elector of Saxony, since 1526. Therefore, it was to be expected that the young Duke William of Cleves (who only began to rule in 1539 after the death of his father, John) would easily gain the support of not just the King of France, but also his brother-in-law John Frederick of Saxony, or alternatively the Schmalkaldic League, in his dispute with the Emperor.

In this situation, Emperor Charles V. utilized important personal information that his intelligence network had collected on the leading figures of the Schmalkaldic League. He made use of the fact that Landgrave Philip of Hesse, one of the main leaders of the Schmalkaldic League, had gotten married for the second time (in March 1540) to the young noblewoman Margarethe von der Saale.[38] This, however, took place while his first wife was alive, which meant that the contemporary view was that Philip of Hesse had committed bigamy. Not only had his first marriage not been annulled from the perspective of ecclesiastical law, but Philip's first wife Christina of Saxony (daughter of the leader of the Catholic side among Imperial princes, Duke George of Saxony † 1539) allegedly did not have any objections to her husband's second marriage. Landgrave Philip then went on to diligently produce descendants with both women; 1541 saw the birth of his two sons named Philip; each with a different wife.

At a time when neither the Emperor nor the Pope made any secret of their illegitimate children, born of different women, the strenuous demands of thirty-six-year-old Landgrave Philip to formalize his sexual relationship with a seventeen-year-old girl may have seemed anachronistic, but this devi-

---

37 Neelak Serawlook Tjernagel, Henry VIII and the Lutherans. A Study in Anglo-Lutheran Relations from 1521 to 1547 (Saint Louis 1965), 204–210.

38 William Walker Rockwell, Die Doppelehe Landgaf Philipps von Hessen (Marburg 1904); Walter Köhler, "Die Doppelehe Landgaf Philipps von Hessen", Historische Zeitschrift 94 (1905), 385–411; J. Whaley, Germany and the Holy Roman Empire, I, 313; F. Brendle, Dynastie, Reich und Reformation, 257–259.

ation from contemporary custom became a powerful weapon for his political opponents. In the end, the Landgrave's behaviour was even publicly criticized by the leading Church representatives in the Lutheran camp. Nobody would have been offended if he had fathered children with the girls in his court, as this was nothing unusual for the Habsburgs or for most of the Imperial princes, whether they were Catholics or Lutherans. But the conclusion of a prohibited second Church marriage was a crime for which, according to the recently adopted Imperial Criminal Code of 1532, he could be punished by death.

In order for Philip of Hesse to avoid the cut-throat court process, which the Emperor threatened him with for the afore-mentioned offence, he concluded an unusual secret agreement with Charles V.. The Landgrave promised the Emperor that he would support the Habsburgs' claims to the afore-mentioned Dutch county of Geldern; in addition, he undertook to prevent the entry of the Duchy of Cleves into the Schmalkaldic League (so that there would be no formal pretext for military assistance by the Schmalkaldic League if the Emperor attacked Williams of Cleves' territory). In return, the Emperor generously accepted Philip of Hesse's second marriage, and stopped the prosecution against him. All the same, this agreement between Philip of Hesse and the Emperor did not remain secret. Other members of the Schmalkaldic League perceived it as a betrayal of common interests, which subsequent developments confirmed.

Even when William of Cleves began his rule of the county of Geldern (as was contractually agreed in January 1538), Emperor Charles V. cast doubt on his hereditary claims from the title of ruler of the Empire. The Imperial Diet, held in 1541 is Regensburg, then confirmed the Emperor's claims to the county of Geldern. On the basis of this legal pretext, Emperor Charles V. utilized his economic resources outside the Empire, and attacked William of Cleves with the help of the Spanish army. The war over the county of Geldern only lasted a few weeks; William of Cleves did not receive help even from his closest relatives from the ranks of anti-Habsburg-oriented monarchs (i.e. Francis I., King of France, and John Frederick, Elector of Saxony), or from the Schmalkaldic League, of which he was not a member at the time. In September 1543 the Emperor forced him to accept an unfavourable peace treaty, under which he not only ceded the county of

Geldern to the Emperor, but also had to promise to change the religious policy in his own county, Jülich-Cleves, to which he was to reintroduce the "old faith", i.e. the Catholic religion.[39] The forced shift of William of Cleves to the Habsburg side significantly weakened the authority of the Schmalkaldic League, as it showed that even the supreme League leadership was not unified in a common interest, and that in urgent cases it could prioritize personal interest, as "demonstrated" by Landgrave Philip.

As a result of the loss of confidence, Landgrave Philip of Hesse was temporarily relieved of his function of one of the commanders of the League army, and the cohesiveness of the Schmalkaldic League was disrupted, manifesting itself in a fundamental way at the time of the military campaign in the Danube region in 1546. Also, League members could not come to an agreement on further action regarding the militarily-occupied Duchy of Brunswick-Wolfenbüttel, which was under the administration of the Schmalkaldic League from 1542 to 1547. Duke Henry strove intensively to regain the lost land, and in 1545 he tried military intervention. However, he was overpowered, captured and put in prison. So, to defend Brunswick-Wolfenbüttel, the Schmalkaldic League had to maintain a permanent and sufficiently powerful military garrison, which was very expensive and a burden on the League's budget.[40] These costs could not even be covered by the economic revenue of the Duchy itself, or by the profits from production of the local silver mines. But the newly-introduced mintage of Schmalkaldic League coins, issued for Brunswick-Wolfenbüttel, had a great symbolic significance. These were mintages that bore the portrait and titulature of John Frederick of Saxony on one side, and Philip of Hesse on the other. Unlike his own concurrently-minted Saxony coins, John Frederick of Saxony did not use the title of Elector on the "League" mintages.

Although later, in the 1640s, Philip of Hesse once again acted as the Habsburgs' main opponent, the Habsburg diplomacy used his example to verify that influencing individual important representatives of the seemingly unified Lutheran camp could significantly weaken the opposition

---

39 Heribert Smolinsky, "Jülich – Kleve – Berg", in in Die Territorien des Reichs, Bd. 3, edd. A. Schindling and W. Ziegler (Münster 1995), 86–106; H. Schilling, Aufbruch und Krise, 227–228.
40 Hans-Achim Schmidt, "Landsknechtwesen und Kriegsführung in Niedersachsen 1533–1545", Niedersächsisches Jahrbuch – Neue Folge der "Zeitschrift des Historischen Vereins für Niedersachsen" 6 (1929), 167–223.

camp, whether by threats (as in the case of Landgrave Philip), enticing promises, or directly by way of well-paid contracts in the Imperial service, i.e. primarily in military service. After all, the Habsburgs desperately needed experienced military commanders, regardless of their confessional orientation. This, however, worked both ways: as long as the Habsburgs paid well, even Lutherans were willing to serve in their army. This not only meant ordinary mercenaries (their religious orientation was of no interest to anyone) but even officers and the commanding corps.

A critical situation occurred at the start of the forties, mainly at the south-eastern border of the Empire, where Ferdinand I. found it difficult to face down Turkish pressure. The siege of Vienna by Turkish troops in 1529 may have been repelled, but other military campaigns by the Ottoman Empire gradually seized Habsburg territories in Hungary. Ferdinand I. suffered a great military defeat in 1541, when he lost a significant portion of Hungarian lands, including his residence in Buda. Turkish troops also used repeated forays to penetrate the southern regions of Styria and Carniola, and threatened to invade the Danube. During this crisis situation, King Ferdinand I. requested the common financing of an Imperial army at the Imperial Diet, which was to be sent (at the Schmalkaldic League members' expense) to the south-west of the Empire to protect Christians against the Turkish danger.

Opposition Estates responded to the request by Ferdinand I. very obligingly: they approved the collection of a relatively high common tax for financing the army, and they managed to collect most of this money.[41] They even concluded a relatively complicated agreement with Ferdinand I. on operational exchange rates between the specific coins of individual local currencies, which the soldiers, sent to the hereditary Austrian lands in 1542, were to use to pay for their needs.[42] The Imperial army campaign, dispatched to defend the south-eastern border of the Empire and into Hungary, did actually take place in 1542; it was even led by an important member of the

---

41 Wolfgang Steglich, "Die Reichstürkenhilfe in der Zeit Karls V.", Militärgeschichtliche Mitteilungen 11 (1972), 7–55; Peter Schmidt, "Reichssteuern, Reichsfinanzen und Reichsgewalt in der ersten Hälfte des 16. Jahrhunderts." In Säkulare Aspekte der Reformationszeit, ed. Hanz Angermeier and Reinhard Seyboth (München, 1983), 153–198.

42 Petr Vorel, "Směnné kursy jako nástroj mocenské politiky v Římsko-německé říši počátkem čtyřicátých let 16. století, Český časopis historický 112 (2014), 379 – 401.

Schmalkaldic League, Joachim II. Hector, Elector of Brandenburg.[43] Despite all the complex and costly preparations, this Imperial army only fulfilled its task to a limited extent, and did not significantly influence the battle with the Ottoman Empire. Or, more precisely: it was withdrawn by the Habsburgs from the battlefield before its strength could be utilized against the Turks.

This was because Emperor Charles V. needed the Imperial army elsewhere, for the war against France, which had started again after a lengthy peace, directly on the Burgundy front. This battlefield, on the wealthy Imperial-French border, was much more attractive for the military commanders than the plundered Hungarian-Turkish border, and the expected penetration into the French interior promised an easy haul. Under the impression of the helpfulness of Charles V. in religious issues (repeatedly declared at the Imperial Diet in Speyer in 1542), the Schmalkaldic League even agreed to participate in the campaign by Emperor Charles V. against France.[44]

This sudden turnaround on the issue of the possible co-operation between the Imperial opposition and the Imperial camp in the defence against France was associated with a distinctive application of the element of national identity which accompanied the expansion of the Lutheran Reformation. It offered a possible path towards the formation of a powerful Empire as a nationally and confessionally homogenous state (i.e. German and Lutheran).[45] At the Imperial Diet in Speyer, the King of France was declared to be "the public enemy of all Christianity, and the German nation in particular" and the Imperial Estates approved the common financing of an army of 24,000 infantry and 4,000 cavalry for a period of six months.[46]

Only large southern German Imperial towns protested against the participation of Schmalkaldic League members in this war; they were aware of

---

43   Christian Meyer, "Die Feldhauptmannschaft Joachims II. im Türkenkriege von 1542", Zeitschrift für Preußische Geschichte und Landeskunde 16 (1879), 480–538; Hermann Traut, Kurfürst Joachim II. von Brandenburg und der Türkenfeldzug vom Jahre 1542 (Gummersbach 1892).

44   Heinrich Lutz, "Kaiser Karl V., Frankreich und das Reich", in Frankreich und das Reich im 16. und 17. Jahrhundert, edd. Heinrich Lutz, Friedrich Hermann Schubert and Hermann Weber (Göttingen 1968), 7–19; F. Brendle,. Dynastie, Reich und Reformation, 329–333.

45   C. Scott Dixon, "Martin Luther and the German Nation, The Reformation and the Roots of Nationalism", in Confession and Nation in the Era of Reformations (Central Europe in comparative Perspective), edd. Eva Doležalová and Jaroslav Pánek (Prague 2011), 123–138.

46   Albrecht P. Luttenberger, "Karl V., Frankreich und der deutsche Reichstag", in Das römisch-deutsche Reich im politischen System Karls V., Schriften des Historischen Kollegs – Kolloquien 1, ed. Heinrich (München – Wien 1982), 189–221.

the danger which could result in the event of a victory by Charles V. in France – the victorious Habsburg could then even utilize French resources against the Schmalkaldic League. However, the leaders of the Estates opposition did not take this warning into consideration, and they approved the financial contribution and the participation in the Imperial army's campaign in France for the Emperor.

This approach had its own practical logic: of all the money collected, it was mainly the military commanders who acquired the biggest portion, and in the case of the Imperial army, from a religious perspective, they belonged exclusively to the Lutheran camp. Of the main commanders, it was the generously paid Margrave Albert Alcibiades of Brandenburg (the main cavalry commander), Moritz of Saxony, Konrad von Bemelberg and William of Fürstenberg; however, the Lutherans also formed most of the lower commanding corps.

Thus, the war on the Imperial-French border between 1542 and 1544 became, in its own way, a "prelude" to the clash between Emperor Charles V. and the Schmalkaldic unity, if in a slightly different sense. The same armies that would clash several years later in Germany set off against France together. The main commander of the "German" part of the army of Charles V. in France was the Lutheran general William of Fürstenberg; the "Romance" (Spanish-Italian) army was commanded by Fernando Gonzaga, Marquis de Gustalla, Charles' governor in Milan.[47]

The Imperial-French war between 1542 and 1544 was one of the phases of the long-time conflict between Charles V. of Habsburg and Francis I., King of France, but their preceding clashes took place mainly in the area of north-west Italy, where both rulers fought for power influence. Although the transfer of the epicentre of this conflict to the western border of the Empire might have been perceived by Lutheran Estates as a greater danger, the military forces of the Habsburgs were bound by this war to such an extent that the Emperor could not even contemplate intervening against internal opposition in the Empire.

So, as long as the Emperor waged wars in foreign lands, the Lutheran opposition could feel relatively safe in the Empire. This isn't some discovery

---

47 Johannes Volker Wagner, Graf Wilhelm von Fürstenberg 1491–1549 und die politisch-geistigen Mächte seiner Zeit, Pariser historische Studien IV (Stuttgart 1966), 244–245.

of modern historiography; this argument already regularly appeared in contemporary journalism in the 1630s. For the Schmalkaldic League, even the fact that the Imperial army in France was commanded by supporters of the Reformation represented a "safeguard" in its own way. The Emperor could not even technically use this army against the Lutheran opposition in the Empire – he did not have a sufficiently reliable commanding corps available for campaigns by the Imperial "German" army in Germany.

However, this situation changed significantly after the capitulation of Francis I., accompanied by the conclusion of peace treaties in Crépy in September 1544. Although Francis I. lost the war with the Empire, the peace conditions were not as devastating and humiliating for him as two decades earlier, after the lost Battle of Pavia (1525). On the contrary – the Crépy peace treaty declared future friendly relations between both rulers, which were even to be confirmed by a dynastic marriage. The rulers agreed on compensation for mutual territorial claims (Francis I. renounced his claims to Naples; Charles V. renounced his claims to Burgundy) and even the spheres of influence in northern Italy were defined: Francis I. was to rule in Piedmont and Charles V. in Milan.

In all probability, neither of the signatories expected that the Crépy peace treaty would be a permanent solution to long-term hostility, but for Charles V. it at least meant a temporary "free hand", as the King of France simultaneously undertook not to interfere in internal Imperial affairs. So, in the language of contemporary diplomacy, he promised not to help the Schmalkaldic League in the event of a conflict with the Emperor, and that his alliance contract with the Schmalkaldic League from 1538 was now invalid. At the time, the alliance contract with the Schmalkaldic League was also weakened by Christian VII., King of Denmark, when he concluded a non-aggression pact with Emperor Charles V.. So, as early as 1544, the Schmalkaldic League lost both of its main foreign allies, i.e. France and Denmark.

The diplomatic preparation of the Habsburg camp also continued during the following year, when the Emperor managed to achieve significant success in his talks with Pope Paul III.. (actual name Alexander Farnese).[48] In his case, the Habsburgs used the centuries-proven approach of family

---

48 Wilhelm Maurenbrecher, Karl V. und die deutschdn Protestanten 1545–1555 nebst einem Anhang von Aktenstücken aus dem spanischen Staatsarchiv von Simancas (Frankfurt a. M. 1865), 58–68.

alliances. In 1538, a "diplomatic marriage" was arranged between Margaret, illegitimate daughter of Emperor Charles V., then sixteen years old (already a widow of Gonzaga, Duke of Florence, for a year)[49] and Octavian Farnese, grandson of Pope Paul III.. Octavian's father, Peter Ludwig Farnese (1503–1547) was born at the time when his father was still "only" a cardinal; despite his illegitimate origins, he used his father's family name of Farnese. The marriage of Octavian Farnese to Margaret of Austria (later named Margaret of Parma) was for several years merely formal; the Emperor and the Pope only lived to see their joint descendant, Alexander, in 1545. On this occasion, Emperor Charles V. had a part of the territory located to the south of the river Po separated from the Duchy of Milan, and he established a new Duchy of Parma here, with its main headquarters in the town of Parma. Emperor Charles V. then bestowed this new Duchy as a fiefdom to Peter Ludwig Farnese, son of Pope Paul III. and father-in-law of his illegitimate daughter Margaret.[50]

Thanks to this unusual helpfulness on the Emperor's part (whose background understandably also included the Emperor's interest in socially adequate security for his eldest – albeit illegitimate – daughter) the Emperor's older disputes with the Papal power centre seemed to be dispelled in the long term, and Pope Paul III. began to act as a clear advocate of Imperial interests. This was also reflected in the Pope's long-awaited consent to the establishment of a Church Council, which was to resolve the drawn-out problem with the Lutheran Reformation in the form of talks.

Both the Emperor and the Pope accommodated the Lutheran opposition's requirement that the Church Council be held on Imperial Territory. That is why the first phase of the municipal Church Council began in 1545 in Trent. This town may have been located in the territory of the Catholic bishopric in the Italian part of the main Alpine pass, but it was clearly still

---

49   Hermann Weber, Zur Heiratspolitik Karls V., in Das römisch-deutsche Reich im politischen System Karls V., Schriften des Historischen Kollegs – Kolloquien 1, ed. Heinrich Lutz (München – Wien 1982), 136–143; Elena Bonora, Aspettando l´imperatore – Principi italiani tra il papa e Carlo V. (Torino 2014), 148–174..

50   Ludvig von Pastor,. Geschichte Papst Pauls III. (1534–1549). Geschichte der Päpste seit dem Ausgang des Mittelalters, Bd. V. (13th ed. Freiburg, 1956), 525–528; Anna Parma, "La Corte Lontana – Poteri e strategie nel Marchesato Farnesiano di Novara", in "Familiglia" del Principe a famiglia aristocratica, ed. Cesare Mozzarelli (Roma 1988), 487–505.

inside the Empire's borders at the time. Seemingly peripheral (but very important for the Habsburgs) was the "act of kindness" performed by Pope Paul III. in the same year, 1545, when he annulled the marriage (concluded in 1541) between Duke Henry of Cleves and French princess Jana, niece of King Francis I.. The purpose behind this act was soon revealed.

All that was left to do was to free the military potential, bound in the long term to the front line with the Ottoman Empire. This was achieved in October 1545, when Charles V. concluded a temporary ceasefire with the Sultan, for a period of 18 months. This agreement was mutually advantageous; the Sultan also needed his soldiers elsewhere, so that he could use them in the war against Persia, and to quash internal disputes within his Empire.

The diplomatic preparation was successfully completed; only weapons could talk now.

CHAPTER 2

THE SCHMALKALDIC WAR IN THE EMPIRE
(1546–1547)

At the same that the Church Council was officially established, whose main aim (as the Emperor declared) was to be an agreement on the relationship between the Catholic Church and the Lutheran Reformation, the Emperor launched an attack against the opposition in the Empire. From a diplomatic perspective, his steps were well thought out and planned. He could not risk a direct frontal military clash with the Schmalkaldic League in 1545, as he was faced with an opponent who (despite all internal antagonisms) unified the interest in defending the Lutheran faith. That's why Charles V. had to outwardly declare that his intervention against the opposition in the Empire was not of a religious nature, and that it merely involved the securing of internal order in the Empire.[1]

In mid-October 1545, Emperor Charles V. set off from his main residence in Brussels in the direction of Regensburg, where in May of the following year (1546) the Imperial Diet was announced. The Imperial Court spent Christmas in the Brabant town of Herzogenbusch; for New Year celebrations it moved to nearby Utrecht, where at the start of January 1546 the Emperor organized the ceremonial admission of new members to the Order of the Golden Fleece. The expansion of the Order to include new members was last performed 15 years ago and, just like in 1531, this expansion again had extraordinary power-political meaning in 1546. For a historian, it's no surprise that the newly admitted Order members included Spanish and Italian commanders who went on to distinguish themselves in the Imperial army during the Schmalkaldic War. The Pope's grandson, Octavian Farnesse, who had married the Emperor's illegitimate daughter the previous year, also attended. Somewhat surprisingly, William of Cleves, former

---

1   F. Hartung, Karl V. und die deutschen Reichsstände, 25–44; J. Whaley, Germany and the Holy Roman Empire, 317–324.

enemy of the Habsburgs in the battle for the county of Geldern at the start of the forties, as well as the young Duke Albert of Bavaria, appeared among the new members of the Order of the Golden Fleece. Both surely already knew back then in Utrecht that wives had been picked out for them from among the Habsburg princesses. However, entry into the Order of the Golden Fleece meant a significant symbolic undertaking of loyalty to Catholic matters for them, and a loyal environment at the opposite sides of the nation was what Emperor Charles V. needed the most in the forthcoming battle with the opposition.

After the end of the Order celebration in Dutch Utrecht, the Emperor and his Court continued across Luxembourg and Lorraine to the Upper Palatine and to Speyer, where the first important political talks of 1546 were held. At that time, however, nothing yet indicated that a dangerous war would flare up in the land. Recruiters working for individual military entrepreneurs may have been hiring mercenaries wherever they could, but that was nothing unusual. There was always a war being waged somewhere, and the preparation of the Imperial army was concealed by the constant and current threat of danger from the Ottoman Empire.

When the Emperor stopped in Speyer in March 1546, on the way to the Regensburg Imperial Diet, both the Emperor's allies and his adversaries gathered – including Landgrave Philip of Hesse. The Emperor negotiated on all sides. He mainly tried to cause a rift in the opposition, which until then had been united, and to acquire some important figures, undoubtedly belonging to the Lutheran camp, for his side. This time, Landgrave Philip of Hesse refused to be convinced or bought, so the Emperor was forced to search for a new ally among the Lutheran princes.

Preliminary talks, which brought about a surprising turnaround in the distribution of political power, took place in utmost secrecy. This already showed during the Imperial Diet which was officially commenced on the 5th of June 1546 in Regensburg.[2] An important part of the Diet talks was the conclusion of the "Treaty of Regensburg" on the 19th of June 1546, in which most of the participating princes (including Lutheran princes and some

---

2   RTA 1546, 391–395; Franz Lau and Ernst Bizer, A History of the Reformation in Germany to 1555 (London, 1969), 194–200.

former open supporters of the Schmalkaldic League) bound themselves to neutrality in the event of a military clash between the Habsburgs and the Schmalkaldic League. For example, this group included Duke William of Bavaria (father of the afore-mentioned Albert) and Duke Moritz of Saxony.

Although the conclusion of the June agreement on neutrality appeared to be a part of the diplomatic measures associated with the sitting of the Imperial Diet, the signatories of this agreement in fact stood on the side of the Habsburgs in the subsequent conflict. The June agreement did not provide any information on what had been promised to whom, but this quickly became apparent.

Even while the Imperial Diet was in progress, two diplomatic marriages took place in Regensburg, by which the Habsburgs publicly manifested important alliances in the forthcoming clash with the opposition. Biological or marriage-created non-blood relationships did not necessarily mean a political alliance by themselves (this can be documented using a number of cases of next of kin who stood on opposite sides of contemporary conflicts), but the planning and realization of both marriages at such a tense time carried extraordinary weight.

At the very end of the Regensburg Diet, King Ferdinand I. married off both his so-far unmarried daughters, who by then had reached marriageable age; eighteen-year-old Anna and fifteen-year-old Maria. The marriages took place within two weeks of each other (the 4th of August and the 18th of August 1546) according to the brides' ages (the eldest one first). Thus, they must have been planned several months in advance; the time and venue (directly at the Imperial Diet) had important symbolism, as such marriages usually took place in rulers' residences, not in Imperial towns (where neither side had "their own" technical facilities at their disposal).

The grooms, however, were even more significant.

Eighteen-year-old Anna of Habsburg was married to Albert, who was the same age – the eldest son of Duke William Wittelsbach of Bavaria (1493–1550). At the time, Duke Williams was the only ruler of Bavaria (with a residence in Munich) as, after the death of his younger brother Ludwig X. Wittelsbach (1495–1545) he also acquired his brother's part of the previously-divided land (with a residence in Landshut). The third of the brothers, Ernest Wittelsbach (1500–1560), was the administrator of two wealthy and territorially extensive southern German bishoprics (Passau and Salzburg). The Bavarian Wittelsbachs may have traditionally belonged to advocates of the Catholic tradition, but they had unresolved "old scores" with the Habsburgs and territorial claims from the first third of the 16th century.[3] Duke William himself was Ferdinand of Habsburg's rival candidate during the election of the new King of Bohemia in 1526.[4] In this situation, the distrustful Emperor chose his proven strategy and used his niece Anna to ensure the Bavarian allies' loyalty, who in any case belonged among the blood-related next of kin of the Imperial princes at the time (William's mother was Cunicunda of Habsburg, daughter of Emperor Frederick III).

This step proved successful; even before the wedding (but when everything had already been arranged), Duke William of Bavaria formally declared neutrality and prevented the southern army of the Schmalkaldic League (which remained deployed at the Bavarian border in the town of Füssen) to proceed further into Bavarian territory. Thus, the Emperor could feel safe in Bavaria although, until mid-August, his own army was numerically quite insignificant.

The second of the Habsburg princesses, fifteen-year-old Maria, was married off at the Regensburg Diet to Duke William of Cleves, who was thirty at the time. Duke William already had certain experience with political marriages, as he himself had formerly been married to Jana, daughter of Henry II., King of France. This, however, took place in 1541, when this marriage was to strengthen his link to the Habsburg opponents' camp. After the military defeat and forced peace treaty with the Emperor in 1543, by which William cut himself off from his previous allies, this marriage (albeit with a girl from the royal family) was no longer comfortable. The political importance of wealthy and influential Duke Henry, whose territory on the French-Imperial border (Duchy of Jülich-Cleves) had a strategic location, was so extraordinary at the time that the Habsburgs offered him a

---

3   Alfred Kohler, Antihabsburgische Politik in der Epoche Karls V. - Die Reichsständische Opposition gegen die Wahl Ferdinands I. zum Römischer König und gegen die Anerkennung seines Königstums (1524–1534), Schriftenreihe des Historischen Komission bei der Bayerische Akademie der Wisssenschaften, Schrift 19 (Göttingen 1982), 22 – 39; Handbuch der bayerischen Geschichte, I. Band, ed. Andreas Kraus (München 1988), 352–360, Kap. IV. § 49 "Bayern im Kreise der reichsfürstlichen Opposition gegen Habsburg (1525–1534)".

4   Vorel, Velké dějiny, VII., 26–29.

different wife of their own royal blood. The previous "uncomfortable" marriage to the French princess was annulled in 1545 thanks to the helpfulness of Pope Paul III., and the sword-enforced alliance between the Habsburgs and William of Cleves in 1543 could now also be confirmed with wedding vows. This marriage was especially important for the Habsburgs in the tense political situation in August 1546, as until then the loyalty of William of Cleves had been very uncertain.

The main "gain" by the Habsburg side was the most important ally in the Schmalkaldic War, Duke Moritz of Saxony (1521–1553).[5] At the Imperial Diet in Regensburg, he was entrusted with imposing the Imperial anathema on the leaders of the Schmalkaldic League together with King Ferdinand of Habsburg. There was absolutely no doubt as to the affiliation of Moritz of Saxony to the Lutheran side; his "involvement" in sanctions against the leading representatives of the Schmalkaldic League was to be proof that the forthcoming military campaign was not of a religious nature or background, and that its aim was not the disruption of former confessional agreements, but "merely" the securing of Imperial peace, which John Frederick of Saxony and Philip of Hesse had disrupted by the military occupation of the Duchy of Brunswick-Wolfenbüttel.

For Duke Moritz of Saxony, serving the Habsburgs was nothing new. He himself was a military commander who had proved himself in Imperial service between 1542 and 1544 in the wars with the Ottoman Empire and on the French battlefield. He also commanded Imperial troops during the short war with William of Cleves over the Dutch county of Geldern, and thus he was directly instrumental in the forced shift of this Duke to the Habsburg side in 1543. However, the year 1546 was about something different than just the well-paid activities of a Lutheran commander in the Imperial service:

In the first half of the 16th century, the Saxon Wettins represented the main family line among German princes, connected with the propagation of the Lutheran Reformation, mainly by the merit of the main, so-called "Ernestine", branch after Ernest, Elector of Saxony, † 1486), which was the

---

5   Johannes Herrman, Moritz von Sachsen (1521–1553) - Landes-, Reichs- und Friedenfürst (Beucha 2003); Petr Vorel, "Sňatkový projekt Pernštejnů se saskými Wettiny z roku 1529", Východočeský sborník historický 24 (2013), 81–98.

bearer of the Electoral title and which also included Luther's main protector, Elector Frederick III. († 1525). The second line of Saxon Wettins, the
so-called "Albertine" line (the descendants of Duke Albert † 1500, younger
brother of the afore-mentioned Elector Ernest) was still wealthy at the end
of the 15ᵗʰ century from the perspective of property tenures, but it had a
claim to the Electoral title only in the event that the older "Ernestine" family branch died by the sword. At the start of the Reformation, the main representative of the "Albertine" Saxon Wettin branch was Duke George, who
(unlike his cousin, Elector Frederick III.) was a fanatical advocate of the
"old faith" and tried everything possible to prevent the propagation of the
Lutheran Reformation. The Reformation also brought about a rift in the
Saxon Duke family, as Duke George (as the head of the "Albertine" family
branch) also tried to influence the religious development of the family of
his younger brother Henry, who leaned towards Lutheranism. Thus, Henry's eldest son Moritz had quite a complicated childhood, as he was separated from his Lutheran parents on his uncle's orders and sent for proper
Catholic re-education to the Court of the Archbishop of Mainz.

This plan by Catholic uncle George failed; young Moritz kept his
father's faith,[6] but he did not get on with his own parents very well. When
uncle George later died (1539), the "confessional guardianship" became
vacant, and the barely adult Moritz began to look for a bride himself, in
the family of Lutheran leader Landgrave Philip of Hesse. Despite the dis-
approval of his parents he married Philip's daughter, Agnes of Hesse, in
1541, and he entered high politics at twenty years of age. He had inherited
a large amount of property. Moritz's cousins John († 1537) and Frederick (†
1539), as well as his uncle George († 1539) died within a short time of one
another without male descendants. Thus, the main ruler of the Albertine
line of Wettins became Moritz's father Henry but he, too, died in 1541.
The monarchal rights were transferred to Moritz, as the eldest living member of this family branch, when he was twenty years of age – not only in
Saxony,[7] but also in Silesia, where this branch of the Wettins ruled in the
princedom of Żagań (Sagan).[8]

---

6   H. Bornkamm, Das Jahrhundert der Reformation, 225–241.
7   Georg Voigt, Moritz von Sachsen 1541–1547 (Leipzig 1876), 7–15.
8   Vorel, Velké dějiny, VII., 605.

A firm Lutheran conviction that survived his Catholic education in the Passau bishopric school, as well as his close relationship with both main Schmalkaldic League leaders (John Frederick, Elector of Saxony, was Moritz's second cousin; Landgrave Philip of Hesse was his father-in-law) indicated that Moritz would remain a firm part of the Schmalkaldic League. After all, this logical prerequisite was also to have been proclaimed by the proposed ceremonial Schmalkaldic League banner, which survived from 1542.[9] It contained the symbols of all contemporary members, i.e. the coats of arms of the princely and count families, and the emblems of member Imperial and Hanseatic towns. Understandably, the dominant positions on the proposed banner were taken up by the League leaders' coats of arms, i.e. John Frederick of Saxony, and Landgrave Philip of Hesse. But the Saxon Wettins' other coat of arms is located immediately in third place, with the inscription "alle Fürsten zu Sachsen" (i.e. "all the Saxon princes"). This had significant symbolism, as in the previous years (until 1539) the Catholic camp also received significant support in the form of Duke George.

Against all expectations, however, Moritz of Saxony himself did not become a member of the Schmalkaldic League in the end. Apparently the main causes were his personal disagreements with John Frederick, Elector of Saxony, which in 1542 (during the Easter holidays) almost escalated into a military clash between these two Saxon princes. Given the extent of the landed property by which Elector John Frederick ruled for years on the one hand, and which Duke Moritz inherited in 1541 on the other, it was a truly insignificant matter: even after the separation of both branches of the Saxon Wettins (which occurred in 1485), the Wurzen monastery remained their joint property. Both branches of the Saxon Dukes shared its administration and revenue (or, rather, their clerical apparatus looked after such matters) even after the secularization of these Church goods. However, the manner in which the Imperial tax for the financing of the anti-Turkish campaign of 1542 was to be levied on this property was not clear. For this reason, Elector John Frederick sent a group of eighty five city militants from his town of Turgau to the dominion of Wurzen to collect the money. Duke Moritz did not appreciate this unilateral intervention, and decided to defend himself

9   H. Schilling, "Aufbruch und Krise", 213, the Picture "Entwur der Schmalkaldischen Bundesfahne, 1542".

with military force. The imminent war between the two princes was only prevented by the mediation of Landgrave Philip of Hesse and Martin Luther; however, after this experience with his second cousin John Frederick, Duke Moritz cancelled the already-advanced talks on his accession to the Schmalkaldic League.[10]

The Habsburg diplomacy was able to make good use of the information, and it was even familiar with the subtle nuances of personal grudges and passions that ruled among the individual members of contemporary ruling families, which were more or less biologically related to one another (after all, Moritz's great-grandmother Margaret of Habsburg was the sister of Emperor Frederick III.). Despite consensus on faith, young Moritz genuinely hated his second cousin Elector John Frederick; neither was he very friendly with his father-in-law Philip of Hesse (whose bigamous lifestyle had brought shame to the family). The twenty-five-year-old youth, who insisted on a wife of his own choosing despite his parents' protests, and whom the imaginary Fortuna still favoured, had high ambitions.

We do not know whether Moritz of Saxony set his "price" himself, or whether someone in the Imperial Court came up with the unusual solution (the Lutheran opposition attributed all "bad" ideas to the Emperor's main advisor, the Spanish Grand Granvelle), but the offer with which Charles V. apparently came up shortly before the Regensburg Diet "could not be refused". The Emperor's offer to the young Duke meant that, if John Frederick of Saxony was defeated, he would be stripped of the title of Elector and the new Elector of Saxony would become Duke Moritz, who would also acquire his defeated second cousin's property.

Thus strongly motivated, Moritz of Saxony agreed to the decision of the Imperial Diet in Regensburg on the 20th of July 1546, by which he and King Ferdinand I. of Habsburg were entrusted with imposing the Imperial anathema on both leaders of the Schmalkaldic League.[11] At the same time, the Emperor announced the mobilization of the Imperial army at the Impe-

---

10 Carl August Hugo Burkhardt, "Die Wurzerner Fehde", Archiv für die Sächsische Geschichte 4 (1865), 57–81; G. Voigt, Moritz von Sachsen, 22–25.

11 Matthias Weber, "Zur Bedeutung der Reichsacht in der Frühen Neuzeit," in Neue Studien zur frühneuzeitlichen Reichsgeschichte, Zeitschrift für historische Forschung (Vierteljahreschrift zur Erforschung des Spätmittelalters und der frühen Neuzeit, Beiheft 19, ed. Johannes Kunisch (Berlin 1997), 55–90.

rial Diet, which was to be dispatched and financed by all Imperial Estates (including Schmalkaldic League members) for the purpose of ensuring "Imperial peace" - i.e. to overpower John Frederick of Saxony and Landgrave Philip of Hesse.

However, Emperor Charles V. must have already had a military solution prepared at the time, independent of the Imperial Diet talks. The purpose of the parliamentary talks and resolution was merely to create a legal pretext that would be at least formal, and that would justify the military intervention within the Empire. Charles V. must have assumed that the pan-Imperial army whose mobilization he had ordered would not convene (but that it would at least be possible, after the anticipated victory, to punish the princes and towns which had not obeyed the mobilization notice). He must have known that the forces of Moritz of Saxony, although he was an experienced military commander, were not sufficient to defeat Elector John Frederick. And surely he was also familiar with the military abilities of his younger brother Ferdinand I. of Habsburg, who had not managed to defend the Hungarian border against Ottoman expansion, even with the help of all the countries he ruled. The important formal positions to which the Imperial Diet had appointed prince Moritz of Saxony and King Ferdinand of Habsburg were merely a diplomatic guise for using a truly effective force that could reverse the power relationships within the Empire.

However, this force had to come from the outside, and it had to originate from sources outside the Empire. By 1546, the Empire itself was mostly Lutheran, any everybody who was even slightly informed about contemporary politics could see what the true objective of the Emperor's efforts was. Nevertheless, until a direct military clash occurred between the Emperor and the Schmalkaldic League, there was still room for a diplomatic solution.[12] An exceptional source that documents this anticipation about whether there would be a forceful or diplomatic solution is the personal record of Augsburg banker Jakob Fugger from the 12th of June 1546, in which Fugger noted the content of his conversations on this topic with two bishops (of Augsburg and Passau) and with the well-informed Imperial diplomat Angelot.[13]

---

12 M. Salomies, Die Pläne Kaiser Karls V., 92–95.

13 Hermann Joseph Kirsch, Die Fugger und der Schmalkaldische Krieg (München – Leipzig 1915), 216–218, Beilage 11, "Aufzeichnungen Hans Jakob Fuggers".

We do not know the precise reasons why Charles V. finally decided to risk a forceful military solution. This fundamental change in long-term Habsburg policy (which in previous decades was of a rather consensual nature)[14] is generally associated with the death of Martin Luther himself († the 18th of February 1546), whose diplomatic mediator's role on the internal Imperial political scene had been noticeably stabilizing.[15] The main architects of the outbreak of the Schmalkaldic War are considered to be the Emperor's Spanish advisers (especially his secretary, Granvelle) as well as the Papal diplomacy.[16]

This reasoning has a certain logic, as the deciding forces that were to rearrange the situation in the Holy Roman Empire of the German Nation, and eliminate the power duality caused by the existence of the Schmalkaldic League,[17] were the "internal" forces. Outside the Empire, Emperor Charles V. understandably had significant economic and human resources at his disposal in Spain, Naples and Milan,[18] as well as rich profits generated at the time by overseas colonies.[19] That is why the Emperor's Spanish, Neapolitan and Milanese military divisions, withdrawing into Imperial territory from surrounding countries, became the main military forces. Key for him at that time was his alliance (albeit temporary) with Pope Paul III. and certain northern Italian princes. They were all able to supply both money and military units. At the start of 1546, Pope Paul III. promised to provide

---

14 Oswald Artur Hecker, Karls V. Plan zur Gründung eines Reichsbundes - Ursprung und erste Versuche bis zum Ausgange des Ulmer Tages (1547). Leipziger historische Abhandlungen, Heft 1 (Leipzig, 1906), 73–100; F. Hartung, Karl V. und die deutschen Reichsstände, 9–25; Albrecht P. Luttenberger, Glaubenseinheit und Reichsfriede, Konzeptionen und Wege konfesionsneutraler Reichspolitik 1530–1552 - Kurpfalz, Jülich, Kurbrandenburg, (Göttingen 1982); Winfried Schulze, "Der deutsche Reichstag des 16. Jh. zwischen traditioneller Konsensbildung und Paritätisierung der Reichspolitik", in Im Spannungsfeld von Recht und Ritual (Köln 1997), 447–464. J. Whaley, Germany and the Holy Roman Empire, 317–320.

15 Martin Brecht, "Martin Luther und Karl V.", in Aspectos históricos y culturales bajo Carlos V - Aspekte der Geschichte und Kultur unter Karl V., Studia Hispanica 9, ed. Christoph Strosetzki (Madrid 2000), 78–96.

16 E. Bonora, Aspettando l'imperatore, 175–178.

17 J. D. Tracy, Emperor Charles V, 211; here the Map "Schmalkaldic League in 1546".

18 Hermann Kellenbenz, Die Römisch-Deutsche Reich im Rahmen der wirtschafts- und finanzpolitischen Erwägungen Karls V. im Spannungsfeld imperialer und dynastischer Interessen, in Das römisch-deutsche Reich im politischen System Karls V., Schriften des Historischen Kollegs – Kolloquien 1, ed. Heinrich Lutz (München – Wien 1982), 35–54.

19 Ramón Carande, "Das westindische Gold und die Kreditpolitik Karls V.", Spanische Forschungen der Görresgesellschaft (Erste Reihe) - Gesammelte Aufsätze zur Kulturgeschichte Spaniens 10 (1955), 1–22; J. D. Tracy, Emperor Charles V, 91–108.

the Emperor with the following for the forthcoming war with the opposition in the Empire: 500 cavalry, 12,000 infantry and a cash loan of 200,000 ducats. This had the potential to decide the situation in the Empire.

Inside the Empire, the Emperor did not have many allies.

Aside from Church Electors and some remaining Catholic Church princes, the Habsburgs only had their own lands available in the Empire; the Netherlands in the west and the hereditary Habsburg lands in the south-east. And they still had an "open account" with their south German bankers. The willingness of the Augsburg Fuggers, Baumgartners, Welsers and other south German bankers to finance the Imperial army with their loans increased significantly when this wealthiest segment of the population left Augsburg (standing as a member town of the Schmalkaldic League on the side of the Imperial opposition) and took shelter under Habsburg protection.[20] The Emperor could even find effective help among Lutheran princes (with the exception of direct members of the Schmalkaldic League), but he had to pay well for it. This mainly involved some experienced military commanders who had already previously worked in the Imperial service during wars with the Ottoman Empire and with France, and who were willing to wage war against anyone, regardless of their confession, in exchange for good pay or other advantages in the Imperial service.

It was mainly the neighbouring powers that bordered the Empire which could effectively intervene in the great anticipated military clash (expecting numerically large armies); they could stage a direct military intervention if necessary and they also had "human resources" at their disposal, i.e. extensive recruitment areas. The role of the western neighbours of the Empire at the time of the Schmalkaldic War, i.e. France and Denmark, is well known. These countries were a potential danger for the Emperor in the forthcoming clash with the Estates opposition which is why, from 1544 to 1545, he strove intensively to eliminate their possible influence.

But the Habsburgs still had one important ally on the European political scene, whose role previous interpretations usually do not take into consideration at all, although it was an important contemporary power, located

---

20   H. Lutz, "Augsburg", 427; Hermann Kellenbenz, "Hugo Angelo – Bürger von Augsburg und kaiserlicher Agent." In Gesellschaftsgschichte – Festschrift für Karl Bosl zum 80. Geburtstag, Band II, ed. Ferdinand Seibt (München 1988), 115–130.

on the eastern borders of the Empire - the Polish-Lithuanian Common-wealth.

On the whole, the Schmalkaldic War in the Empire itself represents a rather marginal theme from the perspective of the Polish view of Central European history,[21] as it did not concern internal Polish history in any significant way.[22] In Polish history, this period is primarily a dynastic milestone, associated with the death of King Sigismund I. of Jagiellonia († 1548). The political priorities of the Royal Court in the mid-1540s were the interests of Sigismund I. on the Hungarian border and relations with the Ottoman Empire, in which the son-in-law of the King of Poland, Duke of Transylvania and properly elected Hungarian "anti-king" John Zápolya, was significantly involved.

Nevertheless, Polish-Habsburg relations were also very important for the development of the Polish state's foreign policy at that time,[23] which understandably had to influence a power-political conflict in the Empire as fundamental as the Schmalkaldic War. That is why these issues also essentially related to Polish affairs, not only with regard to a broader confessional development, but also in respect of the creation of various relationship models between the ruler and the Estates.[24]

In the long term, peace reigned at the border between the Holy Roman Empire of the German Nation and the Polish state, and in principle there was no territorial or dynastic pretext that would cast doubt on the status quo. From a confessional perspective, the Polish king stood clearly on the Catholic side, and he tried to prevent the penetration of the Lutheran Reformation into Polish territory himself, whether from Imperial territory

---

21 Zbigniew Wójcik, Historia powszechna – Wiek XVI-XVII (Warszawa 2008), 189–191; Krzystof Mikulski and Jacek Wijaczka, Historia powszechna – Wiek XVI-XVIII (Warszawa 2012), 195–197.

22 Stanisław Grzybowski, "Dzieje Polski i Litwy (1506–1648)", in Wielka Historia Polski, Tom II, Część II (Kraków – Warszawa 2003), 321–715.

23 Jacek Wijaczka, Stosunki dyplomatyczne Polski s Rzeszą niemecką v czasach panowania cesarza Karola V (1519–1556), Prace Instytutu Historii Wyższej Szkoly Pedagogicznej w Kielcach, Nr 7 (Kielce 1998), 88–96.

24 Jaroslav PÁNEK, "Zemská zřízení v kontextu ústavních proměn ve střední Evropě v 16. a na počátku 17. století – Die Landesordnungen im Kontext der Verfassungsrechtlichem Veränderungen in Mitteleuropaim 16. und zu Beginn des 17. Jahrhunderts – Ustawy krajowe w kontekście zmian konstytucyjnych w Europie Środkowej w XVI i na początku XVII wieku", in, Vladislavské zřízení zemské a počátky ústavního zřízení v českých zemích (1500–1619), Sborník příspěvků z mezinárodní konference konané ve dnech 7.–8. prosince 2000 v Praze, red. Karel Malý and Jaroslav Pánek (Praha 2001), 403–441.

(the territory of the Elector of Brandenburg and Pomerania directly bordered Poland) or from Silesia.

On the political scene, Sigismund I. of Jagiellonia acted as a friendly power towards the Habsburgs, although it was merely a formal alliance that was not backed up with any specific assistance or support. But even that was a relatively advantageous situation for the Habsburgs, as they did not have to fear any danger from the Polish state at the time of the preparation of a forceful intervention against opposition Imperial princes (unlike France or Denmark). More precisely: they did not have to invest diplomatic and financial potential in talks by which they would have to gain the King of Poland for their side. The Royal Court unequivocally approved Charles V.'s intervention against the Schmalkaldic League as, according to Sigismund I. the conduct of the opposition Imperial princes constituted a revolt by vassals, bound by a feudal oath, against their lord. That is why he deemed Charles V.'s approach completely legitimate.

Although the Polish-Lithuanian Commonwealth differed significantly from the Holy Roman Empire of the German Nation in terms of its structure, some elements of Habsburg internal Imperial policy also had an important diplomatic meaning for Sigismund I.. For the Cracow Court, this primarily meant an important precedent in the relationship towards former Order territories in Prussia. After the secularization of the Order territories, Albert Hohenzollern recognized the supreme rights of the King of Poland and accepted Prussia from him in the form of a fiefdom (1525).[25] Thus, even for Sigismund I., Charles V.'s approach towards "disobedient vassals" represented a possible and now also diplomatically justifiable model in relation to Lutheran Prussia, as viewed in this way it was purely an "internal Polish" matter. However, despite all the friendly and encouraging proclamations, Sigismund I. did not intervene in the war in the Empire on the Emperor's side in any way.

In the case of King Ferdinand I., his circle of potential allies and resources for the war in the Empire was significantly more limited. He declared neutrality in his own hereditary Habsburg lands in 1546 (when Schmalkaldic League forces wanted to occupy Alpine passes in Tyrol). By then, a signifi-

---

25   S. GrzybowskI, "Dzieje Polski i Litwy", 372–375.

cant portion of Austrian lands had already been Lutheranized, and most of the nobility refused to wage war against the Protestant opposition in the Empire. Thus, the Schmalkaldic War in the Empire affected the Austrian lands only marginally,[26] although we can assume that certain nobles and their military corps personally participated in Ferdinand's campaign in Saxony, mainly in the positions of commanders of smaller units of mercenaries, as we have documented in the case of John of Lodron.

Outside the Empire, King Ferdinand ruled in lands of the Crown of St. Stephen (i.e. in Hungarian lands) and in lands of the Bohemian Crown.

However, after the Turkish occupation of 1541 he did not have much left of Hungary, and the narrow "Royal Hungary" belt (whose capital, after the Turkish occupation of Budin, became present-day Bratislava, capital of Slovakia) required much greater financial resources for its constant defence than the normal economic profit of this entire territory. It was probably only the gold mines in the Slovak Ore Mountains that slightly equalized this unfavourable balance. However, thanks to the conclusion of the peace treaty with the Ottoman Empire, King Ferdinand was able to withdraw some war-experienced and well-trained frontier cavalry army divisions from Hungary after the end of the Imperial Diet in Regensburg. In the end, this Hungarian cavalry was the main effective military force which King Ferdinand had at his disposal during the invasion of the territory of John Frederick, Elector of Saxony, at the start of November 1546.

In the lands of the Bohemian Crown, King Ferdinand could not expect any great sympathy for his task of imposing the Imperial anathema. In this territory's core, i.e. in the Kingdom of Bohemia and the Margraveship of Moravia, there was a general reluctance to deal with problems that the Empire caused itself by its internal disputes. In the 1540s, the other lands in this commonwealth, Lusatia and Silesia, were already mostly Lutheran, and some of the Silesian princedoms were directly ruled by members of secondary branches of Imperial prince families, predominantly Lutheran ones. It was to be expected that the acquisition of resources in Bohemian lands for military adventure in the Empire would not be easy.

---

26 Thomas Winkelbauer, Österreichische Geschichte 1522–1699 (Ständefreiheit und Fürstenmacht - Länder und Untertanen des Hauses Habsburg im konfessionellen Zeitalter), Bd.1. - 2. (Wien 2003).

During this chaotic situation, the Habsburgs tried to avoid a direct clash will the full military potential of the Schmalkaldic League (which in the summer of 1546 was significantly larger than the Habsburg forces); they tried to buy time to mobilize more distant resources (Dutch, Italian and Spanish) and, from the very start, attempted to divide the opposition forces.

The Emperor already had the foundation of his army with him during the campaign from the Netherlands to Bavaria at the start of 1546, but this army could not have been too large, so as not to arouse fear in the Lutheran opposition before the sitting of the Regensburg Diet. During his campaign from the Netherlands to Bavaria (which took place peacefully), the Emperor was accompanied by only about a thousand soldiers. At that time, however, Habsburg military forces began to shift from more distant areas of Europe, and this understandably could not have escaped the Schmalkaldic League's intelligence network.

The Schmalkaldic League commenced intensive talks after Landgrave Philip of Hesse left the March meeting with the Emperor in Speyer. The League Assembly was convened on the 12th of April in Worms, and then after ten days the venue was moved from the western border of the Empire directly to where the Imperial Diet was to be held, i.e. to Regensburg. The diplomatic talks still indicated a certain mutual desire for a peaceful solution. The League Assembly came up with various ideas; it proposed the establishment of a pan-German Christian Assembly (independent of the Council), which would solve disputes between Catholics and Lutherans. This concerned not only doctrinal matters, but to a large extent also property-legal issues, i.e. what the actual legal status of secularized Church assets was. At the same time, the League Assembly raised an official query with the Emperor – why was Charles V. arming his Spanish and Italian forces, and withdrawing them into the Empire. The Emperor responded to this query in a letter dated the 12th of June 1546 (which was delivered to the Schmalkaldic League on the 16th of June 1546), stating that he urgently needed to have a powerful army with him so that he could punish disobedient princes.[27]

---

27   RTA 1546, 438–442; Ernst Bizer, "Reformationsgeschichte 1532 bis 1555", in Reformationsgeschichte Deutschlands bis 1555 - Die Kirche in ihrer Geschichte (Ein Handbuch), Band 3, Lieferung K, edd. Franz Lau and Ernst Bizer (Göttingen 1964), 140–141.

The Schmalkaldic League viewed this letter as an obvious declaration of hostility by the Emperor (by "disobedient princes" he undoubtedly meant the members and main leaders of the Schmalkaldic League) and, in accordance with the League statutes, it declared the mobilization of a League army to protect its members.

To the Habsburgs' surprise, this mobilization took place very quickly, in a matter of 2–3 weeks. The recruitment areas were local Imperial regions and, thanks to effective religious-political propaganda (making extensive use of leaflet distribution), the Schmalkaldic League managed to interpret military resistance against the Emperor as a defence of the Lutheran faith. Charles V. helped this along greatly in his own way when he made use of an offer of alliance by Pope Paul III.,[28] who made no secret of the fact (in a letter sent to Catholic cantons in Switzerland, whose text the Schmalkaldic League obtained) that the forces he sent were on their way to Germany to eliminate the heretical movement together with the Emperor. In a Papal Bull dated the 15th of June 1546, Pope Paul III. even declared a crusade against Lutheran "heretics", which was not very diplomatic for the Habsburgs at the time.[29]

As early as the start of July 1546, the Schmalkaldic League had a "southern army" numbering 10,000 men at its disposal, financed primarily by wealthy south German towns which (as legal persons) were League members. Command of this army was entrusted to Sebastian Schertlin von Burtenbach (he replaced Landgrave Philip of Hesse as commander of the southern army). Under the leadership of John Frederick, Elector of Saxony, the northern army of the Schmalkaldic League was concentrated in Thuringia; at the start of July it numbered 16,000 infantry and 5,000 cavalry.

Despite this overwhelming military superiority, the Schmalkaldic League did not commence a military conflict with the Emperor during July 1546, although such powerful military corps could have fairly easily overpowered the Imperial Court and its allies, who were still in Regensburg. Only the southern army, under Schertlin's command, was more noticeably active; it occupied the town of Füssen, located on a strategic communication link at

---

28 Henri Hauser, and Augustin Renaudet, L'età del Rinascimento e della Riforma (Torino 1957), 551.
29 L. Pastor,. Geschichte Papst Pauls III., 557–573.

the foot of the Alps, without a fight. The objective was to gain control of Alpine passes in Bavaria and Tyrol, in order to prevent, or at least delay, the concentration of the Emperor's forces and that of his allies from Italian regions. But Duke William of Bavaria and King Ferdinand (who declared neutrality in the forthcoming conflict) did not agree with the League forces' entry into Bavarian or Tyrolean territory, and a campaign against their will would have been a pretext for war; the Schmalkaldic League did not want to be the first to provide such a pretext.

Meanwhile, Emperor Charles V. desperately awaited the arrival of his military reinforcements; he prolonged parliamentary talks, and offered the princely family members who were present (including the "enemy") a wealth of entertainment and distractions in Regensburg. The two "royal" marriages of the daughters of King Ferdinand I., associated with feasts and balls, were moved to the first half of July 1546. They were to create an impression of carefree peace and security, and their participants (although they did not seem to be aware of this) were, in their own way, hostages. How could the Schmalkaldic League justify an attack on an aristocratic society party, nota bene at the time of the sitting of the Imperial Diet?

At the Diet, the Habsburgs managed to push through a resolution by which both leaders of the Schmalkaldic League were declared violators of Imperial peace in connection with the earlier siege of Brunswick-Wolfenbüttel (and the imprisonment of Duke Henry in 1545), and an Imperial anathema was imposed on them. This was already a relatively powerful Imperial political instrument, but not yet a commencement of war, as long as both affected parties were willing to accept and obey the Imperial Diet's decision (as well as return the occupied Duchy, and release Duke Henry from prison). It was not likely, but if the Imperial anathema was not to be a disgrace (this political instrument was last used in 1521 against Martin Luther), the Emperor had to be prepared to enforce this decision with power. But when an army of almost sixty thousand, led by both of the aforementioned princes, lay only six days' military march from Regensburg, the Emperor had to think twice whether declaring an Imperial anathema was appropriate or not.

It was apparently also for this reason that the official declaration of the Imperial anathema against the leaders of the Schmalkaldic League was delayed, and only announced after the two afore-mentioned weddings (on the 20th of July 1546). Thus, the younger Habsburg princess Maria may have felt "cheated", because instead of the feasts and balls at which society was entertained after the marriage of her older sister Anna (after the 4th of July 1546), much less effort was put into her marriage, which consisted only of the ceremony itself, on the 18th of July 1546. The wedding guests could go home now; they were no longer needed, as Charles V.'s first significant reinforcements had arrived. The Imperial anathema could now be declared.[30] At the same time that the Imperial anathema was declared, the Diet entrusted King Ferdinand of Habsburg and Duke Moritz of Saxony with the execution of this decision.

On the 20th of July 1546, before the Diet guests left Regensburg, twelve battalions of Spanish mercenary infantry (i.e. approximately 6,000 men), previously deployed in Hungary, came marching, as well as 500 cavalry, led by Margrave Albert Alcibiades of Brandenburg and Wolfgang, Grand Master of the Order of the Teutonic Knights. At the end of July, 600 Bohemian sappers also reached Regensburg, and ships bearing "Viennese bombs" - metal balls filled with gunpowder and used as siege grenades – came sailing up the Danube.[31]

While the Emperor awaited further reinforcements from Italy, Spain and the Netherlands, the southern Schmalkaldic League army moved from the Bavarian border to the Imperial town of Donauwörth where it awaited the arrival of the northern army, which had set off for the Danube from its marshalling area in Erfurt in Thuringia. At the end of July, both armies merged – their total military potential numbered around 7,000 cavalry and 50,000 infantry; a military force that, at the time, the Habsburgs were still not capable of confronting.

---

30 RTA 1546, 552–562.
31 Nicolao Mamerano Lucemburgo, D. Caroli V. Roma. Imp. Avg. inter ex inferiore Germania ab Anno 1545. Vsq[ue] ad Comitia apud Augustam Rheticam indicta Anni 1547. quo vsq[ue] singulis diebus & ad quor militaria rexerit (Augsburg 1548); Lambertus Hortensius von Montfort, Wahrhaffte und eigentliche beschreibung des Protestierenden kriegs Teutscher Nation, welchen weiland Keiser Carolus der Fünfft diß nammens, Hochlobiger gedechtnus, wider etliche fürnemme Fürsten und Stette vorermelter Landen, gefüret, wie sich derselbig allgemach angespunnen, verloffen, und im Fünfzehenhundert, sieben und vierzigsten jar geendet habe, darinn auch alle umbstende weitleuffiger, dann von anderen bißher beschehen, vermeldet warden, Erst newlich auß Lateinischer Sprach in das recht Hochteutsch mit fleiß vertolmetschet (Basel 1573), 936–937.

The main gathering place for the Imperial army became friendly Bavaria. At the start of August, the Emperor and his Court moved around 70 km south, from Regensburg to the town of Landshut, while the present troops set off to build a field camp between Regensburg and Landshut (around 25 km north of Landshut). On the 13th of August, a large Italian unit (600 cavalry, 11,000 infantry) under the command of Octavius Camerino arrived in Landshut, and here the Emperor also received the news that, on the 14th of August, John Frederick, Elector of Saxony, and Landgrave Philip of Hesse had officially rejected the Emperor's invitation from the Regensburg Diet, whereby they had insulted the Sovereign Majesty. At that stage, the Emperor had his army prepared for a ceremonial parade, which took place near Landshut on the 15th of August 1546. A relatively powerful army marched at the parade near Landshut, formed mainly of Charles' Italian and Spanish infantry, accompanied by smaller cavalry units sent to the Emperor by the Duke of Florence (300 cavalry) and Ferrara (200 cavalry).

After the parade, this predominantly "Romance" army moved from Landshut to the field camp, where the troops that had arrived earlier awaited it. On the 15th of August, the entire army, numbering around 5,000 cavalry and 30,000 infantry, set off on a slow march west in the direction of Donauwörth, as if it was preparing itself for a great decisive battle against the Schmalkaldic League army. However, the League army was still significantly more powerful, which is why the Emperor chose a delaying tactic. The Imperial army crossed the Danube on the 24th of August with the help of pontoon bridges; four days later, the army pitched camp in front of the gates of the town of Ingolstadt, around 60 km from Donauwörth.

At the time, Ingolstadt was an important Danube fortress on which extensive fortification work had started (designed, according to contemporary defensive theories, as a bastion system of poured earth embankments) in 1537. The fortress had not yet been completed; however, in the summer of 1546, a large Schmalkaldic League garrison was found here, which refused to let the Emperor enter the fortress. For this reason, the Imperial army pitched camp in front of the Ingolstadt ramparts and stopped its rapid advance westward.[32] However, the actual objective was not the conquest of

---

32 Eugen von Frauenholz, Das Heerwesen des Reiches in der Landsknechtszeit, Entwicklungsgeschichte des deutschen Heerwesens, Zweiter Band, II. Teil (München 1937), 104.

Ingolstadt (whose military significance in the given context was relatively small), but to gain time so that the main clash with the Schmalkaldic League army would be postponed until further reinforcements arrived. Additional Habsburg troops were on their way from the Danube in the north-west; approximately 17,000 men, who had been recruited for the Emperor from Dutch sources by Maximilian von Egmont. However, the relocation of this army across the whole Empire took several weeks.

So, in Ingolstadt, the Imperial artillery mainly tested the effectiveness of its new siege technology. The technical preparation only took two days, so, on the 30th of August 1546, 111 siege cannons were able to commence a three-day-long continuous artillery barrage against Ingolstadt. The Ingolstadt fortress was able to return the artillery barrage.[33]

Thus, while war had commenced, it did not yet take a fatally destructive form. The troops were rested, well supplied and paid. Someone lost their life every now and again as a result of the artillery barrage, but in comparison with field battles, where the troops got into physical contact, these losses were very small. In front of the gates of Ingolstadt, young men of princely families, for whom this campaign was their first military experience, could still view the whole affair as an interesting, and in its own way quite entertaining, adventure. An example of this was Archduke Maximilian, eldest son of King Ferdinand. In addition to describing his experiences from his first "battle" to his sister, he also sent her an interesting souvenir of a cannonball fired from an enemy cannon which, upon impact, had rolled right into his army tent.

The siege of Ingolstadt lasted two weeks, and did not bring a clear result. The artillery barrage itself had failed to destroy the well fortified (albeit unfinished) fortress, and the Emperor did not want to risk a frontal attack in case he incurred more unnecessary losses. When, in mid-September, Egmont's troops also finally arrived in Ingolstadt, the Emperor ended the siege. On the basis of a concluded agreement, the Schmalkaldic League military garrison could leave the fortress. It was not really about Ingolstadt.

---

33 August von Druffel, ed., Des Viglius van Zwichem Tagebuch des Schmalkaldischen Donaukrieges, (München 1877); F. Lau, A History of the Reformation, 201–204; J. D. Tracy, Emperor Charles V, 212; here Figure 10.1 The Ingolstadt Cannonade.

Thanks to Dutch reinforcements, the military power of both groupings was now balanced.[34] Allied Imperial troops set off from Ingolstadt in a north-westerly direction, but they did not attack the Schmalkaldic League army which was walled in in the environs of Donauwörth. During the second half of September, Imperial troops moved 30 km further north-west, to the town of Nördlingen. The Schmalkaldic League responded to this tactical manoeuvre, and after several week's encampment at Donauwörth the army set off for Nördlingen, where the lure of a great decisive battle was expected at the start of October.[35]

But this assumption was not fulfilled either, and the Imperial army moved again, several dozen kilometres further, this time to the south-west to the town of Giengen an der Brenz. The repeated strategic movements of such large armies began to have a devastating effect. Not only on the extensive Danube region, which the pantry divisions of both warring sides began to pillage. With such a large concentration of population finding itself in camp conditions for weeks on end (the mercenary encampment surrounded "technical facilities" where the soldiers' pay could be spent on alcohol or the services of prostitutes), various diseases and violence quickly spread among the soldiers themselves. Both of the warring sides were also quickly running out of cash – mercenaries in the field had to be paid, even when they only moved and camped.

Before the lure of the great field battle between both armies, the Imperial side chose a different strategy. Small armies separated from the main Habsburg force, led by Moritz of Saxony and Ferdinand of Habsburg, whose task was to attack the then only weakly protected territory of John Frederick, Elector of Saxony, in the north-east of the Empire, i.e. far from the places where both armies had so far merely "circled" each other. Duke Moritz was strongly motivated, as he was occupying his second cousin's Saxon territories "for himself" (their tenure was promised to him as reward for participating in the war on the Habsburgs' side). King Ferdinand declared that his campaign constituted defence of the territory of the Bohemian Crown, whose integrity the Elector of Saxony had violated. They

---

34   Manuel Fernández Álvarez, Carlos V, el César el Hombre (18th ed. Madrid 2006), 681–682.

35   Wieland Held, 1547 – Die Schlacht bei Mühlberg / Elbe - Entscheidung auf dem Wege zum albertinischen Kurfürstentum Sachsen (Beucha 1997), 52–58.

both then simultaneously justified their attack on defenceless Saxony as fulfilment of the will of the Imperial Diet, at which they were appointed executors of the Imperial anathema.

This unexpected strategic move by the Habsburgs caused disputes in the Schmalkaldic League commanding corps. Elector John Frederick requested that his attacked territories be effectively defended (to which he was entitled in accordance with the League statutes); Frederick of Hesse wanted to first use the common military forces to defeat the main Imperial army, and only then intervene in the "secondary" battlefield in Saxony. However, the Elector's interest prevailed, and on the 16th of November 1546 his "northern army", forming the larger part of the Schmalkaldic League army, withdrew from the Danube to the north-east to defend Saxony.

The thus weakened remainder of the Schmalkaldic League army now avoided direct clashes with the significantly numerically stronger Imperial troops. There was no money left for continuing to aimlessly maintain mercenaries, and so the hired League armies were disbanded for the winter, without any significant clash taking place in the Danube region with the Emperor. In mid-November, Landgrave Philip of Hesse, who had almost been captured by Imperial troops on the 23rd of November 1546 during an unexpected night-time raid on the south German monastery of Herbertingen where the Landgrave was spending the night at the time, also left the Danube. After quickly fleeing the battlefield, Landgrave Philip of Hesse did not participate in any further military actions (he no longer had any money left to pay his troops) and he merely tried to negotiate some peaceful solution with the Emperor through his son-in-law, Moritz of Saxony.

So, by autumn 1546, the Schmalkaldic League no longer had a military presence in southern Germany. The Emperor took advantage of this situation (he still had a powerful army in the field) and began to gradually break the active resistance of the south German Schmalkaldic League members. He focused mainly on forcing peace treaties with princes (by which he could easily exploit individuals), while in the towns (whose leadership was of a corporate character) he wagered on a direct military threat.

Thus, by the end of 1546, the Emperor had gotten rid of two dangerous opponents, being Frederick, Elector of Palatine, and Ulrich, Duke of Württemberg.

At the end of 1546, both of these princes signed a "neutrality agreement" with the Emperor, which also meant a significant financial burden for them. The Emperor made sure that his "forgiveness" was well paid. For the Elector of Palatine, his timely capitulation also had another dimension: in his case, too, the "play" was for the title of Elector, which one of the Emperor's main allies, Duke William of Bavaria, was very interested in. Both belonged to the Wittelsbach family; the transfer of the Elector' vote from from one family branch to another could therefore take place (after the victorious war) similarly to the case of the Saxon Wettins. The neutrality of the Elector of Palatine was very important for the Habsburgs, as the Palatine contingent, comprising an entire cavalry battalion and two infantry battalions, represented a significant part of the Schmalkaldic League army.[36]

Imperial south German towns that were members of the Schmalkaldic League met a similar fate. At the turn of 1546 and 1547, under the threat of siege by the Imperial army, they gradually capitulated one by one (with one exception, which was Konstanz). Even these "voluntary" capitulations cost all the affected towns significant financial sums.[37] At the end of January 1547 even the town of Augsburg, which the Imperial garrison had occupied in February, gave itself up to the Emperor's mercy. This wealthy Imperial town (to which Imperial bankers also returned from their short exile together with Imperial troops) later became the Emperor's long-term residence during two long Imperial Diets (1547/1548 and 1550/1551), when the time for "settlement" came.[38]

In autumn 1546, the main battlefield between the Habsburg side and the opposition in the Empire quickly moved to Saxony.[39] In mid-October, after the signing of an alliance contract in Prague on the 14th of October 1546,[40] Duke Moritz formally declared war against Elector John Frederick

---

36 Adolf Hasenclever, Die Kurpfälzische Politik in den Zeiten des schmalkaldischen Krieges - Januar 1546 bis Januar 1547 (Heidelberg 1905), 90–91.

37 Eberhard Naujoks, Kaiser Karl V. und die Zunftverfassung, ausgewählte Aktenstücke zu den Verfassungsänderungen in den oberdeutschen Reichsstädten 1547–1556 (Stuttgart 1985).

38 Lutz, "Augsburg", 428–429.

39 J. D. Tracy, Emperor Charles V, 214–217.

40 Christian Winter, "Prag 1546. Die sächsisch-böhmische Erbeinung zwischen Herzog Moritz und König Ferdinand." In Eger 1459 – Fürstentreffen zwischen Sachsen, Böhmen und ihren Nachbarn: Dynastische Politik, fürstliche Repräsentation und kulturelle Verflechtung / Cheb 1459 – Setkání

and, after moderate resistance, occupied the "Ernestine" part of Saxony by the start of November. Together with him, King Ferdinand also entered the territory of Saxony, and he began to occupy the so-called Vogtland region, i.e. the territory that was held by the Saxon Wettins as one of the fiefdoms subject to the authority of the King of Bohemia.

The legal pretext for this campaign consisted of the fact that Ferdinand I., from the title of the King of Bohemia, took away this fiefdom (which was part of the lands of the Bohemian Crown) away from the prince who was guilty of violating the feudal oath. The argument of the legal affiliation of the part of the territory, over which the Elector of Saxony ruled, to the lands of the Bohemian Crown (i.e. outside the legal system of the Holy Roman Empire of the German Nation) was often used by the Habsburgs as a diplomatic argument at the time of the Schmalkaldic War, as I will try to explain below in the broader context of the Bohemian lands.

Both "pro-Habsburg" armies that attacked Saxony proceeded at the start without any significant mutual coordination. Moritz of Saxony commanded his troops himself; Ferdinand of Habsburg's army corps (which only operated on the Elector's territory, formally appertaining to the lands of the Bohemian Crown) were commanded by west Bohemian noble Sebastian of Weitmille and Bohuslav Felix Hasištejnský of Lobkovice.

At the end of October 1546, Sebastian of Weitmille's divisions occupied the town of Plauen (the main centre of the so-called Vogtland);[41] Moritz of Saxony gradually occupied only more weakly defended regions; of the more important towns, he only captured Zwickau. He did not dare attack better-fortified towns such as Gotha, Eisenach, Coburg or even the seat of Wittenberg.

The Habsburgs may have ceremonially declared victory over John Frederick of Saxony on the 9th of November 1546 (they had occupied most of his territory), but their superiority in Saxony did not last long. Ferdinand I.'s army withdrew from the Vogtland for the winter. The large army of Elector John Frederick, which began to move away from Nördlingen in southern

---

panovníků Saska, Čech a jejich sousedů: Dynastická politika, panovnická reprezentace a kulturní vazby. Saxonia. Schriften des Vereins für sächsische Landesgeschichte e. V., Bd. 13, ed. André Thieme and Uwe Tresp (Wettin-Löbejün, 2011), 354–380.

41 Erich Wild, Das Vogtland im Schmalkaldischen Kriege (Plauen, 1939).

Germany after mid-November 1546, gradually not only forced Moritz of Saxony out of the Elector's occupied territories, but at the end of the year also began seizing the other parts of the Saxon lands, where Duke Moritz ruled. War activities continued even during the winter, which was unusual for the time. Moritz of Saxony quickly retreated until the 6th of January, when he and the remainder of his (albeit still numerous) troops were surrounded in Leipzig. He had 10 battalions of infantry knechts at his disposal (around five thousand soldiers), with whom he managed to defend Leipzig. The unsuccessful Elector may have ended the siege of Leipzig after three weeks, but he had gained a decisive superiority on the battlefield.

In desperation, Moritz of Saxony and King Ferdinand asked Emperor Charles V. for direct military intervention. Charles V. pledged to provide it, but no earlier than the start of March. Until then, they had to fend for themselves. At that time, the Habsburg side found itself in a difficult situation, and King Ferdinand tried to mobilize the military potential of the Kingdom of Bohemia against the will of the Estates. Not only did he not succeed, but he also provoked the mostly non-Catholic nobility and towns to passive resistance, and talks on possible mutual assistance with Elector John Frederick.

In such a complicated positional clash (after all, no major field battle had occurred so far) all resources (human, food and financial) were quickly running out. Thus, the Elector of Saxony, who controlled the Saxon battlefield, focused on controlling the available resources during the winter months (when the movements of large armies were much more complicated than in the summer). While the Elector relocated to his seat of Altenburg in Thuringia for the winter, the army, under the command of William of Thumshirm, crossed the Bohemian border in the Ore Mountains, and occupied not only the border towns of Loket and Chomutov, but most importantly took control of the mining area in Jáchymov, where it also seized significant supplies of metallurgical silver.

King Ferdinand only sent his own army to help Duke Moritz at the end of February 1547. It was a relatively powerful army, numbering 1,500 cavalry and 10 infantry battalions (approximately 4,000 men). Command was entrusted to one of the other Lutheran princes, Albert Alcibiades Hohenzollern, Margrave of Brandenburg; Moritz's peer and friend from his youth with whom he had participated in a number of military campaigns in the Imperial service. Margrave Albert commenced talks with Elector John Frederick, but before any official agreement could take place, his army was disabled in a battle near Rochlice (around 60 km south-east of Leipzig) which took place on Saturday the 2ⁿᵈ of March 1547.

The Margrave and his royal army (six battalions) pitched camp directly in the town of Rochlice; the Imperial divisions (four battalions) remained in the suburbs. The Elector of Saxony sent the infantry divisions to Rochlice, and he himself only left Alteburg, located around 35 km west of Rochlice, late on Friday afternoon, accompanied by several other prominent Schmalkaldic League members (Duke Ernest of Lüneburg and Counts Vollrath of Mansfeld and Wolf of Schönberg). After a night ride, the Elector launched a surprising pre-dawn attack, during which his army overcame and almost massacred the Imperial divisions in the suburbs, in just a few hours and without any significant losses. Landgrave Krystof of Leuchtenberg, later celebrated as a hero by the Lutheran side, devised and led this strategic approach.

There was no need for the Elector to complicatedly besiege the town of Rochlice itself as, by noon, Margrave Albert's soldiers had capitulated. After the battle, around a thousand dead soldiers were gathered up in the town's environs; a further three hundred corpses were fished out of the river Mulden, which flows around Rochlice and which was part of the fortification system. Surviving mercenaries of German origin were released after they put down their weapons if they promised not to fight against the Elector for a period of six months (most of them were eligible for hiring by the Elector's army); Spanish and Italian soldiers, however, remained in captivity.

Margrave Albert Alcibiades was also captured, but in his case it was not completely clear whether his army's "capitulation" had been arranged with the Elector of Saxony in advance. After all, the course of the battle also corresponded to this, as the vast majority of the dead were Italian and Spanish Imperial soldiers whose unprotected suburban camp had been attacked before the morning with great superiority, while Margrave Albert's German mercenaries stayed within the safety of the town ramparts. Whether this was the case or not, Margrave Albert stayed "out of the game" until the Battle of Mühlberg, and the Habsburg side was significantly weakened by the defeat at Rochlice. Apart from the actual military potential that the

Elector of Saxony gained at Rochlice (i.e. six infantry battalions of Margrave Albert's German Landsknechts, which he was able to hire himself for a good soldier's pay), fourteen artillery barrels of various sizes also fell into the anti-Habsburg side's hands.

Although it was a short clash lasting only a few hours, it was actually the first important battle of the entire Schmalkaldic War that ended (unlike the siege of Ingolstadt) in a clear result. That is why the Schmalkaldic League's victory in the battle at Rochlice was used extensively in contemporary printed propaganda.[42]

After this defeat, Moritz of Saxony and Ferdinand of Habsburg withdrew from Saxony to Cheb in Bohemian territory, where they expected help from the Emperor, and where the King negotiated with Bohemian Estates about which of them, and possibly under what conditions, would be willing to offer him military assistance. In the end some Bohemian troops did gather together, although King Ferdinand paid most of them from money that he had acquired by using the property of Catholic Church institutions, which at that time still held out in the immediate sovereign princedoms in Silesia.

The main Imperial army only set off from Nuremberg in the direction of the Bohemian border at the end of March 1547. It relocated to Cheb (Eger),[43] where it merged with King Ferdinand's army. Only during April did the united Habsburg armies, numbering around 27,000 men, commence their campaign towards Saxony.

Elector John Frederick retreated with a smaller army of approximately 7,000 men from Meissen to the north-west. On the 23rd of April he crossed the Elbe, and continued along the right bank of the river. He did not expect an attack by the Imperial army, and relied on the natural barrier that the rather wide river Elbe formed in this part of Germany in the spring. After all, the Saxon army had torn down all the bridges over the Elbe during their retreat along the river's flow. That evening, the Elector pitched camp on the

---

42 Von Marggraf Albrecht von Brandenburg Whrhafftige Zeitung, Der sich unbedacht seiner Ehren und Pflicht, Under Erdichtem Schein, mutwilliglich und freuenlich. Wider den Churfürsten zu Sachsen und Burggraffen zu Magdeburg, zuuerdrückung Warer Christlichen Religion, als eyn Feind, eingelassen, durch Gottes gnedige schickung, sampe dem Lantgrauen von Leuchtenburg, mit allem irem Kriegsvolck, zu Roß und fuß, um bund bei Rochlitz erlegt, und gefangen worden seind (1547).

43 M. F. Álvarez, Carlos V, 693–694.

bank of the Elbe, near the town of Mühlberg. But Imperial sappers managed to find a suitable place to ford the river (one local villager, whose horses the Elector's soldiers had previously requisitioned, allegedly divulged it to them) and build a pontoon bridge. Thus, early on the morning of the 24th of April 1547, the Habsburg army crossed the river Elbe and attacked the Elector's field camp with great superiority. The Saxon army, taken by surprise, did not have time to move to one of the nearby fortified towns (Torgau or Wittenberg), where it could have resisted even a long siege, but instead was destroyed in the short and bloody battle. The injured Elector gave himself up, and was imprisoned by the Emperor.[44]

---

44 Max Lenz, Die Schlacht bei Mühlberg - Mit neuen Quellen (Gotha 1879), 91–147; E. Frauenholz, Das Heerwesen des Reiches, 104–117; W. Held, 1547 – Die Schlacht bei Mühlberg, 114–123.

The Emperor's temporary victory, and the war of the princes in the Empire (1547–1555)

The capture of John Frederick, Elector of Saxony, broke most, but not all, of the Schmalkaldic League's military resistance. The Imperial army did not do well in northern Germany; a part of the League army numbering approximately 7,000 men still operated here, commanded by Albert of Mansfeld. He demonstrated his qualities in the minor Battle of Draken-burg (23rd of May 1547), in which he crushed the equally powerful Imperial army commanded by Duke Eric of Brunswick-Calenberg.[1]

After this defeat Imperial troops withdrew from northern Germany completely, and Charles V. focused on a political "settlement" with the rebels whom he had under his power. He left the remainder of the still resisting rebels, mostly members of the Schmalkaldic League which ceased to exist in 1547, until later. There were three important Imperial towns whose sieges were long and costly; Konstanz in the south (only conquered in 1548) and Magdeburg in the north (only conquered in 1551).[2] The harbour town of Bremen remained the only Schmalkaldic League town which never submitted to the Emperor, and which he did not conquer.[3]

However, after the Battle of Mühlberg, the other Schmalkaldic League leader, Landgrave Philip of Hesse, still eluded the Emperor. He had lost any

---

1   Wie Hertzog Erich von Braunschweig, in die flucht geschlagen, durch Grauen von Mansfeld, Grauen von Altenburg, und Thomshirn, und widerumb durch den Christoff Bußberger, mit seinem gerügten volck, das feld behaltem, wie folget, M.D. XLVII.

2   Römischer Kaiserlischer Maiestat Achterclärung gegen der Alten Statt Magdenburg M. D. XL-VII. Augsburg, 1547. Friedrich Huelsse, Die Stadt Magdeburg im Kampfe für den Protestantismus während der Jahre 1547–1551, Verein für Reformationsgeschichte (Schriften für das deutsche Volk), Heft 17 (Halle,1892).

3   Helmut Lucke, Bremen im Schmalkandischen Bund 1540–1547, Schriften der Wittheit zu Bremen, Reihe F, Veröffentlichungen aus dem Staatsarchiv der Freien Hansenstadt Bremen, Heft 23 (Bremen, 1955).

chance at military resistance; he squandered most of his financial resources in the summer phase of the military campaign in 1546 and, after the capture of John Frederick, Elector of Saxony, he could no longer expect effective help from anyone. After negotiating preliminary conditions (agreed with the Emperor by his son-in-law Moritz of Saxony and Joachim, Elector of Brandenburg, on his behalf),[4] he surrendered voluntarily to the Emperor, expecting only a symbolic punishment as, after the disintegration of the League army in southern Germany in autumn 1546, Philip of Hesse himself had not actually fought against the Emperor. That is why, on the 19th of June 1547, he himself voluntarily came to Halle in Saxony and surrendered to Charles V.[5]

However, despite all expectations, the Emperor threw the captured Landgrave into jail. He went on to hold both of the former leaders of the Schmalkaldic League in jail as his "personal prisoners" for the following five years, and had them transferred between Brussels, Augsburg and Innsbruck. The Emperor's treatment of the imprisoned princes was (among others) one of the princely opposition's arguments in the subsequent conflict with the Emperor, but back in 1547 nobody dared to criticize Charles V. openly.[6]

All of the Emperor's defeated opponents in the Empire (i.e. mainly members of the Schmalkaldic League who financed the League army's campaign in 1546) were affected financially; the sovereign sanctions were directed mainly at "disobedient" Imperial towns. The ones that surrendered voluntarily during 1546 (Ulm, Frankfurt, Augsburg etc.), were punished more leniently; the ones that the Emperor had had to conquer later (Konstanz in 1548, Magdeburg in 1551) received very drastic punishments. However, the Emperor charged them all significant financial sums, which he needed to pay his debts. War is always a costly affair, and war damages are paid by the losers. The case of the Schmalkaldic League was no different.

Unlike the towns, however, the Imperial princes (as long as they surrendered to the Emperor's "mercy") were punished relatively leniently. Ulrich

---

4   J. D. Tracy, Emperor Charles V, 217.

5   Carl von Heister, Die Gefagennehmung und die Gefangenschaft Philipps des Grossmüthigen Landgrafen von Hessen - 1547 bis 1552 (Marburg and Leipzig, 1868); Gustav Turba, Verhaftung und Gefangenschaft des Landgrafen Philipp von Hessen 1547–1550, Archiv für österreichische Geschichte, Bd. 83 (Wien, 1896).

6   J. Whaley, Germany and the Holy Roman Empire, 325–330.

of Württemberg was even allowed to keep his Duchy. Those who had not submitted to the Emperor by April 1547, or even stood against the Emperor in the field at the Battle of Mühlberg and failed to surrender, lost both their freedom and their property. This was also how Wolfgang of Anhalt-Bernburg lost his princedom (his property was used by King Ferdinand to pay for the services of Henry of Plauen, one of his most important allies in the Kingdom of Bohemia).

But one of the Imperial Estates never submitted to the Emperor: this was the former Imperial commander William of Fürstenberg, who had commanded the Habsburg army in the previous war with France (1542–1544) and ended up in a French prison, from which he was released only after the payment of an exceptionally high ransom (32 thousand Rhenish guilders). The Habsburgs did not help him financially in the attainment of his freedom; his relatives had to club together for the ransom, and the Schmalkaldic League also contributed (especially the town of Strasbourg). Thus, William of Fürstenberg became a sworn enemy of the Habsburgs; he wanted to actively fight against them, and offered the Schmalkaldic League his experience as a commander during the war. The payment of the ransom had ruined him financially, so he offered to command the anti-Habsburg army for free, as long as the Schmalkaldic League accepted his potential high officer's pay (which he valued at 400 Rhenish guilders per month) instead of the regular League membership contribution. The League leadership considered this experienced general's offer, but in the end it was not accepted, due to William of Fürstenberg's advanced age and his inadequate health which had been weakened in the French prison.

However, after 1547, Emperor Charles V. no longer considered William of Fürstenberg to be dangerous, and in the end he did not even insist that this man surrender to his "mercy". A declaration by William's brother Frederick of Fürstenberg (who had faithfully served the Habsburgs; in the Schmalkaldic War he had been a member of Archduke Maximilian's commanding staff), that he would hold William under "house arrest" in the family manor until his death to prevent him from participating in political life, was sufficient.

Understandably, the main punished party was John Frederick, Elector of Saxony. He was sentenced to death by the Emperor for his offences; however, he would be spared this cut-throat punishment as long as he agreed with the conditions that the Emperor stipulated for him if he wanted to save his life. These were specified in the so-called Capitulation of Wittenberg of the 19ᵗʰ of May 1547. Firstly, John Frederick of Saxony gave up his title of Elector (it was later transferred to Moritz of Saxony) and also significant parts of his landed property (most of it was taken over by Moritz of Saxony). However, in the end, Moritz of Saxony did not feel satisfied with the property.

When the captured Elector's property actually began to be divided up, it was discovered that a significant part of his territory was a historical part of the lands of the Bohemian Crown, and the Elector held them in the form of a fief from the King of Bohemia. The Capitulation of Wittenberg could not cover these territories (they were not de jure part of the Holy Roman Empire of the German Nation), as they appertained back to the feudal lord, i.e. Ferdinand of Habsburg, as the King of Bohemia. For quite a long time afterwards, Moritz of Saxony also argued with King Ferdinand about the legal status of specific small pastures and individual villages, and regarded the Habsburgs' procedure in this matter as very unhelpful.

In comparison with Moritz of Saxony, who felt cheated by the Habsburgs (he even had to cede the Princedom of Żagań in Silesia to Ferdinand), Duke Henry of Brunswick, whose dispute with the Schmalkaldic League and his imprisonment in 1545 was the formal reason for the commencement of the Schmalkaldic War, fared much better. He was reinstated as ruler of the Duchy of Brunswick-Wolfenbüttel, to the full extent, as early as the end of 1546 / start of 1547.

Understandably, the sovereign sanctions against the defeated parties resulted in a wave of religious-political emigration, directed mainly towards nearby northern Protestant countries (Denmark, Sweden), but also towards France and England.[7]

Immediately after the material punishment of the offenders (thanks to which the Emperor acquired sufficient financial resources to finish the military campaign against the remainder of the opposition between 1548 and 1551), Charles V. used his absolute political superiority (he did not know

---

7   Henry John Cowell, Strasbourg Protestant Refugees in England 1547–1553 (London, 1932).

that this was merely a temporary situation) to enforce two fundamental amendments with which he wanted to change the Empire.[8]

For this purpose, he also convened another Imperial Diet in 1547, this time held in Augsburg and under the control of the Imperial army. That is why this Diet, which was extended until 1548,[9] became nicknamed even in the 16th century as the "Armed Diet". It's clear that, in the new power constellation, the Diet approved anything the Emperor proposed.

The first proposal related to the internal political arrangement. The proposal to establish an Imperial League ("the Reichsbundprojekt") significantly strengthened the Emperor's influence, to the detriment of estate institutions.[10] It was a path to a monarchy controlled in an absolutist manner. However, it remained a mere proposal; it was rejected by the Imperial princes, and practically none of its parts became effective.

The second proposal concerned the religious situation. Regardless of the course of the Council of Trent (which was even interrupted due to the disputes between the Emperor and the Pope), the Imperial Diet approved a temporary religious measure known as "the Augsburg Interim" in 1548.[11] In its own way, given the contemporary Imperial environment, this measure was surprising. Inside the Empire during the 1540s, intensive talks were taking place (regardless of the Papal Curia's opinion) on the possible bringing together of the Catholic Church and the Lutherans. The main platform presented complex arguments by both Church and political representatives of both sides, which took place in 1541 and 1546 in Regensburg.

---

8   Horst Rabe, Reichsbund und Iterim - Die Verfassungs- und Religionspolitik Karls V. und der Reichstag von Augsburg 1547/1548 (Köln and Wien, 1971).

9   Römischer Kayserlicher Maiestat und deß heyligen Reychs Landfriden auff dem Reychstag zu Augspurg declariert, erneüweret. Auffgericht, unnd beschlossen, Anno Domini M. D. XLVIII. (Meyntz: Juon Schöffer, 1548); Karl Zeumer, ed. Quellensammlung zur Geschichte der deutschen Reichsverfassung in Mittelalter und Neuzeit, II. Teil – Von Maximilian I. bis 1806. (2nd ed. Tübingen,1913), 330–340; RTA 1547/1548.

10   Salomies, Die Pläne Kaiser Karls V., 107–147; Wolker Press, "Die Bundespläne Kaiser Karls V. und die Reichsverfassung", in Das römisch-deutsche Reich im politischen System Karls V., Schriften des Historischen Kollegs – Kolloquien 1, ed. Heinrich Lutz (München and Wien, 1982), 55–106; Heinz Angermaier, Die Reichsreform 1410–1555 - Die Staatsproblematik und Deutschland zwischen Mittelalter und Gegenwart (München, 1984), 297–315; F. Heer, The Holy Roman Empire, 166–167.

11   Der Römischen Keiserlichen Maiestat Erklärung, wie es der Religion halben, imm Heyligen Reich, biß zu Auftrag deß gemeynen Concilij gehalten werden soll, uff dem Reichßtag zu Augspurg, den XV. Maii, im M. D. XLVIII. Jar publiciert und eröffnet, unnd von gemeynen Stenden angenommen. (Meyntz: Juon Schörfer, 1548); Lau, A History of the Reformation, 208–218; RTA 1547/1548, 83–91, 1910–1947.

However, these talks ended in 1546 without a result; from both a theological and political perspective, the differences after three decades of Reformation were too deep, and the willingness to compromise was negligible.[12] That is why, after his victory in 1547, Charles V. implemented a political decision that was to result in the Lutheranized parts of Germany being gradually returned to the administration of the Catholic Church, as neighbouring Bohemia had managed to do, with various degrees of success, with the local Calixtines ("old Utraquists") during the previous century.

With the help of the Augsburg Interim, a religious model systemically based on the so-called Compacts, i.e. on the agreement between the Council of Basel and the Bohemian Hussites in 1436, was to be implemented in the Empire. In a slightly modified form, this Compact was one of the basic State laws in Bohemia, and in its own way it was also a very convenient diplomatic instrument for King Ferdinand in the prevention of the direct and unrestricted expansion of the Lutheran faith, as was shown in Bohemia in 1543. We know, even directly from Habsburg sources, that Karl Ferdinand advised his brother Charles to use his experiences from Bohemia, where the coexistence of two official religious directions had been practised quite successfully for over a hundred years, to suppress religious opposition. Late medieval Bohemian Utraquism, which regarded itself as part of the Catholic Church and recognized Papal succession, was no longer a danger to the Catholic Church (even in comparison with the Lutheran Reformation, let alone the Reformation's more radical forms).[13] That is why even Cardinan Loaysa, who was certainly not a supporter of any deviations from official Catholic rite, advised Charles V. to proceed similarly to his brother Ferdinand: "...accept the heretics and have them be subjects to your brother, as the Bohemians are...".[14]

However, given the situation in the Empire, the Augsburg Interim, which was directly inspired by the Bohemian Compacts, was acceptable for neither

---

12 Horst Rabe, Reichsbund und Interim - Die Verfassungs- und Religionspolitik Karls V. und der Reichstag von Augsburg 1547/1548 (Köln and Wien, 1971), 195–239; Schmidt, Konfessionalisierung, 3; Luise Schorn-Schütze, ed., Das Interim 1548/50 – Herrschaftskrise und Glaubenskonflikt, Schriften des Vereins für Reformationsgeschichte, Band 203 (Heidelberg, 2005); Tracy, Emperor Charles V, 217–220.

13 David, Finding the Middle Way, 45–79.

14 Hans J. Hillerbrand, The World of the Reformation (New York, 1973), 90.

Catholics nor Lutherans in the long term,[15] as (unlike Bohemia), the many generations of forced coexistence between several different confessions were missing here. After all, even in Bohemia itself, the Compact, which was over a hundred years old at the time, represented an inconvenient archaism from the perspective of confessional development which the Protestant Estates had already unsuccessfully tried to change during the 1540s (in 1543). Given the primary interest Emperor Charles had in the stabilization of the religious situation, part of the Empire (especially Imperial towns) still adopted the afore-mentioned Augsburg Interim and practised it for several years (during the time of Emperor Charles V.'s power superiority).

Emperor Charles V. tried to use his years of power superiority in the Empire (1547–1551) not only to enforce state and religious reforms, but also to establish a single Imperial currency.[16] His draft II. Imperial Mintage Act was one of the main points of another "Habsburg" Imperial Diet that was held in 1550 and 1551, also in Augsburg.[17] However, this Diet was a breakthrough milestone; after it, the Imperial Estates' resistance against the Emperor's reforms grew to such dimensions that it again stimulated the Estates opposition to military resistance. A direct stimulus became the criticism of the Emperor's plans to restrict the princes' influence in the administration of the Empire, and the attempt to enforce the long-term succession of the Spanish branch of the Habsburgs in the Imperial government.

Thus, as early as the end of 1551, plans were created for a military resistance against the Emperor, whose main architect was the new Elector of Saxony, Moritz.[18] At the start of 1552, the league of Protestant Imperial princes even received direct French support, confirmed by a contract dated the 15th of January 1552. In addition to Moritz, Elector of Saxony, the newly-formed Imperial opposition was also led by Duke John Albert of Mecklenburg and Landgrave William of Hesse, son of the imprisoned Philip of Hesse.

---

15 Günther Wartenberg, "Philipp Melanchton und die sächsisch-albertinische Interimspolitik," Lutherjahrbuch 55 (1988), 60–80.

16 Petr Vorel, Monetary Circulation in Central Europe at the Beginning of the Early Modern Age – Attempts to Establish a Shared Currency as an Aspect of the Political Culture of the 16th Century 1524–1573 (Pardubice, 2006), 61–102.

17 RTA 1550/1551, 60–62, 1619–1629.

18 Christian Winter, "Kurfürst Moritz von Sachsen als Haupt der reichsständischen Opposition genen Kaiser Karl V.", in Kaiser und Kurfürst – Aspekte des Fürstenaufstandes 1552. Geschichte in der Epoche Karls V., Band 11, ed. Martina Fuchs and Robert Rebitsch, (Münster 2010), 51–70.

With significant French financial support which allowed it to hire a new army, the opposition princes organized a new military campaign against the Emperor. In mid-March 1552, the Estates army began to march from Leipzig in Saxony in the direction of Augsburg, which it occupied at the start of April, after brief negotiations and without a fight. Emperor Charles V., who had still felt quite safe in the Empire at the Imperial Diet in Augsburg in 1551, did not have an army at his disposal that could face up to the Estates army. He began to hastily negotiate the dispatch of military reinforcements from Italy; however, the Estates opposition did not allow him time to form a truly effective defence.[19]

Under the pressure of a military threat, negotiations began with both Habsburgs about a new arrangement of power relationships in the Empire. As early as the end of April 1552, preliminary talks about the possible compromise resolution of contentious issues took place between Elector Moritz and King Ferdinand in the Upper Austrian town of Linz. The date for official diplomatic talks was agreed as the 26th of May 1552, in Passau.[20] However, the other Habsburg, Emperor Charles V., was not willing to compromise on the achieved positions, confirmed at the two previous Imperial Diets (1548 and 1551). So, in mid-may 1552, the Estates army began a surprising and rapid campaign from Augsburg in the direction of Innsbruck, where both Habsburgs stayed at the time while they awaited military reinforcements. Contrary to all expectations, by the 18th of May 1552 the Estates army managed to use military cunning to very quickly take control of a well-fortified stronghold (Ehrenberg Castle) which guarded the entrance to an Alpine pass approximately 90 km north-west of Innsbruck. But the report of the loss of this main defensive element on the route to Innsbruck only reached the Emperor after a considerable delay, shortly before the Estates army itself arrived. The hasty and badly-organized evening departure by the Imperial Court from Innsbruck resembled a fast escape taking several days, headed in the direction of safety in Villach in Carinthia.[21]

---

19   Lau, A History of the Reformation, 225–239.
20   Julius Witter, Die Beziehungen und der Verkehr des Kurfürsten Moritz von Sachsen mit dem Römischer Könige Ferdinand sei dem Abschlusse der Wittenberger Kapitulation bis zum Passauer Vertrage (Neustadt a. d. Haardt, 1886), 76–88.
21   Tracy, Emperor Charles V, 233–238; Robert Rebitsch, "Der Kaiser auf der Flucht. Die militärische Niederlage Karls V. gegen die deutsche Fürstenopposition im Jahre 1552", in Kaiser und Kurfürst –

The Emperor's escape from Innsbruck to Villach represented the symbolic end of his power superiority in the Empire, as it was evident that without the permanent presence of his Spanish and Italian troops he was not able to control the Empire. This new situation also contributed to a more significant deepening of the conflicts which divided the Habsburg brothers themselves on a number of issues. The younger Ferdinand, who for dynastic and power reasons had had to stand for many years in the imaginary shadow of his elder brother Charles, could now demonstrate his monarchal qualities more distinctly. That is why further talks with the Imperial opposition were led only by King Ferdinand, whose compromise monarchal and confessional policy made him a more acceptable partner for the Imperial opposition than Emperor Charles V.[22]

So it was King Ferdinand rather than the Emperor who subsequently concluded a peace treaty with opposition princes on behalf of the Habsburg side, which entered history in 1552 as the so-called "Peace of Passau."[23] For Emperor Charles V., this compromise agreement meant a significant concession on the positions obtained in the Empire after 1547.[24] Most of the reforms which the Emperor had enforced were stopped; the recently-adopted (1551) II. Imperial Mintage Act under which Habsburg policy supporters, at least, began minting common Imperial coins, was enforced only with difficulty. The leaders of the Schmalkaldic League, imprisoned by the Emperor since 1547, were released, and the Emperor had to renew certain important opposition leaders' property holdings. That is how, for example, prince Wolfgang, one of the founding members of the Schmalkaldic League, was reinstated as ruler of the Anhalt-Bernburg princedom.

However, even after the conclusion of the "Peace of Passau", which in many respects returned the Empire's internal structure to the way it had been before 1547 and guaranteed the princes their former rights, the situa-

---

Aspekte des Fürstenaufstandes 1552. Geschichte in der Epoche Karls V., Band 11, ed. Martina Fuchs and Robert Rebitsch, (Münster 2010), 119–138.

22 Gerhard Fischer, Die persönliche Stellung und politische lage König Ferdinands I. vor und während der Passauer Verhandlungen des Jahres 1552 (Königsberg, 1891).

23 Gerhard Bonwetsch, Geschichte des Passauischen Vertrags von 1552 (Göttingen, 1907); K. Zeumer, ed. Quellensammlung zur Geschichte, II, 340–341; F. Brendle, "Um Erhalt und Ausbreitung", 84–89.

24 Heinrich Lutz, Christianitas afflicta - Europa, das Reich und die päpstliche Politik im Niedergang der Hegemonie Karls V. 1552–1556 (Göttingen, 1964).

tion in the Empire remained tense. For Emperor Charles V., the renewal of disturbances was complicated significantly by the simultaneous renewal of the war with France, whose new ruler Henry II, against all of the Emperor's expectations, used military force to occupy Lorraine and renewed French territorial claims in northern Italy and in the Empire (partially also on the basis of the afore-mentioned contract from January 1552, on whose basis he provided substantial financial support, in the form of 100 thousand gold French crowns, to the Imperial opposition).

The main protagonist of the new war in the Empire became Margrave Albert Alcibiades, member of the secondary branch of the Brandenburg Hohenzollerns, who ruled in the county of Kulmbach in Franconia.[25] Margrave Albert was Moritz of Saxony's peer, friend and long-time comrade-in-arms on military battlegrounds. At the time of the Schmalkaldic War he commanded the Habsburg army, which in early spring 1547 marched to help Moritz of Saxony; during this campaign, he was defeated by Elector John Frederick and captured during the battle of Rochlice on the 2nd of March 1547. After the Habsburgs' victory, Margrave Albert was obviously released from the Saxon prison and got his satisfaction, but he later decisively rejected Charles V.'s reforms in the Empire, and in 1551 he joined the side of the opposition princes.

However, his resistance did not finish with the Peace of Passau in 1552; Margrave Albert continued his intensive military activities even in subsequent years. Outwardly, he declared his actions to be a battle against the expansion of Catholicism, but in reality they mainly involved material interests. His army operated mainly in the area of Franconia (which is where Albert's seat, the Margraveship of Kulmbach, was found), where it mostly used military force to occupy dominions that Church princes still controlled there. The Margrave either directly subordinated the occupied territories to his rule (with the aim of creating a territorially-extensive Duchy of Franconia under his rule), or he demanded exceptionally large sums of cash from the bishops, abbots or towns, as ransom or protection

---

25   Andrea Badea, "Es trieb ihn längst zum Krieg in der Unruhe seines Geistes." Markgraf Albrecht von Brandenburg-Kulmbach und der Fürstenaufstand," in Kaiser und Kurfürst – Aspekte des Fürstenaufstandes 1552. Geschichte in der Epoche Karls V., Band 11, ed. Martina Fuchs and Robert Rebitsch (Münster, 2010), 99–118.

money. The bishops of Würzburg and Bamberg met this fate. During the summer of 1552, he even demanded pecuniary "ransom" from Church Electors (of Mainz and Trier), whom he threatened with pillaging their dominion if they refused to pay the "protection money". These were not merely idle threats, as the Margrave's troops demonstrated in the case of the Bishop of Speyer who had refused to pay a large sum of money for protection (150 thousand Rhenish guilders). In this way, Margrave Albert even extorted money from Imperial towns in Franconia (Speyer, Worms), and used military force to occupy the town of Schweinfurt, which then became an important foothold for him. He even dared to besiege the town of Nuremberg, which he had twice vainly tried to conquer. He ended the devastating siege of the town only after pillaging the extended surroundings (i.e. most of the territory controlled by the town of Nuremberg) and received payment from its citizens.

So, in the first phase of his military activities, Margrave Albert Alcibiades did not wage war against the Emperor; rather, it was an internal anective war that affected Habsburg interests indirectly, as it significantly economically weakened the Habsburg allies in the Empire, i.e. mainly Church (Catholic) princes. Church and secular princes and towns from the Franconia region which felt threatened by Margrave Albert, quickly merged into defensive sub-coalitions, until they created the relatively powerful so-called Heidelberg League. The most important member of this League became the town of Nuremberg, which financed its own relatively powerful army commanded by Haugh von Parsberg.

For some time, Charles V. did not tactically interfere with these disputes, as it was evident that, under certain circumstances, Margrave Albert's military assistance could be useful to him in the war against France. For example, this happened during the French siege of the fortress of Metz, when the Emperor promised Margrave Albert a confirmation of his territorial gains in Franconia in return for operative military assistance.[26]

However, from the perspective of a long-term strategy, Margrave Albert's activities were dangerous for the Habsburgs. If they were allowed to take their course, not only would they lead to the creation of a new powerful

---

26   Tracy, Emperor Charles V, 239–240.

Lutheran princedom in the last remaining significantly Catholic Imperial region (i.e. in Franconia), but they would also weaken the Catholic side's positions at the Imperial Diet. But the military forces of Charles V. were tied up in the renewed military conflict with France, which is why the approach chosen to suppress Margrave Albert's expansion was similar to the one used in 1546 against the Schmalkaldic League. Margrave Albert was declared a violator of Imperial peace, and an Imperial anathema was imposed on him. The implementation of this anathema was again entrusted to Moritz of Saxony and Ferdinand I. of Habsburg (similarly to the case in 1547).

But, this time, other secular and Church princes and towns also provided troops. In this phase of the war, it was mainly the town of Nuremberg that became involved against the Margrave, as well as Henry of Brunswick-Wolfenbüttel from the ranks of the secular princes and the bishops of Bamberg and Würzburg from the ranks of the Church princes. Part of the military corps was also provided by the Kingdom of Bohemia. From the Bohemian perspective it was important that Margrave Albert had also destroyed the territory around Nuremberg which was, being a so-called external fiefdom, part of the lands of the Bohemian Crown. Particularly significant was the damage that the Margrave caused to the towns of Lauf and Altdorf, which the Luxembourgs had connected to the Bohemian lands as far back as the 14th century, and which the town of Nuremberg held as a fiefdom from the King of Bohemia. That's why, in this stage of the war, King Ferdinand of Habsburg once again turned to the Bohemian Estates to help him with the military campaign whose aim was to defend the territory which may have been located inside the Empire, but which was de jure part of the Bohemian Crown.

On the 9th of July 1553, in the mutually destructive and bloody Battle of Sievershausen, Margrave Albert was defeated. However, he himself escaped from the battle, while the victorious Moritz of Saxony died from the consequences of his injuries, just like another important pro-Habsburg protagonist of the Schmalkaldic War, Duke Henry of Brunswick-Wolfenbüttel.

The victorious Habsburg troops then continued to march on the territory of Margrave Albert, which they systematically pillaged (even the towns of Hof and Bayreuth were besieged and destroyed), just like the Margrave's troops had liquidated the economic facilities of the town of Nuremberg a year earlier. Margrave Albert withdrew his remaining military forces into his well-fortified residencies, being the town of Kulmbach and the nearby castle of Plassenburg.[27] The siege of these two fortresses constituted the final phase of the war against Margrave Albert. Kulmbach was conquered on the 26th of November 1553; its siege was led by (similarly to the siege of the town of Hof shortly before that)[28] Henry of Plauen († 1554), supreme Chancellor of the Kingdom of Bohemia.

The allies then used their remaining forces to attack the last of the Margrave's fortresses that still resisted – Plassenburg. The well-fortified castle, whose garrison was commanded by Joachim von Zedtwitz, resisted successfully until June 1554. During that time, Margrave Albert himself stayed in the safety of fortress Schweinfurt, where from spring 1554 he gathered forces and recruited new troops. However, during the march to help the besieged Plassenburg, the Margrave's army was defeated in June 1554 at the Battle of Schwarzach, mainly through the efforts of the Bohemian army of King Ferdinand I., under the leadership of Utraquist leader Bohuslav Felix Hasištejnský of Lobkovice. After this defeat of the Margrave's army, Plassenburg's defence also surrendered, and it was occupied and destroyed. Margrave Albert once again escaped from the battle and retired into exile in the court of his brother-in-law Charles of Baden (husband of Albert's sister), but he no longer interfered in Imperial politics, and died in seclusion. His own territory (the Margraveship of Brandenburg-Kulmbach) was taken over by the Emperor into forced administration, which until 1557 (until this Margraveship was transferred to George Frederick from the Ansbach branch of the Hohenzollerns) was performed under the authorization of King Ferdinand by Albert Slik of Pasoun, who held the office of the Supreme Chancellor of the Kingdom of Bohemia after the death of the afore-mentioned Henry IV. of Plauen.

Breaking Margrave Albert's military resistance restored a state of peace to the Empire, but it did not mean victory for the Habsburg camp. The Lutheran princes' political superiority in the Empire was so significant that the Habsburgs were forced to conclude new peace treaties, which entered

---

27 Sabine Weigand-Karg, Die Plassenburg – Residenzfunktion und Hofleben bis 1604 (Weißenstadt n.d., cca 1985), 389–419.

28 Kurt Stierstorfer, Die Belagerung Hofs 1553 (Hof, 2003).

history as the so-called Religious Peace of Augsburg.[29] The agreement about the new religious-political and power arrangement of the Empire was accepted at the Imperial Diet in Augsburg in 1555.[30]

Emperor Charles V. never agreed with this treaty, which had understandably been prepared some time before the Imperial Diet was held, and regarded it merely as a forced temporary concession that could be rectified in the future. His war in France and northern Italy continued, and the Emperor did not have the strength to try to reverse the power relations in the Empire once again. This situation was also relatively well reflected in the personnel representation of the new members of the Order of the Golden Fleece, whom Emperor Charles V. (as Grand Master of the Order) appointed at the Order ceremony held nine years later (from 1546) in the Dutch town of Antwerp at the start of 1555.

The Antwerp meeting of the Order of the Golden Fleece at which Charles V., as Grand Master of the Order, accepted new members, who were to fight in the interest of the "Catholic issue" in the future, was the symbolic end of the Emperor's political career. The subsequent talks on religious peace at the Imperial Diet in Augsburg took place outside his control, and meant the end of the Emperor's plan for the confessional reunification of the Empire.[31] In 1556, he resigned from his rule of the Empire (he gave up the Imperial title), and retired to monastic seclusion. In March 1558, the collegium of Electors approved Charles V.'s resignation, and confirmed Charles' younger brother Ferdinand of Habsburg as the new Emperor.[32]

In many respects, Emperor Ferdinand of Habsburg was a more acceptable partner for the Lutheran opposition in the Empire, both thanks to his helpful consensual policy (which it had the opportunity to get to know in 1552 during the talks on the Treaty of Passau), and thanks to the fact that, after 1555, there was no more danger of Charles' son Philip II trying to gain

---

29 Zeumer, Quellensammlung zur Geschichte, II, 343–347.
30 Bornkamm, Das Jahrhundert der Reformation, 242–252.
31 Ferdinand Seibt, "Karl V. und die Konfession", in Aspectos históricos y culturales bajo Carlos V – Aspekte der Geschichte und Kultur unter Karl V., Studia Hispanica 9, ed. Christoph Strosetzki (Madrid 2000), 146–158.
32 Ernst Laubach, Ferdinand I. als Kaiser. Politik und Herrscherauffassung des Nachfolgers Karls V. (Münster, 2001), 207–254.

control of the Empire.[33] On the contrary, the young Archduke Maximilian (who at that time had already been elected King of Bohemia) promised, as the future Emperor who would succeed Ferdinand I., a completely different religious model for the Empire.[34]

In this way, rule in the Empire was practically seized in 1556 by Ferdinand I., King of Rome, and the period of his Imperial rule (1558–1564) and the rule of his son Maximilian II. (1564–1576) represented a period of unusually peaceful and positive development in the Empire's early modern history. After the complete fiasco of the world rule efforts of Charles V., which only brought destruction to the Empire and, for the first time in its history, an extensive invasion by foreign (Spanish and Italian) troops deep into the German interior, the era of Charles V. was an expensive lesson in the problems that even a wealthy and powerful country can have if its fate is connected to a foreign power that's striving for world rule. Towards the end of the first half of the 16th century, Spanish interests, and the principle of confessional policy connected with them, prevailed in Habsburg policy. The subsequent destructive war showed that such an approach was not acceptable in Central Europe.

Two generations later, towards the end of the 16th century, when most of the Empire was already non-Catholic from a confessional perspective, the threat of a superpower (Spanish) meddling in Central European affairs returned once more. That was the price that Europe paid for a system of government which several feuding monarchal families had held in their hands for centuries. Therefore, it was always easy to find a pretext for war, whether it hid behind the defence of the "true faith" or behind the expansion of the ruling house's glory.

The house of Habsburgs, divided into the Austrian and Spanish branches, may have suffered a symbolic defeat in 1555, but Emperor Charles V. left his successors in the battle for power in the Empire, among others, two important allies: The Order of Jesuits and the Order of the Golden Fleece. Both of

---

33 Laubach, "Karl V.", 48–51, Alfred Kohler, Ferdinand I. 1503 – 1564 / Fürst, König und Kaiser (München, 2003), 225–257.

34 Helmut Neuhaus, "Von Karl V. zu Ferdinand V. - Herrschaftsübergang im Heiligen Römischen Reich 1555–1558", in Recht und Reich im Zeitalter der Reformation (Festschrift für Horst Rabe), ed. Christine Roll (Frankfurt am Main – Berlin – Bern - New York - Paris –Wien, 1996), 417–440

these institutions played an important power role at the start of the second half of the 16th century in a place where, around 1543, few probably would have expected it: in predominantly Utraquist Bohemia.

At the afore-mentioned last meeting of the Order of the Golden Fleece, chaired by Emperor Charles V. at the start of 1555 in Antwerp, the newly-accepted members consisted mainly of Catholic nobles from France, Spain and Italy. New Order members were chosen completely pragmatically, with regard to current political interests. By then, for Charles V., these were outside the Empire. That is why, among new Order members from the ranks of the Imperial princes (aside from the marital or non-marital members of the Habsburg family), we find only the young Duke Henry of Brunswick-Lüneburg (born 1533), eldest son of one of the founding members of the Schmalkaldic League, Ernest of Brunswick-Lüneburg († 1546). However, that was a mistake on the Habsburgs' part, and brought the "Catholic issue" little benefit.

In 1555, for the first time in its history, the Older of the Golden Fleece was expanded to include a member of the Bohemian Estates. Vratislav of Pernštejn (born 1530), son of sometime Bohemian Neo-Utraquist political leader and long-time Estates opposition leader John of Pernštejn († 1548) became a member of the Order. This apparent detail, which barely drew any special attention in Antwerp at the time, is, for several reasons, a basic key to understanding the role of the Kingdom of Bohemia in both the Schmalkaldic War and in subsequent military conflicts which took place in the neighbouring Holy Roman Empire of the German Nation during the years 1546–1555.

THE HISTORICAL ROOTS OF THE KINGDOM OF BOHEMIA'S SPECIFIC POSITION IN CENTRAL EUROPE IN THE FIRST HALF OF THE 16TH CENTURY

To understand the relationship of the Bohemian lands to the Lutheran opposition in the Holy Roman Empire of the German Nation in the second quarter of the 16th century, one must at least briefly explain some basic relationships and regional peculiarities which had their roots deep in the past, at the time of the Bohemian state's greatest power expansion in the second half of the 14th century. That is why, first of all, I will take the liberty of briefly recapitulating the four basic thematic spheres, which I consider to be particularly important in the given context or which are so far undervalued in present specialized literature, in a broader chronological context.

The issue of the actual constitutional law relationship of the Bohemian lands to the contemporary Holy Roman Empire of the German Nation is absolutely essential to the given theme.

The property rights tenure of the King of Bohemia in the Imperial territory (the so-called Bohemian fiefdoms in the Empire) is an issue which most German works on the Schmalkaldic War do not take into consideration at all. Nevertheless, in terms of Ferdinand I.'s participation in that military conflict, it was an absolutely fundamental factor.

In comparison with neighbouring countries, the religious situation in the Bohemian lands was completely specific, as here the principle of politically-forced confessional plurality had already been practically applied within the scope of several distinct Christian churches for several generations. That is why the reaction to the Lutheran Reformation was different here to that in the neighbouring German lands or in Poland. The Bohemian side did not view the Lutheran opposition in the Empire as "co-religionists". Most of the Bohemian political representation may have been non-Catholic, but only a small (not decisive) part of it directly identified with the Lutheran Reformation at the end of the 1540s.

A system of Estates monarchy, in which the king was considerably dependent on the Land Diet's decision, had already employed in the land for several generations. However, the actual structure of the Estates in Bohemia was significantly different from the system employed in the Holy Roman Empire of the German Nation at a whole, or in individual Imperial territorial princedoms.

Of the afore-mentioned four thematic spheres, I consider basic constitutional law relationships to be the most important. Their erroneous interpretation (with which we constantly meet, even in specialized historical literature) greatly complicates the correct understanding of the role of the Bohemian lands in the context of 16th century European history.

Within the scope of the late medieval Holy Roman Empire, the Kingdom of Bohemia in its way represented the most important state structure, which with its territorial area, compactness and economic resources (thanks primarily to systematic and highly profitable silver mining) greatly exceeded any secular or Church territorial sub-princedom. In the long term, no state existed within the medieval Holy Roman Empire that was more extensive and more territorially consolidated than the Bohemian state. From the very beginnings of the continuous development of the Bohemian state in the 10th century, the Bohemian power elites participated in the creation of the internal structure of the Holy Roman Empire, and represented important partners (or opponents) for its rulers. A basic prerequisite for the long-term functioning of these relationships was their exceptional military potential: without this quality, the Bohemian princes would not be able to defend themselves against the pressure of their expansive western neighbour's power; without this quality, the alliance with the Bohemian princes would not even be useful for the Emperor. For medieval Emperors, the only partners were those whom they could not subjugate with military force. Also, medieval Bohemian princes did not acquire the royal title merely on the whim of some Emperor or other; they took it by force (and only at a time when the Bohemian state was perceived to be a part of the Empire, which is a significant difference in comparison with the development of Polish or Hungarian statehood) as a condition for staying in alliance relationships.

This situation is especially well documented at the turn of the 12th and 13th centuries, when the Bohemian ruler Ottokar I. of Bohemia acquired the hereditary royal title. He would see the start of two centuries of completely obvious dominance by the Kingdom of Bohemia within the Holy Roman Empire, when the King of Bohemia stood out considerably from all territorial Imperial princes in terms of his power influence and the economic and military resources at his disposal. Apart from Imperial might, the King of Bohemia represented the main long-term stable power element within the Empire. This developmental bipolarity is particularly evident during the period when the Emperor was significantly weakened, or when there was complete anarchy.

These older developmental tendencies culminate in the mid-14th century in the person of Charles IV. of Luxembourg, who was the first of the Bohemian kings to acquire direct rule of the Empire. The status quo, which Charles IV. tried to incorporate into basic Imperial law (the "Golden Bull" of 1356), not only reflected the contemporary dominant position of the Bohemian state in the Empire, but this ruler's period also explains the significance that the militarily and economically powerful Bohemian state had played in the previous periods. On the one hand, the Bohemian state was to a large extent independent of the development in the Empire; nevertheless, there is no doubt that it and supra-state structure had belonged together in medieval times. At the same time, the Bohemian state represented one of the few fixed power constants in the Empire's medieval history, whose support was sought out by potential interested parties in the battle for the Imperial crown (as long as they had something to offer the Bohemian monarchs), just like when in the battle for power in Bohemia, in certain phases of historical development, domestic princes tried to win the support of Imperial power (as long as they had something to offer the Emperor).

The Kingdom of Bohemia (unlike most medieval Imperial territorial princedoms) did not repeatedly break up into territorial sub-units as a result of the division of assets in the monarchal family. From the 13th century it was the only hereditary kingdom within the Holy Roman Empire, it always basically maintained the same borders (defined by the natural formation of the terrain) as well as the city of the monarchal seat, which since the 10th century has been permanently located in Prague.

Within the scope of the complicated internal political relationships in the medieval Empire, the Kingdom of Bohemia represented a stabilizing element which, if necessary, Imperial power could rely on in its battle against the Imperial opposition, during defence against a common enemy, or during territorial expansion. That is why the strengthening of the Bohemian monarch's influence was perceived among the Imperial princes as a latent danger which had to be faced. When, however, the Bohemian King Charles of Luxembourg (1346–1378) finally acquired the Imperial crown (and became Emperor Charles IV.), for the Empire it meant a relatively long period of stable and mostly peaceful life (in comparison with the immediately preceding and immediately following periods). In the late medieval period, the Empire got used to coexisting with the powerful Bohemian state, and accepted the King of Bohemia as one of the most powerful rulers within the Empire, whether it liked it or not. During the period of Charles IV., this long-term development was also completed by the transfer of the main centre of the Empire to Bohemia, and the clear strengthening of the King of Bohemia's position as the head of the seven so-called Electors of the new ruler of the Empire.

The basic principle of Charles IV.'s geopolitical construction was represented by a strengthening of the function of the Luxembourg family domains, spaced out along the horizontal geographical axis of the Empire from the Duchy of Luxembourg in the west to the Margraveship of Moravia in the east. In the mid-14th century, the Luxembourg ruling family's domains were de jure amalgamated into an independent supra-state structure within the Empire called the "Lands of the Bohemian Crown". The most important part of this multi-state coalition was the Kingdom of Bohemia itself; all of the "secondary lands" included among the "Lands of the Bohemian Crown" were also subordinated to the King of Bohemia. The capital city of the Kingdom of Bohemia (Prague) was built over several decades by the Emperor and Charles IV. of Luxembourg, King of Bohemia, as the seat of his kingdom, but also as the permanent capital city of the entire Empire. This was because, before Charles IV.'s long reign, the Holy Roman Empire did not have any permanent seat with a long-term Imperial residence,[1] which is why the Bohemia-centric

---

[1] Ferdinand Seibt, "Die Krone auf dem Hradschin. Karl IV. bündelt die Macht in Prag", in Die Hauptstädte der Deutschen - Von der Kaiserpfalz in Aachen zum Regierungssitz Berlin, ed. Ewe Schultz (München, 1993), 67–75.

model of Charles IV.'s government was a fundamental new element in Imperial history.

During his reign, Emperor Charles IV. went on to systematically attach other Imperial territories in the vicinity to the "Lands of the Bohemian Crown", including the Margraveship of Brandenburg with its seat in Berlin. At the beginning of the reign of Charles' eldest son and successor Wenceslaus IV. of Luxembourg (1378–1419) the territory of the "Lands of the Bohemian Crown" covered around a quarter of the entire Holy Roman Empire, Bohemian money (silver Prague groschen) was a universally recognized means of payment across the entire Imperial territory, the Imperial Court resided in Prague, and Czech was used as a universally accepted language of international diplomacy (the obligation by all secular Electors to have a command of Czech was enshrined by Charles IV. in the main Imperial law, the "Golden Bull" of 1356).

This Bohemia-centric model of Luxembourg government in the Empire[2] ensured the Emperor's considerable independence from Imperial princes. The wealthy Emperor, who had sufficient money at his disposal without having to collect any special taxes, as well as his own large territory which he ruled directly, could not only finance the Empire's administration and reward those loyal to him, but could also operatively mobilize a powerful army. He had sufficient money to pay the soldiers; he also had sufficient human potential from which he could draw young and well-trained fighters from the ranks of minor nobility. The great advantages which the specific economic and demographic potential of the Kingdom of Bohemia provided in this respect were well known in European politics even at the time of King John of Luxembourg (1310–1346). This aspect became even more highlighted in the mid-14th century, as the great wave of the Black Death, badly afflicting Western Europe including the German lands which immediately bordered Bohemia, practically avoided the Kingdom of Bohemia.

The Kingdom of Bohemia itself, consolidated within it natural borders and centralized relatively early, was distinguished from neighbouring Imperial territories not only by its long-term territorial integrity and above-standard own economic resources (acquired through the exploitation of several

---

2   Petr Vorel, "Český velmocenský komplex pozdního středověku", in Velmocenské ambice v dějinách (Tři studie), edited by Jaroslav Pánek, Jiří Pešek and Petr Vorel (Praha, 2015).

rich domestic silver deposits), but also by its distinctively profiled state ideology, linked to the person of the historical Přemyslid monarch Prince Wenceslaus († 935); several years after the death of the canonized. The bearer of statehood at the time was not just the monarchal family (as was usually the case in feudal Imperial structures), but historically speaking it was very soon also the domestic elite from the ranks of clerical and military aristocracy (later established as the Estates). Thanks to this, the Bohemian state as a whole managed to "survive" even deep power crises and long periods of actual non-existence of monarchal power without fundamental changes; this aspect gained special importance both at the turn of the 13th and 14th centuries, and in the fifteenth century.

That is why the Bohemian nobility viewed the political crisis of 1400, during which reign in the Empire was seized from Wenceslaus IV. of Luxembourg, King of Bohemia, on the basis of a decision by the four Rhenish Electors, as harmful to themselves and damaging to their interests. The Prague Court de jure ceased to be the centre of the Empire, but during the time of Wenceslaus' successors (Rupert of Palatine, Jobst of Luxembourg and Sigismund of Luxembourg), no comparable power centre came into existence in the Empire.

The central role of Prague within the Empire understandably receded into the background completely at the time of the Hussite Revolution (1419–1436)[3] and was not restored even during the short period when Emperor Sigismund was accepted as king in Bohemia (1436–1437) or during the reign of Sigismund's son-in-law Albert of Habsburg (1437–1439). The premature death of Ladislaus of Habsburg (†1457), at the time the only living male biological descendant (grandson) of Emperor Sigismund of Luxembourg and expected future Emperor (who would simultaneously rule the lands of the Bohemian Crown, Hungary and part of the hereditary Austrian lands), made it impossible to directly continue the older Luxembourg model of the Empire. Thus, for over half a century, reign in the Empire stayed in the hands of Austrian Archduke Frederick III. of Habsburg (1440–1493), who had originally (as guardian and close relative of Bohemian prince royal Ladislaus) represented only a provisional solu-

---

3   František Šmahel, Die Hussitische Revolution. I-III. (Hannover, 2002).

tion for the Empire, as he himself did not have any significant power base in the Empire.

As a result of the weak reign of Emperor Frederick III. (who to a large extent, even after 1457, remained dependent on his alliance with the new King of Bohemia George of Poděbrady, elected to the throne from the ranks of domestic nobility after Ladislaus' death)[4] the Holy Roman Empire experienced a deep decline, and one of the most complicated periods in its history, during the third quarter of the 15th century. The most powerful monarch in the south-east of the Empire became the Hungarian king Matthias Corvinus (†1490), who as part of the peace treaty with the Jagiellons received a part of the lands of the Bohemian Crown (Moravia, Silesia and Lusatia) in 1477 as collateral, and from the end of the 1470s gradually began to use military force to occupy Habsburg territories in Danube, including the seat in Vienna. The Habsburgs were not able to confront Corvinus' military power, which was based on rich gold deposits in the area of present-day Slovakia.

At the end of 1485, at the peak of Corvinus' military offensive in the Danube, Emperor Frederick III. gave in to the Rhenish Electors' pressure and agreed to the upcoming implementation of fundamental internal Imperial reforms, which weakened the Emperor's power in favour of the Electors and other Imperial Estates. The medieval Empire was to become an Estates monarchy in which the main legislative power would be transferred from the Emperor to the newly-established Imperial Diet; others Estates institutions were also to be established to execute the judicial agenda and administer the Empire. As consideration, Emperor Frederick III. obtained the Electors' agreement to the election of his son Maximilian as King of Rome (and future Emperor) and, most importantly, the pledge of military assistance by the pan-Imperial army, which was to liberate the Austrian lands from Hungarian occupation in the spring campaign of 1486. The main architect of the new model of the Empire was one of the Church Electors, Berthold of Henneberg, Archbishop of Mainz. The basic formal bond of the newly-formed Empire became the tax register from the turn of 1485 / 1486, according to which individual parts of the Empire were to pay money to finance a com-

---

4   Otakar Odložilík, The Hussite King – Bohemia in European Affairs 1440–1471 (New Brunswick, 1965).

mon pan-Imperial army. Only tax payers were then entitled to request military protection in the event of an attack, such as was the Habsburgs' situation, from whom Matthias Corvinus, King of Hungary, had seized a significant part of the hereditary Austrian lands.

Archbishop Henneberg's proposal did not include the already-restored Empire within its original borders, as we know it from the time of Emperor Charles IV. of Luxembourg, but common military protection was to be mutually provided only by territories that were defined, in contemporary view, as "German" in terms of language. This new (nationalistic) element in international policy received a significant state-forming response (German princes were even willing to support the establishment of a powerful "national" state financially), and it was also to be a safeguard against the efforts of other neighbouring rulers to seize the Imperial throne.

For the newly-constructed Empire, based on a common tax system (which de facto replaced the old medieval feudal ties), the old Luxembourg Bohemia-centric model no longer had any meaning. The Bohemian lands were also not suitable for the reformatory project because they were not "German". Various dialects of contemporary German were understandably used as a native language by inhabitants of mountains in the border areas, descendants of settlers to whom the so-far uncultivated forest land in the foothills and the mountains was offered for cultivation at the time of rapid economic development in Bohemia in the 13th and 14th centuries. However, they had no political rights in medieval Bohemia. The ruling class of nobles in the Kingdom of Bohemia was linguistically Czech (or often bilingual); if someone from the German language neighbourhood married into the Bohemian nobility, then their descendants had to have a command of the State language, otherwise they would be shut out from the highest level of politics and administration of the country. Also, most politically active royal towns in Bohemia at the end of the 15th century were linguistically Czech, whether their town councils were affiliated with Catholicism or Utraquism. The consequences of the Bohemian reformatory movement also created an important psychological barrier to negotiations on the Bohemian lands' future relationship with the reformed Empire. The saying "If they're Bohemian, they're a heretic" applied in Western Europe at the time. This was also one of the reasons why the main participants in Imperial reform at the end of the 15th century (Church Electors from the Rhine; i.e. Catholic prelates who rejected Bohemian Utraquism as a heretical movement) did not want the already complex negotiations about the future arrangement of the Empire to complicate the specific Bohemian confessional situation. Moreover, at the turn of 1485 / 1486, it became evident that the Bohemian state would still not be willing to pay the newly-introduced Imperial tax to finance the common army. That is why the Bohemian lands were not listed in the contemporary tax register at all.

At the start of 1486, the four Electors from the Rhine (with the consent of both of the east German Electors) agreed that the lands of the Bohemian Crown would no longer be represented even in the restored "German" Empire, and that the King of Bohemia (formerly the head of the secular Electors) would not be invited to the election of Archduke Maximilian as King of Rome in Frankfurt am Main in February 1486. This unexpected decision led to a sharp diplomatic reaction by the Bohemian side; nevertheless, common interest prevailed in the end, and within a few years it became clear how the new constitutional law arrangement in the relationship between the Empire and its former main medieval centre (the Kingdom of Bohemia) would function in the future: the Bohemian lands would not be part of the restored Empire, but the King of Bohemia would retain the title of Elector, which however in his case would not grant him any rights in the Empire, only the right to a vote in the event that a new ruler of the Empire was being elected.[5]

This newly-established constitutional law situation was then upheld at the Imperial Diet in Worms in 1495, which is rightly considered to be the year of the creation of the new early modern Empire, which began to label itself the "Holy Roman Empire of the German Nation" (abbreviated to the "Roman-German Empire"). The Bohemian lands had no representation in the newly-established Imperial Diet; the King of Bohemia did not even become a member of the collegium of Electors at the Imperial Diet (it had only six members).[6]

---

5 Petr Vorel, "Česká účast-neúčast na volbě římského krále Maxmiliána I. ve Frankfurtu nad Mohanem roku 1486", in Středověký kaleidoskop pro muže s hůlkou (Věnováno Františku Šmahelovi k životnímu jubileu), ed. Eva Doležalová and Petr Sommer (Praha, 2014), 678–693.
6 Petr Vorel, "Státoprávní vyčlenění českých zemí ze Svaté říše římské (Důsledky říšské reformy Maxmiliána I.)", Český časopis historický 111 (2013), 743–804.

During the life of Emperor Maximilian I. († 1519), this newly-established legal situation was never called into question: the Lands of the Bohemian Crown were not part of the Empire which Maximilian I. ruled as Emperor. Certain doubts on the Imperial Estates' side (but not in Bohemia) only came about after the Emperor's death, at a time when Habsburg power was becoming weak (the young Charles V. had problems in his Spanish and Dutch domains after his election as King of Rome in 1519), the Imperial Estates were discussing a new tax collection system. In order to reach any agreement at all, old written documents were inspected in a search of material containing a precedent which showed how contributions to common expenses were arranged in the past. This material became the overview of the procurement of a military escort for the newly-elected king of Rome during his planned journey to the Imperial coronation in Rome, drawn up some time in the second half of the 14ᵗʰ century.

Thus, a new Imperial tax unit came into existence, called the "Imperial month", which covered the monthly cost of maintaining a precisely stipulated number of soldiers, who were to be sent from individual parts of the Empire, together with the newly-elected King, on his coronation journey to Rome. One of the people who sent their soldiers on the "Rome" journey during the Luxembourg period was understandably also the King of Bohemia who, given his wealth and the territorial extent of the lands of the Bohemian Crown, armed by far the largest military contingent. This medieval "military obligation" by the King of Bohemia (which however related merely to the coronation journey to Rome, i.e. an event that in the Middle Ages was not held more than once over the course of an entire century), may even have been transcribed into the new Imperial tax register (the so-called Imperial Register) of 1521, but, from the Bohemian side, this newly-established tax obligation was neither recognized nor discharged, even later under the Habsburgs' reign.[7]

As a result of the above-described illogicality of its creation, the Imperial Register of 1521 was as a whole anachronistic and difficult to use in practice (in addition to the Bohemian lands it also included a number of

---

[7] Johannes Sieber, Zur Geschichte des Reichsmatrikelwesens im ausgehenden Mittelalter (1422–1521)", Leipziger historische Abhandlungen, Heft XXIV (Leipzig, 1910); Handbuch der deutschen Geschichte ed. Grundmann Herbert, Bd. 2 (Stuttgart, 1970), 769–784.

other territories, which in 1521 were no longer part of the Empire). However, the very fact that this oversight led to the inclusion of the Bohemian
lands in the list of permanent Imperial tax payers again raised the question
of whether they were part of the Empire or not. Archduke Ferdinand of
Habsburg tried to utilize the Bohemian lands' former medieval affiliation
to the Empire in 1526, when he was trying to win the Bohemian royal
throne, and asked his brother Charles V. to grant him the Kingdom of
Bohemia as a so-called "dead Imperial fiefdom", whose ruler had died without male descendants. However, Charles V. himself refused this, with the
justification that the Kingdom of Bohemia did not fall under his authority
because it was not part of the Empire.[8] When Ferdinand of Habsburg
later acquired the Bohemian royal crown by free elections, it was more convenient for him to accept the Bohemian legal opinion, according to which
the lands of the Bohemian Crown (including the so-called German fiefdoms) were not part of the Empire. This interpretation was then taken into
account during the revision of the Imperial Register, from which the Bohemian lands were struck off (similarly to other areas of France, Switzerland
and Italy, which at that time already lay outside the Empire).[9] The fact
that, from a constitutional law perspective, the Bohemian lands were not
part of the contemporary Roman-German Empire, was also upheld at the
Imperial Diet in Worms in 1545.[10]

Subsequent disputes within the Empire, which culminated in the
Schmalkaldic War during the years 1546–1547 and military secession by
the opposition Imperial nobility against the Emperor during the years
1552–1554, confirmed to the Habsburgs that it is more politically convenient for them when the lands of the Bohemian Crown are not part of the

---

8   Vorel, Velké dějiny, 18–19.
9   Johannes Müller, "Veränderungen im Reichsmatrikelwesen um die Mitte des sechzehnten Jahrhun-
    derts", Zeitschrift des Historischen Vereins für Schwaben und Neuburg 23 (1896), 115–176; Erwein
    Eltz, "Zwei Gutachten des Kurfürstenrates über die Wormser Matrikel und den Gemeinen Pfennig
    (Ein Beitrag zur Reichssteuerproblematik von Reichstag in Speyer 1544)", in Aus der Arbeit an den
    Reichstagen unter Kaiser Karl V. (Sieben Beiträge zu Fragen der Forschung und edition), Schriften
    des Historischen Kommision der bayerischen Akademie der Wissenschaften, Band 26, edd. Hein-
    rich Lutz and Alfred Kohler (Göttingen, 1986), 273–300.
10 RTA 1545, 1124–1126; Petr Vorel, "Die Länder der böhmischen Krone und das Heilige Römische
    Reich in der Frühen Neuzeit", in Neue tschechische Interpretationen der Fragen des tschechisch-
    deutschen Zusammenlebens (47. Deutscher Historikertag / Dresden 2008 - Die Vortragende der ts-
    chechischen Gastsection), edd. Jiří Pešek and Petr Vorel (Magdeburg, 2011), 21–32.

Roman-German Empire. Needless to say, Ferdinand I. of Habsburg and his successors on the Bohemian throne participated both in Imperial Diet and in other political talks within the Empire. However, these activities were in no way connected with their reign in the Bohemian lands which, since the accession of Ferdinand I. of Habsburg to the Imperial throne, had only a common monarch with the Roman-German Empire. Nothing changed about this fact later, either (until the turn of the 17th and 18th centuries), even when, after 1583, Prague again became the main diplomatic and cultural centre of the Empire during the reign of Emperor Rudolf II., and some Imperial offices were located in Rudolf's Court in Prague. However, it was this very fact that was criticized by the Imperial opposition, and the transfer of the Imperial offices from Prague to the Roman-German Imperial territory was one of the conditions for the election of Matthias II. of Habsburg as Emperor in 1612.[11]

The so-called "Bohemian fiefdoms in the Empire", referred to by the Bohemian side as the "German fiefdoms" or the "external fiefdoms" (i.e. located outside the borders of the five founding Bohemian Crown lands, which were Bohemia, Moravia, Silesia and Upper and Lower Lusatia), still remained the imaginary "inheritance" of the Kingdom of Bohemia's dominant position during the Luxembourg period in the 14th century. Although these property-legal relationships were almost two centuries old, at the time of the Schmalkaldic War (1546–1547), they represented a fundamental diplomatic context.

The significant power superiority which Emperor Charles IV. of Luxembourg achieved during his reign in the Empire, enabled him to expand his directly-controlled territorial domain. Firstly, he was interested in larger territorial units that immediately bordered the core of his Bohemian lands (formed by the Kingdom of Bohemia and the Margraveship of Moravia): Lusatia, Silesian sub-princedoms, Vogtland in Saxony, the Upper Palatinate and the Margraveship of Brandenburg. In addition to this, he systematically expanded the belt of smaller and larger territories (castles, dominions, towns), with which he linked the western (Luxembourg) and eastern (Bohemian lands) family domains across the entire territory of the Empire.

---

11 Petr Vorel, "Císařská volba a korunovace ve Frankfurtu nad Mohanem roku 1612 a česká účast na těchto událostech", Theatrum historiae 10 (2012), 59–166.

Regardless of the territorial distance or small economic significance, Charles IV. de jure incorporated all of the newly-acquired territories in the Empire into the supra-state structure of the "Lands of the Bohemian Crown."[12] Members of prominent contemporary Bohemian noble families (whose coats of arms Emperor Charles IV. had painted in the still-preserved interior décor of the Upper Palatine castle Lauf, near Nuremberg)[13] then often operated as administrators of some of these dominions in the Empire. Most of these small territories were granted by Charles IV., as King of Bohemia, to other Imperial princes, minor nobles and Imperial towns in the form of fiefdoms, by which he strengthened their dependency on the Prague power centre. Thus, all three secular Electors, as well as some important Imperial towns – in particular Nuremberg – found themselves feudally dependent on the King of Bohemia. These circumstances also played a significant role in forming the nobles' own sense of power and importance, which was present in the Bohemian aristocratic environment for several decades in the second half of the 14th century.

The afore-mentioned "German fiefdoms" remained part of the lands of the Bohemian Crown even during the 15th century, but their number no longer increased. In the case of most of these medieval fiefdoms, formal feudal dependency on the King of Bohemia was preserved, but, as a result of long periods of anarchy in Bohemia, this system was non-functional from a power and influence perspective. However, there were certain phases during which these property-legal relationships were revised in the Bohemian Royal Court. From this perspective, the year 1459 represented an important period, when thanks to the active Imperial policy of George of Poděbrady, King of Bohemia (1458–1471), most of the older feudal relationships were restored.[14] Another important period from this perspective was

12 Lenka Bobková, "Vedlejší země České koruny v politice Lucemburků a jejich následovníků (1310–1526)", in Korunní země v dějinách českého státu I. – Integrační a partikulární rysy českého státu v pozdním středověku (Sborník příspěvků přednesených na kolokviu pořádaném dne 4. června 2002 na FF UK), ed. Lenka Bobková (Praha, 2003), 9–31.

13 Franz Xaver Lommer, Die böhmischen Lehen in der Oberpfalz. Bd. I. (Amberg, 1907); Aleš Zelenka, Der Wappenfries aus dem Wappensaal zu Lauf - Zum 600. Todestag Karls IV. 1378/1978 dargestellt in maßstabgerechten Zeichnungen und kommentiert (Passau, 1978).

14 Jiří Veselý, "Obnova zahraničních lén České koruny za Jiříka z Poděbrad", Právněhistorické studie 8 (1962), 261–279; Lenka Bobková, and Jana Hanousková, "Die böhmischen Lehen in Mitteldeutschland und die Erneuerung der Böhmischen Krone durch Georg von Podiebrad im Lichte der Vorträge von Eger", in Eger 1459 – Fürstentreffen zwischen Sachsen, Böhmen und ihrer Nach-

the turn of the 1470s / 1480s, when the so-called "secondary lands of the Bohemian Crown" (Moravia, Silesia and both Lusatias) were acquired as collateral in 1477 by Matthias Corvinus, King of Hungary. Vladislaus II. Jagiellon, King of Bohemia, directly ruled just the Kingdom of Bohemia for a relatively long time, but also kept the afore-mentioned "German fiefdoms" in the Empire. That is why, at the start of the 1480s, a thorough inventory of this property was performed, individual bearers' (including both east German Electors) feudal obligations were restored, and a new office was established in Prague which was to represent the Bohemian monarch's interests in relation to his property in the Imperial territory; a so-called German fiefdoms authority.[15]

The restoration of old property-legal relationships, in which the King of Bohemia operated as the feudal lord of an extensive network of sub-domin-ions in the territory of the Empire, was also commenced by King Ferdinand I. of Habsburg immediately after his accession to the throne, and he was also supported in this activity by the Bohemian Estates.[16] Thanks to this, the so-called German fiefdoms of the Kingdom of Bohemia, located in Imperial territory, also played a fundamental role at the time of the Schmal-kaldic War and subsequent military events in the Empire. This was because the military clashes in Saxony during the years 1546–1547, and later in Franconia around Nuremberg during the years 1552–1553, to a large extent took place directly in the territory of these Bohemian fiefdoms, which King Ferdinand used as a reason for the need and legal justification of sending his troops into these areas.

The complicated religious situation, which in the case of the Kingdom of Bohemia at the end of the 1540s was fundamentally different from the development in the neighbouring Roman-German Empire, also had deep roots dating back to the Luxembourg period. Wenceslaus IV., King of

---

barn: Dynastische Politik, fürstliche Repräsentation und kulturelle Verflechtung / Cheb 1459 – Set-kání panovníků Saska, Čech a jejich sousedů: Dynastická politika, panovnická reprezentace a kul-turní vazby. Saxonia. Schriften des Vereins für sächsische Landesgeschichte e. V., Bd. 13, eds. André Thieme and Uwe Tresp (Wettin-Löbejün, 2011), 241–262.

15 Franz Haimerl, Die deutsche Lehenhauptmannschaft (Lehenschranne) in Böhmen – Ein Beitrag zur Geschichte des Lehenwesens in Böhmen mit urkundischen Beilagen (Praha, 1848); Jiří Veselý, "O soudech hejtmanství německých lén", Právněhistorické studie 16 (1971), 113–124.

16 Milan Skřivánek, "K některým aspektům lenní politiky za prvních Habsburků", Sborník prací východočeských archívů 1 (1970), 59–79.

Bohemia, refused to recognized the four Rhenish Electors' decision in the year 1400 to remove him from the Imperial throne, and Prague and its university (at the time the oldest and most important in Central Europe) remained a very important power centre, even in a pan-Imperial context. Even after the year 1400, with regard to its earlier privileged position, the Kingdom of Bohemia defined itself as a superior entity, preferring its own interests, in relation to the "rest of the Empire". This manifested itself most distinctively in the highest spheres of power politics, where the King of Bohemia, with the support of his diplomats and Bohemian noblemen, continued to be actively involved in the battle for control of the Empire, but also in the intellectual sphere, i.e. in the university environment (the Decree of Kutná Hora in 1409) and most of all in the religious sphere.[17]

It was thanks to this unusual power constellation that the Bohemian environment reacted to the contemporary deep internal crisis in the Catholic Church, manifesting itself both in the Papal Schism and in the decline of the moral authority of Church institutions.[18] Thanks to the surviving awareness of own uniqueness and the former extraordinary influence of the intellectual centre which surrounded the Prague Imperial Court, an independent reformatory movement came into existence in Bohemia. Ideologically, it pledged allegiance to its European predecessors (mainly to the proposed Church reforms formulated by English theologian John Wycliffe, †1384), but one of its advantages was also direct political support by King Wenceslaus IV. The Bohemian reformatory movement also gained a distinctive leading personality, comparable to the importance of Martin Luther in reformatory Germany one hundred years later, in University of Prague rector and preacher Master Jan Hus. The proclamation of Master Jan Hus as a heretic, and his burning to death on the decision of a Church Council in Konstanz in 1415, significantly strengthened Bohemian resistance against contemporary Catholic Church authorities, and the rapid expansion of the Bohemian Reformation, supported by the Bohemian Monarchal Court.

17 Robert J. W. Evans, "Language and Politics, Bohemia in International Context 1409–1627", in Confession and Nation in the Era of Reformations (Central Europe in comparative Perspective), eds. Eva Doležalová and Jaroslav Pánek (Prague, 2011), 155–182.

18 Jaroslav Pánek, "Nation and Confession in the Czech Lands in the pre-White Mountain Period", in Confession and Nation in the Era of Reformations (Central Europe in comparative Perspective), eds. Eva Doležalová and Jaroslav Pánek (Prague, 2011), 139–154.

The main requirements of the subsequent Hussite movement, formulated in the so-called Four Articles of Prague, were already applied in the Bohemian environment during the life of King Wenceslaus IV. (†1419), including the extensive secularization of Church property. This was because, for a number of years before the Hussite Revolution (1419–1436), the monarch had used the property tenures of most Bohemian Church institutions to pay his loans in the form of temporary liens or property shares, thanks to which the domestic nobility gained control of Church property.

Attempts at military suppression of the Bohemian Reformation by the Papal Curia and Emperor Sigismund of Luxembourg (who, after the death of his elder brother Wenceslaus IV., was prevented from assuming reign of Bohemia by the Bohemian Estates) took the form of so-called crusades, repeatedly directed at Bohemian territory. The first anti—Bohemian crusade of 1420 began the long-time internal Imperial war, led by Emperor Sigismund and the rest of the Empire against the Kingdom of Bohemia. All of the crusades during the years 1420–1431 ended in victory by the Bohemian side. In 1431 talks began about a diplomatic solution to the situation, both from a religious point of view and in terms of Sigismund's succession to the Bohemian throne.[19]

From a religious perspective, the ecclesiastical division within the Empire ended with the formal recognition of the Bohemian reformatory movement, upheld at the Council of Basel. The so-called Basel Compacts of 1436 accepted the so-called Four Articles of Prague (the original main requirements of Bohemian religious reform) and granted the Bohemians the right to an independent form of contemporary Christianity. Bohemian Utraquism formally remained part of the Catholic Church, but differed by several external elements, both in terms of religious rite (the so-called acceptance of Utraquism – the "body and blood of the Lord" - during mass) and in terms of normal ecclesiastical life (Utraquist priests were allowed to marry). Later, Pope Pius II. declared this agreement null and void (1462), and at the time of George of Poděbrady's reign (1458–1471), the Papal Curia and its Catholic allies (in particular Matthias Corvinus, King of Hungary) made many more vain attempts to suppress Bohemian Utraquism by force.

---

19 K. Krofta, "Bohemia", 65–155; Winfried Eberhard, "Der Weg zur Koexistenz (Kaiser Sigmund und das Ende der hussitischen Revolution)", Bohemia 33 (1992), 1–43.

In the Kingdom of Bohemia, the Basel Compacts of 1436 remained one of the main State laws. Their validity was also upheld by the so-called Religious Peace of Kutná Hora of 1485.[20] This was a state law, accepted by the Bohemian Estates regardless of the stance of Church institutions, which granted both confessions in the land (Utraquism and Catholicism) equal rights, and defined the issue of confessional affiliation as a private matter which should not, for example, be taken into consideration during appointments to Land offices. In the aristocratic environment, this principle actually prevailed. On the contrary, in the corporately structured urban environment, confessionally-closed communities were formed; i.e., every large town was religiously united, Catholic or Utraquist. A member of a different faith could not become a rightful citizen, or acquire real estate. That it why the religious division of the urban environment in Bohemia was relatively stable, unlike the aristocratic environment, where intergenerational changes in the religious orientation of entire families, or the confessional conversion by individuals for career or other reasons, were relatively common.

However, during the second half of the 15th century, another version of reformatory movement, based on more radical religious traditions from the Hussite period, developed simultaneously; it completely distanced itself from Papal succession and, unlike Utraquism, did not consider itself to be part of the Catholic Church. This reformatory movement was formally established in 1457, and adopted the title Unity of the Brethren.[21] It was an independent Bohemian Christian Church, whose direct successors are the so-called Moravian Brethren, who in later centuries significantly contributed to the settlement of the American continent, and still belong among influential cultural-social structures in the USA today.

The original Unity of the Brethren was based on the teachings of Bohemian thinker Petr Chelčický; it rejected the ownership of property and participation in municipal self-government, in the armed forces etc.. At the time of the conclusion of the afore-mentioned Religious Peace of Kutná

---

20 Winfried Eberhard, "Entstehungsbedingungen für öffentliche Toleranz am Beispiel des Kuttenberger Religionsfriedens von 1485." Communio viatorum 19 (1986), 129–154; František Šmahel, "Pax externa et interna - Vom Heiligen Krieg zur erzwungenen Toleranz im hussitischen Böhmen (1419–1485)", In Toleranz im Mittelalter. Vorträge und Forschungen des Konstanzer Arbeitskreises für mittelalterliche Geschichte 45, ed. A. Patschkowsky and H. Zimmermann (Konstanz, 1998), 221–273.
21 Josef Theodor Müller, Dějiny Jednoty bratrské, I. (Praha 1923), 65–90.

Hora (1485) the Unity of the Brethren was still perceived in Bohemia as a completely marginal issue of a small religious group, which is why contemporary political representation did not concern itself with its role in the country's confessional structure. It was only after the internal reforms at the start of the 1490s that the Unity of the Brethren also became attractive for wealthier aristocratic and urban social classes, and its influence and number of followers began to grow significantly. The contemporary Catholic monarch (Vladislaus II. Jagiellon) reacted to this development by issuing the so-called St. Jacob's mandate of 1508, under which the Unity of the Brethren was prohibited as an illegal ecclesiastical movement. However, this prohibition was not applied in practice, as it was the individual landed nobles, i.e. specific aristocrats, who decided on the religious situation in their dominions. At the start of the 16th century, the Unity of the Brethren also had a number of supporters, and even actual members, among important magnates. Thus, the main centres of religious and cultural life of the Unity of the Brethren became Mladá Boleslav (the dominion of the Krajíř family from Krajk) and Litomyšl (the dominion of the Kostka family from Postupice).[22]

At that time, however, relatively extensive areas of Bohemia also remained mostly Catholic. This was mainly southern Bohemia and the Rosenberg family's dominion (in the Austrian border area, which was linguistically predominantly German); as well as all border areas that were linguistically German and which had not adopted Bohemian Utraquism. However, in connection with the expansion of the Lutheran Reformation in neighbouring Saxony and other nearby German areas, these originally Catholic parts of the Bohemian territory were very quickly Lutheranized during the 1520s.

The Lutheran Reformation pledged direct allegiance to the spiritual legacy of the Bohemian reformer Jan Hus,[23] and also recognized other Bohemian Utraquist achievements (the secularization of Church property, the

---

22 Josef Petráň, "Stavovské království a jeho kultura v Čechách 1471–1526," in Josef Petráň - České dějiny ve znamení kultury (Výbor studií), ed. Jaroslav Pánek and Petr Vorel (Pardubice 2010), 60–122.

23 Siegfried Hoyer, "Jan Hus und der Hussitismus in den Flugschriften des ersten Jahrzehnts der Reformation," in Flugschrift als Massenmedium der Reformationszeit. Spätmittelalter und Frühe Neuzeit – Tübinger Beiträge zur Geschichtsforschung, Band 13, ed. Hans-Joachim Köhler (Stuttgart, 1981), 291–307; Zdeněk V. David, "Perennial Hus: Views from the Protestant Reformation to the Enlightenment." Comenius – Journal of Euro-American Civilization 2 (2015), No. 2.

abolition of priestly celibacy)[24] but, from a confessional perspective, it was not in concord with Bohemian Utraquism. Thus, in 1526, King Ferdinand as the new Bohemian monarch assumed reign of a very confessionally complex territory. Formally, the Compacts applied in Bohemia, guaranteeing dual Utraquist-Catholic faith, but in reality the confessional map of the land was significantly more complicated. A slight majority of the population pledged allegiance to traditional Bohemian Utraquism. The influence of the Unity of the Brethren, whose main centres were located in the east and north-east of Bohemia, increased significantly (especially among the nobility). A part of the Bohemian nobility continued to pledge allegiance to the Catholic faith, thanks to which the Catholic religion was also preserved in some rural areas, especially in southern Bohemia; some important Bohemian towns also defined themselves as Catholic (especially the west Bohemian town of Plzeň). The Bohemian border area, which was linguistically mainly German and which remained Catholic during the post-Hussite period, were quickly Lutheranized at the start of the 1520s.[25] An economically (but not numerically) significant part of the population was also formed by Jewish inhabitants, who did not create a compact territorial enclave in Bohemia, but instead lived dispersed throughout the urban environment, both in royal towns (with certain restrictions) and in servile noble towns (with greater freedom in craft and commercial activities).

The religious situation in contemporary Bohemia was also complicated by fact that, since Hussite times, the office of the Archbishop of Prague, to which both Catholic and Utraquist priests were subject, had remained vacant. The Bohemian Estates managed to solve the long-term absence of the Archbishop's office by establishing alternative institutions; the so-called Upper Consistory (for Catholics) and Lower Consistory (for Utraquists).[26] However, the specific extent to which statutory religious plurality was

---

24 Eva Doležalová, "National and religious aspects of the Czech reform movement in the 14th and 15th centuries and of the Hussite revolution in the mirror of Western historiography", in Confession and Nation in the Era of Reformations (Central Europe in comparative Perspective),eds. Eva Doležalová and Jaroslav Pánek (Prague, 2011), 63–75.

25 Winfried Eberhard, "Konfesionelle Polarisierung, Integration und Koexistenz im Böhmen von 15. bis zum 17. Jahrhundert." In Religion und Politik im frühneuzeitlichen Böhmen (Der Matestätsbrief Kaiser Rudolfs II. von 1609), Forschungen zur Geschichte und Kultur des östlichen Mitteleuropa, Band 46, eds. Jaroslava Hausenblasová, Jiří Mikulec and Martina Thomsen (Stuttgart, 2014): 25–45.

26 David, Finding the Middle Way, 143–167.

applied was largely influenced by specific nobles, who owned extensive landed property and found themselves in positions of landed nobility. At the time, not even the King had any tool at his disposal with which he could intervene in the religious situations in individual aristocratic dominions, which were the free property of individual members of the Estates.

In terms of Bohemian involvement in the Schmalkaldic War (1546–1547) the Kingdom of Bohemia's long-formed Estates structure represented one of the important circumstances that was difficult to understand for the Imperial princely opposition in the first half of the 16th century. The Bohemian state's estate system differed significantly from neighbouring Imperial territories in several respects. Firstly, no class of territorial princes existed here, and Imperial titulature did not have any legal weight in Bohemia. If one of the members of Silesian or Imperial princely or count families married into Bohemia, or attempted to buy landed property in Bohemia, they could be accepted into the lordly estate (as long as the lordly Curia of the Land Diet had granted them habitation rights in Bohemia; a so-called incola), and they could even use their princely or count title, but in terms of social structure, their origin brought them no benefits. Thus, an illogical situation came about, as the title of "freeman" (baron) was used in the Roman-German Empire for minor nobility, while in Bohemia and Moravia this title was reserved for only a few dozen of the most powerful families (the lords),[27] whose property or political influence often exceeded that of less important Imperial or Silesian princes.

From the end of the 15th century, Bohemian nobility was divided into just two Estates that enjoyed full political rights, being the upper nobility (the lords) and the lower nobility (the knights). The lowest class of rural military gentry, still very active in the second half of the 15th century and forming a third noble estate in Bohemia from a political perspective, was deprived of political rights at the end of the 15th century, and within a few decades practically disappeared from the country's social structure. The right to participate in political life (e.g. in the form of appointment to Land offices and execution of voting rights at the Land Diet) was pre-

---

27 Petr Vorel, "Pernstein", in Höfe und Residenzen im Spätmittelalterlichen Reich – Grafen und Herren. Residenzforschung (Herausgegeben von der Residenzen-Kommision der Akademie der Wissenschaften zu Göttingen), Band 15. IV, Teilband 2, ed. Werner Paravicini (Ostfildern, 2012), 1098–1103.

served only for members of the lordly and knightly estate, but aside from family origin it was also contingent on the ownership of unrestricted (so-called unburdened) property, whose tenure was registered at the level of the entire state in the so-called Land tables. Property circumstances were also verifiable according to the so-called tax registers, i.e. declarations of the value of landed property which individual Estates themselves submitted in connection with tax collection.[28] The vast majority of landed property in the Kingdom of Bohemia was not of a feudal nature; instead, it was free aristocratic property, or lien property (short-term lien tenure of free goods) or registered property (long-term tenure of chamber or former Church property, to which the supreme ownership rights were usually held by the monarch).

Subsequently, three Land Diet Curiae were formed in accordance with the Estates key; two noble (lordly and knightly) and one urban. Without the majority consent of the Land Diet, the King could not introduce new legal norms or taxes. In noble Curiae, the possible number of members was limited only by family origin and the tenure of any (even small) free landed property. In theory, every vote had the same weight in the relevant Curia; however, the actual social and political influence of individual nobles was evident thanks to the seating arrangement at the Diet talks. The most influential and most wealthy were the first to vote; the specific order in the seating arrangement was then determined by biological age (according to the "the elders have priority" principle). Royal towns were represented in the third Diet Curia; they were represented by trusted delegates (in this Curia, each town had only one vote). These were the Bohemian towns that were not subordinate to any nobility – in terms of the Estates structure they were "free", formally subject only to the King. The decisive vote in this Curia was held by Prague (or rather the allied Prague Towns), whose delegates were always the first to vote. The Prague Towns' standpoint was usually accepted by all other smaller royal towns, of which in Bohemia in the mid-16th century there were slightly less than forty. The King could not treat this group of provincial royal towns (which had obtained exceptional

---

28 Josef Heřman, "Zemské berní rejstříky z let 1523 a 1529", Československý časopis historický 10, (1962), 248–257; Josef Petráň, "Stavovské království a jeho kultura v Čechách (1471–1526)", in Pozdně gotické umění v Čechách (Praha, 1984), 14–72.

legal privileges at the time of the Hussite Revolution) as his own property, but their relationship with the King of Bohemia was similar to the Imperial towns' relationship with the Emperor.

However, constant tension reigned between the nobility and the royal towns in Bohemia at the start of the 16th century, as a result of growing economic competition. The development of aristocratic enterprise, and the emergence of large dominions with a newly-built closed market system, caused the royal towns to lose their former dominant production and commercial positions. Direct military confrontation between the towns and the nobility may have been prevented by the so-called Peace of St. Wenceslaus of 1517 but, in internal politics, the nobility and the towns remained in positions of latent hostility even after these main disputes were settled. Both aristocratic Estates made constant long-term efforts to restrict the royal towns' political rights at the Land Diet and to strengthen the role of the large aristocratic manors (including the development of the servile towns and townlets themselves) at the expense of the royal towns. These old and still not surmounted political-economic antagonisms were not significantly influenced by the Lutheran Reformation, and manifested themselves very distinctly in connection with the Bohemian state's relationship to the Habsburgs' war against the Imperial opposition during the years 1546–1547.

CHAPTER 5

THE KINGDOM OF BOHEMIA AT THE BEGINNING OF FERDINAND I.'S REIGN (1526–1546)

The power clash between the Schmalkaldic League and the Habsburgs, which significantly influenced the Imperial political scene after the year 1530, was watched with great interest in contemporary Bohemia, but only as events that took place in "neighbouring lands" and which practically did not affect the Bohemian state at all. Nevertheless, during the period when the Habsburgs began to lose the decisive military conflict with the Imperial opposition (the start of 1547), the majority opinion that prevailed in Bohemia was that this could be a suitable time to revise the existing relationship with King Ferdinand. During the first two decades of his reign in Bohemia, he had managed to significantly strengthen his monarchal influence, and push through certain systemic changes which the domestic Estates regarded as a danger to their older freedoms and as a breach of the pre-election capitulation, which the newly-elected King had to take an oath to adhere to before he could enter Bohemian territory at the start of 1527.[1]

The young Archduke Ferdinand (*1503), who had been freely elected King of Bohemia in autumn 1526, could not have been aware of the complex internal political, economic and religious relationships, by which the Kingdom of Bohemia differed from neighbouring countries, immediately after his election. He had no suitable advisers by his side who would have been familiar with the Bohemian environment, and he did not know the language of the decisive class of domestic aristocracy (Czech). Even his wife, Bohemian princess Anna Jagiellon, could not help him; she was not very familiar with the Bohemian environment either, as she had spent the period from her childhood until her marriage to Archduke Ferdinand (1520) in Tyrolean Innsbruck.

---

1   Pánek, "Regierungsstrategie und Regierungsformen", 323–331.

In autumn 1526, most of the domestic Bohemian nobility leaders did not have any serious reservations against Archduke Ferdinand of Habsburg, but this was only after he finally (under threat of military resistance) agreed that he could only become King of Bohemia in the form of free elections – i.e. not a hereditary king (as he himself had originally declared), but an elected one, which from a legal perspective was quite a fundamental difference. King Ferdinand never forgave the contemporary representatives of Bohemian political life (aristocratic magnates and royal towns) this "humiliation" which he experienced at the very beginning of his reign. The property and political sanctions, which he applied in Bohemia in 1547, were in their own way also "retaliation" for the hard times he had experienced at the end of 1526.

Archduke Ferdinand was a peer and brother-in-law of deceased King of Bohemia Ludwig Jagiellon (†1526), and he did not rule his own (Austrian) lands for very long. However, in the previous five years he had proved that he was capable of firmly intervening against an extensive subject rebellion, which affected the western part of the Habsburg hereditary lands at the time of the so-called German Peasants' War. His effort to consolidate central monarchal might, which he made in the Austrian lands, took place in accordance with the interests of local nobility and was directed against provincial royal towns. This suited Bohemian aristocratic leaders as early as 1526, and King Ferdinand took advantage of the constant latent tension between the nobility and towns in Bohemia at the time of the Estates Revolt in 1547.

An important role in the development of the Bohemian state was played during the entire 16ᵗʰ century by the monarch's indebtedness; this factor also played a fundamental role in Bohemian participation in the Schmalkaldic War during the years 1546–1547. At the time of Ferdinand I.'s accession to the Bohemian throne, his sister Maria (widow of deceased King Ludwig Jagiellon) estimated that direct royal debts in Bohemia may amount to around 150 thousand ducats (an annual interest of 10% was payable on this sum). Overall, monarchal liabilities were estimated at twice that sum (300 thousand ducats), but this sum also included the anticipated costs of disbursing long-pledged chamber and Church dominions back to monarchal property, which was an activity that the domestic nobility certainly had no interest in.

The problem was not so much the actual amount of the debt, but rather in the fact that, in 1526, the monarchal chamber in the Kingdom of Bohemia had practically no regular income at its disposal. Older sources of money were under long-term lien, just like most of the income from the main royal mint in Kutná Hora, a significant amount of silver mining still took place at the time. Therefore, the first problem King Ferdinand had to contend with in Bohemia was the procurement of monarchal income. He saw a way forward in the reform of the state financial administration, in the thorough application of monarchal property rights, and in the reform of the tax system. The quickest solution (i.e. using royal might to confiscate property from its owners, under some pretext) was not an option in the Bohemian lands at the time; the Estates opposition was too powerful for that. King Ferdinand I. had to wait twenty years - until 1547 - for such an opportunity in Bohemia.

The first significant governmental measure by the new King of Bohemia was the issue of the so-called Court Order on the 1st of January 1527. This document formally established several important central institutions, whose authority also extended to the Bohemian lands: the Privy Council, the Court Council, the Court Office and the Court Chamber. At the start of Ferdinand's reign, the Bohemian lands were directly affected by the establishment of the Court Chamber; a central authority that was to administer the monarch's financial affairs. From January 1527, it was to serve as the central institution for all the lands that King Ferdinand ruled. A separate office was established for the lands of the Bohemian Crown in Prague, called the Court Chamber's Bohemian division ("the Bohemian Chamber" in short).[2] At its head, the King appointed John of Wartenberg; other members included Sebastian of Weitmille, Henry Hložek of Žampach, Volf Planknar of Kyšperk, Christopher Gendorf of Gendorf, chief accountant Mikuláš Hýzrle of Chody and secretary George Žabka of Limberg.[3] This was the first group of the King's "loyal men" whom we

---

2   Václav Pešák, Dějiny královské české komory od roku 1527, část I. Začátky organisace české komory za Ferdinanda I., Sborník Archivu Ministerstva vnitra Republiky československé, svazek III. (Praha, 1930), 19–21.

3   Thomas Fellner and Heinrich Kretschmayr, eds., Die österreichische Zentralverwaltung I/2, Aktenstücke 1491–1681 (Wien, 1907), 167–171; Franz Bernhard Buchholz, Geschichte der Regierung Ferdinand des Ersten, IV. (Wien, 1834), 469.

later meet in important positions on the royal side at the time of the Estates Revolt in 1547.

The newly-appointed officials' first task was to be the revision of the monarchal debts; i.e. the precise specification of sums, creditors, reason for the incurring of the debt and its legal documentation. This reduced the amount of the expected demands by creditors, as part of them could be rejected as being legally inconclusive. The Bohemian Chamber officials also performed an inventory of all potential sources of royal income, and verified who controlled them and why. However, this approach did not have any great effect, as the domestic nobility had most of the former royal chamber dominions and fixed-income assets (so-called chamber salaries) long-secured with monarchal deeds which were hard to contest. However, at the start of Ferdinand's reign, the monarchal chamber managed to find one significant "weakness", which was the private mintage of silver coins in Jáchymov in the Ore Mountains, in the dominion of the Slik family of Pasoun.

The Slik silver mines, at the production of a great mass of coins associated with them, minted according to metrological patterns from neighbouring Saxony, represented the most profitable business activity in the Bohemian lands in the 1520s,[4] but the legal circumstances of this entire enterprise were highly debatable. After all, the profit from the Jáchymov mining enterprise had been directly dependent on the political situation from the very start of 1516. It was to be expected that the change in the political situation in 1526 would also bring about a new division of the profits from this precious metal mining income source; it was the most profitable of those operating at the time, not just in Bohemia but in the whole of Central Europe.[5]

The forced agreement on the nationalization of coin production and the silver trade was concluded between the King and the operator of the Jáchymov enterprise on the 18th of September 1528. Ten days later, a decision by

---

4 Petr Vorel, "The political context of the origin and the exportation of thaler-coins from Jáchymov (Joachimsthal) in the first half of the sixteenth century", in Proceedings of the XIVth International Numismatic Congress Glasgow 2009, II, ed. Nicholas Holmes (Glasgow, 2011), 1778–1782.

5 Josef Janáček, "Die Fugger und Joachimstal." Historica 6 (1963), 109–144; Petr Vorel, From the Silver Czech Tolar to a Worldwide Dollar. The Birth of the Dollar and its Journey of Monetary Circulation in Europe and the World from the 16th to the 20th Century. (New York: Columbia University Press, 2013), 27–52.

the Bohemian Land Diet upheld this agreement. For King Ferdinand, this was a significant diplomatic victory, by which he gained control of an important source of Bohemian royal income, which until then had been fully controlled by the Slik family of Pasoun, or rather, through their mediation, by the rulers of neighbouring Saxony and other foreign investors who had invested their funds into the start of this mining enterprise. They continued to receive their shares after 1528, but the entire enterprise was no longer as profitable; before 1528, combined mining, metallurgical and minting operations facilitated wheeling and dealing with large volumes of precious metals. The nationalization of the mint simplified control over the mining and export of silver. After 1528, miners could only legalize precious metals they had mined by supplying them to the state mint at the standard purchase price, which significantly restricted tax evasion.

However, for the Royal Chamber, it was even more important to control the market mechanisms in the Ore Mountains silver trade. Until 1528, the decisive share in the Bohemian portion of the silver mined in the Ore Mountains was sent to the Saxon market, to Leipzig. The entire trade took place under the control of Saxon miners, who paid shares to the Sliks as landed nobility, and to a small group of contemporary Bohemian politicians as the guarantors of the legal framework for their activities in Bohemia. The combined revenue from the Jáchymov mines, smelting plant, coin mintage and silver trade amounted to several hundred thousand Rhenish guilders per year in the mid-1520s. Zdeněk Lev of Rožmitál, who was financially involved in the Jáchymov enterprise and who had an overview of the profits, estimated the net profit from Jáchymov to be around 70 thousand Rhenish guilders for the second quarter of 1527 alone; i.e. over a quarter of a million Rhenish guilders per year.[6] These sums also had a significant influence on the monarchal budget. In the first half of the 1540s, according to the preserved ledgers of the Court Chamber in Vienna, the annual budget of King Ferdinand I.'s Royal Court was less than one million Rhenish guilders.

The first steps to controlling the Ore Mountains silver trade were a very significant - but actually the only - evident success that King Ferdinand

---

6   Pešák, Dějiny královské české komory, 141–145; Nemeškal Lubomír, "Jáchymov v hospodářských dějinách 16. století", Folia Historica Bohemica 11 (1987), 213 – 232.

achieved at the start of his reign in his effort to diversify permanent sources of monarchal income. This came about thanks to the support displayed for his efforts by a significant part of the Bohemian Estates. The Ore Mountains enterprise was not a collective Estates entitlement, but business activity by a small group of domestic nobility which, with the help of Saxon mining investors and thanks to the well-organized (and partly illegal) export of silver, had for several years enriched itself at the expense of the monarch (and therefore also the state budget).

The transfer of these activities under the monarch's control to none of the Bohemian Estates (apart from those who were directly involved in this trade) was in no way financially demanding. On the contrary; the idea of the King's increased solvency thanks to the Ore Mountains silver may have been attractive, as the King could begin repaying old debts more quickly. However, in the late 1520s, Causa Jáchymov had a much broader background, because it was in fact a mining enterprise realized under Saxon direction.[7] Ferdinand's actions in the case of the nationalization of the Jáchymov mint and the silver trade significantly influenced the Saxon market for this precious metal. More precisely, the great volume of commercial silver which flowed from the Bohemian side of the Ore Mountains to the precious metal market in Leipzig in Saxony until 1528 was restricted by King Ferdinand, and to a large extent turned in the other direction: to Habsburg creditors in Augsburg and Nuremberg.

Ferdinand's actions in Bohemia (although they may have been completely justified in terms of state laws and the logic of the matter) understandably caused resentment on the Saxon side, and became one of the arguments of the Lutheran opposition in the Empire, which feared a significant growth in the influence of the younger of the Habsburg brothers in Imperial politics. Even in the Roman-German Empire, the highly profitable mining and monetarization of silver was a sensitive issue. Unlike gold, silver was still not imported to Europe from overseas in great quantities at that time (this phase only began in the 1540s), and the price of silver against gold on the international market was rising.[8] That is why German miners

---

7   Lubomír Nemeškal and Petr Vorel, Dějiny jáchymovské mincovny a katalog ražeb I. 1519/1520–1619 (Pardubice, 2010), 9–7.

8   Petr Vorel, Stříbro v evropském peněžním oběhu 16.-17. století 1472–1717 (Praha, 2009), 123–156.

feared the growth of the political influence of the Habsburgs and the south German banking houses linked to them (the Fuggers, and others) as the proposed Imperial monetary reform also contained ideas about the introduction of a single purchase price for silver, which would have been disadvantageous for the miners. So, in talks on the introduction of the I. Imperial Mintage Act (1524), the political and economic interests of the "miners", i.e. mainly those in Saxony, still prevailed.[9]

However, the restriction on the trade with Bohemian silver in 1528 also strengthened the domestic Bohemian Estates opposition. The reasons which brought part of the Bohemian Estates into the royal opposition camp were varied, and changed gradually; understandably, they also had a religious-political dimension. But it was in 1528 that the most active core of anti-Habsburg opposition in Bohemia came into existence, bringing together a group of nobles connected to the Saxon Court who lost an important source of income as a result of the nationalization of the Jáchymov mint and the export of silver. These included some representatives of the Slik family of Pasoun, Hanuš Pluh of Rabštejn, Christopher of Švamberk, and others.

This interest group became significantly radicalised after 1545, when the administration of the Jáchymov government mint was also taken away form the Slik family by court order, and their share of the profit from the mining activity ceased to be paid to them.[10] Christopher Gendorf of Gendorf was appointed the new royal administrator of the mining district in Jáchymov, who (as Supreme Governor) was to oversee that the king did not incur any losses during the mining of silver, its metallurgical processing, its trade, or monetarization.[11] This, however, led to the emergence of a relatively complex credit problem. Until the 1520s, an exceptionally large debt of 90 thousand Rhenish guilders was owed to the Sliks by the Jáchymov mining district. After the death of Stephen Slik († 1526), it was passed on to his then under-age son Moritz. This sum (composed mainly of investments by Saxon mining entrepreneurs) was to have been paid over the long term

9   Vorel, From the Silver Czech Tolar, 56–60.
10 Nemeškal, Dějiny jáchymovské mincovny, 47–76.
11 Nemeškal, Dějiny jáchymovské mincovny, 47–76.

from the very shares that were paid to the Sliks every year.[12] When King Ferdinand stopped this regular flow of money in 1545, is became clear that this twenty-year-old debt would not be paid unless some fundamental political change came about in Bohemia. That is also why John Frederick, Elector of Saxony, directly supported this group of radical (and, from a confessional perspective, mostly Lutheran) part of the Bohemian Estates opposition, involved in the Jáchymov mining enterprise and represented on the political scene mainly by Kašpar Pluh of Rabštejn.

By the time of Archduke Ferdinand's accession to the Bohemian throne, the Habsburgs had many years of experience battling Estates opposition in the Netherlands, in Spain, and most recently also in the hereditary Austrian lands. The process which King Ferdinand began to apply in the Kingdom of Bohemia was very similar to the earlier approach of his brother Charles V. in Western Europe. It consisted of the gradual and systematic restriction of the actual influence of the lower Estates (i.e., in Bohemia, the knightly and urban Estates) in favour of the upper nobility (the lordly estate). It was easy to tie the numerically small, but exceptionally influential group of domestic magnate families to the Monarchal Court and use various means to weaken their opposition role. Or, if necessary, to remove a specific political opponent from the power scene. It was not possible to deal with the numerically powerful Estates grouping in this individual manner, which is why the royal towns and the knightly estate represented a greater possible danger as political opponents than the small group of influential magnates. That is why the first measures which the King implemented in political practice in the Kingdom of Bohemia were purposefully focused on restricting the knightly and urban Estates' ability to take action.

One of these measures became the prohibition on organizing Regional Assemblies without the monarch's explicit consent in 1528. Thus the King eliminated most of the minor and less affluent rural nobility from political life. In previous decades, before the statewide Land Diet was held, it was common procedure to hold preliminary regional talks in each of the fourteen regions, into which the Kingdom of Bohemia had been traditionally

---

12 KomS, Book No. 49, fol. L 13.

divided since the 15th century for tax and military purposes (the Land army was convened according to regions in the event of an external threat to the state, and declaration of mobilization).[13] At the regional level, the Estates agreed on their standpoints on the most important issues, which the forthcoming Land Diet was to address, and authorized a specific representatives who were to defend this standpoint at the Diet.

This traditionally tested procedure was particularly important in the case of the very large rural nobility. The vast majority of minor nobility members could not turn out for the Land Diet in Prague due to technical or existential reasons (long journey, high accommodation costs, etc.), but they could all convene in a nearby regional town without any major problems. The Regional Assembly's resolution, interpreted by an authorized delegate, had a much greater weight at the Land Diet than an individual's opinion. This system worked in Jagiellonian Bohemia, and the rural gentry was accustomed to expressing itself in this manner in relation to important statewide issues.

The royal decision of 1528 did not mean the complete end of Regional Assemblies in Bohemia, but they could no longer be held without the King's consent and therefore outside his control. They were still sometimes convened in subsequent years, if necessary. However, a significant change in the country's political system was brought about by the purposeful disruption of the regular organizing of Regional Assemblies as regional platforms from which standpoints emerged for talks at the Land Diet.[14] In the 1520s, the knightly estate in Bohemia was still a politically influential and powerful grouping, which played a significant role in the fragile power equilibrium between the magnate aristocracy and the wealthy royal towns. After 1528, it took just a few decades of absence of Regional Assemblies for the numerically powerful but less prosperous rural gentry as a whole to be de facto pushed to the margins of active political life. In the second half of the 16th century, participation in public political affairs ceased to be a normal part of a rural knight's life; rather, it was an occasional distraction whereby

13   Jan Pelant, "České zemské sněmy v létech 1471–1500", Sborník archívních prací 31 (1981) 340–414.
14   Jaroslav Pánek, "Český a moravský zemský sněm v politickém systému České koruny doby předbělohorské", in Sejm czeski od czasów najdawniejszych do 1913 roku, ed. Marian J. Ptak (Opole, 2000), 31–47.

he left the comfort of his rural stronghold and set off to attend the Land Diet session in Prague. But the vast majority of rural nobles had no interest in their mundane lives being livened up in this way; travel expenses and long-term accommodation in Prague were becoming more and more expensive, and the actual participation in the Diet (apart from a certain life experience) did not bring the rural noble any immediate benefit. That is why, from the start of King Ferdinand's reign, the structure of the Land Diet's Knightly Curia gradually began to change.

Another one of the new monarch's measures that was to influence the urban estate's political activity was a prohibition on meetings of "large municipalities" (i.e. the community of all fully-fledged citizens) in royal towns without explicit royal consent (1528). In the relationship with royal towns, this was analogous to abolishing the Regional Assemblies, as the prohibition on Regional Assemblies did not fundamentally affect political life in the towns (only elected representatives of royal towns participated in their talks, just like in Land Diets). However, it was the very gathering of "large municipalities" that represented the basic political platform in the royal towns themselves. Their prohibition resulted in the elimination of most fully-fledged citizens ("neighbours") comprising the urban municipality from the political life of specific towns, regardless of their property background. The purpose was similar to that in the case of the Regional Assemblies – reduce the number of politically active persons to a smaller group which will be easy to manipulate. The prohibition on the free convening of "large municipalities" resulted in the growth of town councils' power influence in royal towns, which is why the monarch's battle to control royal towns (as important parts of the Estates opposition) became purposefully focused on the personnel composition of town councillor committees in royal towns. However, it was several more years before the King managed to appoint his own "loyal people", through whom he could directly influence the very personnel composition of the town councils, to key functions in the Estates government system.[15]

After all, in the battle with the Estates opposition, Ferdinand I. of Habsburg had experience not only from his own hereditary Austrian lands,

---

15 Petr Vorel, "Politická komunikace české stavovské opozice roku 1547 (Regionální aspekt a role "Přátelského snešení" ve stavovském odboji)", Theatrum historiae 15 (2014): 51–96.

but also from the environment of the Imperial Estates, towards whom he acted as the Imperial governor of his brother, King of Rome (and later Emperor) Charles V. of Habsburg in the first half of the twenties. He was well aware that, as King, he could easily deal with one, or even several, rebellious princes. However, if the opposition were to unite at Diet level, it would not be easy for the King to enforce his will in the Estates monarchy system. This was also another reason why it took a relatively long time for King Ferdinand to recruit his "loyal people" among members of the old domestic families for whom, in the second half of the 1520s, common long-term Estates corporate interests represented a more important value than the monarch's personal favour. During individual talks with specific Estates leaders, King Ferdinand used several power instruments, regardless of the confessional orientation of the person in question. It was two "coercion" models that manifested themselves most distinctly.

One consisted of the offer of careers for the noble families' up-and-coming young generation. This was a tried-and-tested strategy which had also been used by Charles V. with the Spanish and Imperial nobility. The young sons of aristocratic leaders (including those of the opposition) were invited to come to the Monarchal Court and act as noble company for the members of the Habsburg family. Such an offer was difficult to resist; the experience of generations showed that this was the way highest offices and power influence could be attained in the future. That is why, at the start of the forties, when Ferdinand I.'s sons began to reach boyhood, he also began to apply this strategy in Bohemia. The same then applied for Habsburg princesses, who were to have their own "women's society" composed of young ladies from influential Bohemian noble families.

The domestic magnates could not raise any objections to such a request – after all, they themselves wanted the King's children to grow up in the company of their Bohemian peers, if only to learn to speak Czech well. Thus, during the first half of the forties, the Habsburg Court was expanded to include a relatively large group of young men and women from the most eminent domestic Bohemian and Moravian families. These then became de facto hostages during the tense crisis in the Empire at the end of 1546 and in the spring of 1547 – so their fathers had a good reason to be involved in opposition activity as little as possible.

The second coercion model related to land tenure. King Ferdinand conveniently made use of the specific property-legal situation in Bohemia (and partly also in Moravia) where, from the end of the 1430s, a significant part of medieval Church and monarchal (chamber) property had been transferred to aristocratic tenure in the form of long-term liens, whose disbursement was also restricted by some other conditions. Such dominions were referred to in Bohemia as "registered" and, from a legal perspective, they were perceived as being almost at the level of unburdened (free) tenure.[16] In the case of this form of land tenure, its future disbursement back to monarchal hands was always theoretically taken into consideration (even in the case of the former property of defunct monasteries). Given the gradual devaluation of the currency, the original lien sums from the 15th century represented relatively small amounts of money. That is why the possibility of the reverse disbursement of extensive dominions represented a real threat for many magnates, which King Ferdinand had purposefully taken into account from the very beginning of his reign, when he was actively interested in the legal context of land tenure in the Bohemian lands.

The problem which the domestic nobility faced with the old lien tenures was specific only to the Kingdom of Bohemia and partly also to the Margraveship of Moravia. In the mid-16th century, no similar land tenure structure existed in other Crown lands or in the immediate vicinity, as its basis was the secularization of Church property in Hussite times, as well as the subsequent extensive liens of chamber property during the Jagiellons' reign. For King Ferdinand, the existence of such a property structure was more convenient than the remainders of medieval feudal structures that survived in many other places, as he could effectively utilize the fears about the disbursement of old liens to obtain cash funds.[17]

In most cases, the King could not immediately disburse the old liens, as the influential magnate families had managed to insure the thus-acquired property with certain legal mechanisms in Jagiellonian times. For example, a common measure which complicated the potential reverse disbursement of Estates under lien was the condition that the lien sum was to be paid only in cash, usually in gold, which could have meant a technical problem even

16   Vorel, Velké dějiny, VII., 110–118.
17   Pešák, Dějiny královské české komory, 89–90.

for the monarchal chamber. Another level of "protection" was the promise that King may not transfer the lien to a third party; he could only disburse it for himself in the future. In the case of Church property, an important condition was that the property could only be disbursed by the original Church institutions, and only for their own needs. In particular, this related to dominions in Bohemia that had formerly belonged to monasteries which no longer physically existed in the 16th century.

However, King Ferdinand found a way to exact the financial contributions. He used the obvious difference between the original lien sum, maybe as old as the first half of the 15th century, and the current market value of the dominion in his time. He did not refund the money which he was to pay the Bohemian magnates for demonstrated services (usually the dispatch of an army, or its maintenance in the field) in cash; instead, he merely increased the old lien sum by the appropriate amount. So the contemporary monarchal deeds, on which the King "credited" thousands of extra three-scores groschen to old liens, were not a manifestation of monarchal favour, but usually a form of forced and de facto non-refundable financing of the monarchal budget. Royal deeds with this content represent the most numerically-extensive documentary agenda of the Court Chamber's Bohemian division from the years 1527–1547.[18]

Magnates whose dominions were to a large extent formed by old liens were the ones most threatened by this process. They faced combined pressure in the form of higher and regular tax rates, whose extent was derived from the actual value of the landed property, and the above-described form of forced and non-refundable loans. Holders of lien dominions could not defend themselves against these practices effectively, as they could not utilize the Estates principle of protecting common interests. The conditions in every lien deed were different, and the King dealt with every such noble separately, away from the Diet floor. In theory, the noble could refuse the King the afore-mentioned increase in the lien sum (i.e. the non-refundable loan), but in such a case it was to be expected that the monarch would exercise their rights to reverse disbursement as soon as possible, even if the monarchal treasury was completely empty. The cheaply-dis-

---

18 Pešák, Dějiny královské české komory, 190–191, 371–377.

bursed dominion could be immediately sold on to another interested party at a higher price.

The extent to which this economic pressure was perceived in Bohemia as a danger is also evidenced by the exceptional case of the largest financial transaction, realized in Bohemia in the late thirties. This was the lien on Kłodzko (Glatz) county which, on the basis of a large financial sum, was taken over in 1537 at a value of 113,464 Rhenish guilders for a period of six years by the wealthiest domestic magnate, John of Pernštejn. The transaction was distinctly disadvantageous for him, as he himself had to borrow money, on which he was paying interest of 10%, to place a lien on the county. At the same time, the direct revenue from the county (on which little chamber property was found) was less than the interest that Pernštejn had to pay on these loans. Nevertheless, he agreed to this transaction, as he had managed to include an important condition in the lien contract: during the period that Kłodzko was under lien, all other landed property belonging to Pernštejn in Bohemia and Moravia would be regarded as free property; i.e. the King could not increase the lien sum even for Church and chamber dominions that were under lien.[19]

The King's actions in relation to John of Pernštejn (1480–1548) were also highly unusual for the reason that, at the turn of the 1530s / 1540s, this noble stood at the head of the Bohemian Estates. He was predetermined for this position not only by his ancestry and his extensive experience from political life, in which he had actively participated since the start of the 16th century in the role of Moravian provincial governor, but mainly by his enormous landed property; the largest land tenure concentrated in the hands of a single person throughout all of the lands of the Bohemian Crown.[20] Both his unburdened dominions, and those under lien, were spread around both parts of Moravia and eastern Bohemia and, as a result of long years of guardianship administration of the Princedom of Cieszyn (Teschen), Pernštejn's influence even reached deep into Silesia. On the basis of these property connections, John of Pernštejn had long-term personal contacts with the

19 Petr Vorel, "Hrabství kladské a finanční politika krále Ferdinanda I. ve druhé třetině 16. století", Východočeský sborník historický 12 (2005), 3–14.

20 Petr Vorel, "Vývoj pozemkové držby pánů z Pernštejna v 15. - 17. století", in Pernštejnové v českých dějinách (Sborník příspěvků z konference konané 8. - 9. 9. 1993 v Pardubicích), ed. Petr Vorel (Pardubice, 1995), 9–76.

Estates municipalities of the afore-mentioned three Crown lands, and he was generally recognized as a political authority. From a religious perspective, he was one of the most important bearers of the domestic tradition of so-called supra-confessional Christianity, whose external manifestation was a relatively high tolerance towards dissidents within the Christian community.[21]

Although, at that time, the main criterion of the power stratification of society in the Bohemian lands was still Estates affiliation, the forties saw the start of a more distinctive forming of foundations of differently structured interest groups, which brought together a confessional sense of belonging, at a political level. This was a natural reaction to the opportunistic religious policy of the Monarchal Court, which rejected any changes to the legal situation with references to the validity of the old Compacts, as well as a reaction to the rapidly advancing confessionalization of political life in neighbouring Imperial territorial princedoms.[22]

In the Bohemian lands, the principle of confessional affiliation still did not control the main power structures, this only came about half a century later; nevertheless, efforts to change the legal situation in the area of religion accompanied the emergence of supra-estate "associations".[23] John of Pernštejn stood at the head of the Utraquist nobility, influenced by the Lutheran direction of the Reformation (so-called Neo-Utraquists). The other three basic political camps of that time were formed by supporters of the Unity of the Brethren, the so-called Old Calixtines, who recognized the Utraquist faith in accordance with the Compacts, and Catholics.

---

21 Josef Válka, "Politika a nadkonfesijní křesťanství Viléma a Jana z Pernštejna", in Pernštejnové v českých dějinách (Sborník příspěvků z konference konané 8. - 9. 9. 1993 v Pardubicích), ed. Petr Vorel (Pardubice, 1995), 173 – 186.

22 Heinrich Richard Schmidt, Konfessionalisierung im 16. Jahrhundert (München, 1992), 2–4; Anton Schindling and Walter Ziegler, eds., Die Territorien des Reichs im Zeitalter der Reformation und Konfessionalisierung (Land und Konfesion 1500 - 1650), Bd. 1 – 7 = Katholisches Leben und Kirchenreform im Zeitalter der Glaubensspaltung - Vereinsschriften der Gesellschaft zur Herausgabe des Corpus Catholicorum, Heft Nr. 49 - 53, 56 – 57 (Münster, 1992 – 1997); Joachim Bahlcke Joachim and Arno Strohmeyer, eds., Konfessionalisierung in Ostmitteleuropa (Wirkung des religiösen Wandels im 16. und 17. Jahrhundert in Staat, Gesellschaft und Kultur), Forschungen zur Geschichte und Kultur des östlichen Mitteleuropa, Bd. 7 (Wiesbaden, 1999).

23 Petr Vorel "Die Außenbeziehungen der böhmischen Stände um die Mitte des 16. Jahrhundert und das Problem der Konfessionalisierung." In Konfessionalisierung in Ostmitteleuropa. Wirkung des religiösen Wandels im 16. und 17. Jahrhundert in Staat, Gesellschaft und Kultur, ed. Joachim Bahlcke and Arno Strohmeyer, (Stuttgart, 1999), 169–178.

Members of other religions, for example Lutherans in German-speaking areas of north-western Bohemia, had not yet formed power groupings with their own programme on the Bohemian political scene; instead, they focused directly on the Saxon Lutheran Court, which also manifested itself at the time of the Estates Revolt of 1547. For example, the Lutherans in the Bohemian Estates included some of the Sliks, the Pluhs of Rabštejn, lords of Biberstein, counts of Plauen, and other nobles, mostly from areas adjacent to Saxony and Lusatia.[24]

The main political figure of the Unity of the Brethren at the start of the 1540s was Kunrát Krajíř of Krajk; Bishop John Augusta stood at the head of the Brethren Church. Nobody from the group of politically-active Catholics or Compacts-abiding Old Calixtines particularly stood out on the Bohemian political scene, as from their perspective there was no reason for any great activity in religious issues on their part. Both of these confessions were legalized by the Compacts, and no sanctions threatened them from the Monarchal Court. On the contrary, from a legal perspective, supporters of the Lutheran Reformation and the Unity of the Brethren were above the law. This is why, even under the influence of the expanding Reformation in the neighbouring German lands, non-Catholics in Bohemia, for whom Compacts Utraquism was not acceptable from a doctrinal perspective, tried to form new legislation governing the religious situation that would offer them a broader range of options for defence against possible forceful intervention by the Monarchal Court.[25]

The protracted religious and economic problems became the subject of talks at the Bohemian Land Diet in 1543. In terms of economic issues, the Diet mainly addressed the monarch's high indebtedness; nevertheless, the solution approved by the Diet at the time led to a rapid and deep credit crisis. Before 1543, the credit system in Bohemia had functioned without any major problems, and the economic situation also attested to the fact that Bohemian lands' credit potential still had significant reserves. In the contemporary context, lodging "money on interest" with an eminent noble-

---

24   František Hrubý, "Luterství a novoutrakvismus v českých zemích v 16. a 17. století", Český časopis historický 45 (1939), 31–44; Jiří Just, "Luteráni v našich zemích do Bílé hory", in Luteráni v českých zemích v proměnách staletí, eds. Jiří Just, Zdeněk R. Nešpor, Ondřej Matějka et all. (Praha 2009), 23–120; Eberhard, "Konfesionelle Polarisierung", 34–36.

25   David, Finding the Middle Way, 133–142.

man represented a sign of social prestige and an expression of belonging to a certain interest group. It also brought with it traditional forms of social communication.[26] Thus, from the end of the 15th century to the mid-1540s, an older type of clientelistic system was created which had a stable form and was usually anchored territorially: the clientelistic network of an eminent nobleman was formed mostly of aristocrats in the immediate surroundings of his dominion, who were often also simultaneously his financial chamber's creditors, receiving regular cash payments from it twice a year (two annual payments of 5% of the "principal sum", i.e. 10% per year). Thus, eminent noblemen's financial chambers performed the function of a relatively stable banking sector, as financial deposits were guaranteed by landed property (aside from the noble's social reputation). The State law also took this fact into account: if someone borrowed an amount of money greater than the value of the landed property with which they guaranteed the loan, they could face capital punishment.

However, the Land Diet of 1543 announced a mandatory reduction in the legally-limited highest possible interest rate from the previously normal 10% to 6%. Apparently, the new highest interest rate value was derived from the financial market in Spain, where it was also set centrally, and moved within the range of 5–7% in the 16th century;[27] the six percent interest rate also became standard for business relationships in the German Lutheran environment. After all, at that time, all monarchs needed to borrow money for war, so why not simplify credit conditions by a political decision?

In Bohemia, the calculated reduction of the maximum interest rate merged the monarch's needs with the great land magnates' interests. The greatest demand for financial loans came from the Royal Court, which is why the monarch himself also had an interest in radically reducing the cost of credit. But, at the same time, this measure may have made things easier for the large aristocratic dominions' credit-burdened financial chambers, which is why this draft Diet resolution mainly found active support in the Land Diet's Lordly Curia. The justification for the new measure had its

---

26 Václav Bůžek, Úvěrové podnikání nižší šlechty v předbělohorských Čechách (Praha, 1989); Petr Vorel, "Petr Hamza ze Zábědovic a regentská správa pernštejnských dominií v Čechách v letech 1550 – 1552", Sborník vědeckých prací Univerzity Pardubice C/2 (1996), 115 – 142.

27 Bartolomé Bennassar and Bernard Vincent, Spanien 16. und 17. Jahrhndert (Stuttgart, 1999), 146.

own logic, and was difficult to call into question: its arguments were Christian morals (loans with a higher interest rate were reserved only for Jewish traders) and the monarch's great expenses in the war against the Turks.

However, under Bohemian conditions, the Land Diet's decision caused the rapid collapse of the credit market. Given a one-off reduction in the interest rate to 60% of its original value, nobody was willing to lend cash funds at such a low interest rate. Many debtors got into big trouble in a very short time, as the formerly common promissory note renewal cycle was suddenly disrupted. Even small creditors wanted their money back in cash rather than accepting a renewed promissory note with just six percent interest. But the magnates' financial chambers were not prepared for the one-off reimbursement of old loans, and nobody wanted to provide new loans at the low interest rate.

The situation was also complicated by the fact the large banking houses of that time, whose branches operated throughout all of Europe and significantly influenced the market in precious and coloured metals and other commodities, maintained the interest rate at the original high level. If one of the Bohemian nobles borrowed funds from the Augsburg Fuggers in cash, they continued to pay them interest of 10% even after the year 1543, just like if the Court Chamber in Vienna provided the loan to them. In this context, the forced reduction of the interest rate in the Bohemian lands had a counterproductive effect on the free circulation of cash, and resulted in not even the Bohemian nobility being willing to lend their King cash after the year 1543.

The one-off reduction in the interest rate caused a significant disparity with the official market value of landed property, calculated on the basis of fixed revenue coefficients. Shortly after the year 1543, before the price situation which had been rocked by the interest rate change stabilized, it was exceptionally advantageous to invest free financial resources in landed property, as the revenue from dominions (even the ones with no developed indirect production) was suddenly higher than the profit from interest. That is also why owners of cash were reluctant to lend it, as they preferred to save it for the operative purchase of any landed property.

The temporary credit system crisis in the Bohemian lands also increased the importance of Jewish financiers, for both domestic magnates and for the monarchal chamber. Thanks to their domestic and foreign contacts, the Jewish bankers were able to satisfy the demand for cash at practically any time if required, but under different conditions than those stipulated by the legal norm. Interest rate limits did not apply to them in this regard; they had the right to lend money "at an extortionate interest rate", i.e. basically under whatever conditions were agreed upon with the debtor; this included usury, which Christians regarded as a crime if the interest rate was higher than 6%. That is why, after the year 1543, the restrictive measures against the Jewish population, which began to be partially realized in the year 1541, had to be moderated in practice.[28]

However, the Land Diet of 1543 went down in Bohemian history mainly as a milestone in religious reformation, as it was this very Diet that saw the public presentation of a project for forming a new domestic Church structure, joining together the Neo-Utraquists and the Unity of the Brethren. In the religious situation in contemporary Europe, this was an extraordinary solution. In the normal religious practice of confessionalized Imperial territorial princedoms and towns, a more common approach was to try to suppress other religions and enforce one's own confessional model (even among non-Catholic churches), than to look for a common foundation. Understandably, the draft Bohemian religious reform from 1543 was adapted to the domestic religious situation, and it also had to take into consideration the existence and strong influence of the independent domestic church, the Unity of the Brethren.

If the reform plan managed to be pushed through in Bohemia, then the thus-constructed provincial non-Catholic Church would be especially suitable for Moravia, where the Neo-Utraquists had not created their own church structure. For both Lusatia and Silesia, the "Bohemian" way of formally uniting reformed churches was out of the question at the time, as the religious development of these two Crown lands chose the path of confessionalization, based on the neighbouring Imperial lands' model, and primarily under the influence of the radical Lutheran Reformation.[29]

---

28 Vorel, Velké dějiny, VII., 147–148.
29 Franz Machilek, "Schlesien", in Die Territorien des Reichs, Bd. 2, 102 – 139; Karlheinz Blaschke, "Lausitzen", in Die Territorien des Reichs, Bd. 6, 93 – 113.

After complex negotiations, the Church reform programme was drawn up and presented in text form by John of Pernštejn to King Ferdinand for approval at the Land Diet on the 30th of April 1543.[30] After several days' consideration, King Ferdinand diplomatically rejected the programme with a reference to the existence of the older Compacts, which he had undertaken to adhere to when he acceded to the Bohemian throne. That is why the non-Catholic opposition, participating in this Diet, chose a different tactic and focused on a new interpretation of the Compacts. On the 6th of May 1543, the non-Catholic Estates submitted a new interpretation of the Compacts according to which, from that point on, only two equal versions of religious affiliation could continue to legally exist in Bohemia – the Catholics and the Calixtines. However, in this new interpretation of the Compacts, the Calixtine Church was defined as an umbrella provincial church with its own structure independent of apostolic succession, whose confessional definition was worded so loosely that both Lutherans and members of the Unity of the Brethren could pledge allegiance to it.[31]

King Ferdinand found himself in an unenviable situation. He could not refuse directly, as the camp of seemingly unified Estates that stood behind the programme was too large. He formally accepted the proposal, but he postponed his official response until other matters important for the Monarchal Court were discussed and approved at the Diet, especially those of a financial nature. The King's obliging attitude aroused false hope about the issue of religious reform, which is why the Diet approved other royal proposals without any major problems. Only after the end of the Diet did the King have the presenter of the original proposal summoned, and rejected any change to the framework of the Basel Compacts' original wording from 1436.

King Ferdinand was obviously well aware that the actual religious situation was completely different by the start of the forties; on the other hand, however, he did not have sufficient power resources to prevent the rapid expansion of the influence of the Unity of the Brethren and the Lutheran

---

30   Petr Vorel, Páni z Pernštejna - Vzestup a pád rodu zubří hlavy v dějinách Čech a Moravy (2nd ed. Praha, 2012), 161–167.

31   Jiří Rak, "Vývoj utrakvistické správní organizace v době předbělohorské", Sborník archívních prací 31 (1981), 182–184; Jaroslav Kadlec, Přehled českých církevních dějin 2 (Roma, 1987), 18–19; J. Just, "Luteráni v našich zemích", 167–169; David, Finding the Middle Way, 111–142.

Reformation, not only in the lands of the Bohemian Crown, but also in the case of Reformation in the hereditary Austrian lands and in Hungary. Supporters of the Reformation did not try to bring about a new change in the legal situation on the issue of religion until Ferdinand's death. The peculiar system of unclear confessional boundaries was preserved, in which the term "Utraquist" could mean advocates of the Utraquist Compacts faith or non-Catholics who had adopted the principles of the Lutheran Reformation, but also those who pledged allegiance to other European Reformation movements and those who saw absolutely no need for a confessional definition of their faith. However, the King's approach during the discussion of the draft religious reform of 1543 caused quite a stir in the land and brought about a general lack of trust of the King's verbal promises, which also significantly influenced the Bohemian Estates' attitudes towards the King during the year 1546.

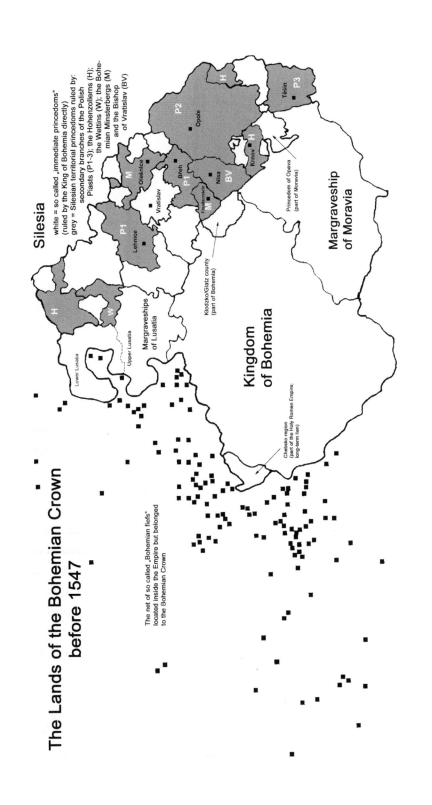

The Lands of the Bohemian Crown
before 1547

Silesia

white = so called „immediate princedoms"
(ruled by the King of Bohemia directly)
grey = Silesian territorial princedoms ruled by:
    secondary branches of the Polish
    Piasts (P1-3); the Hohenzollerns (H);
        the Wettins (W); the Bohe-
        mian Minsterbergs (M)
        and the Bishop
        of Vratislav (BV)

P2

Opole

H

Těšín   P3

Krnov   H

M
Olešnice

Břeh
P1

Nisa   BV

Frankenstein

M

Vratislav

P1
Lehnice

Princedom of Opava
(part of Moravia)

Kłodzko/Glatz county
(part of Bohemia)

H

W

Upper Lusatia

Lower Lusatia

Margraveships
of Lusatia

Margraveship
of Moravia

Kingdom
of Bohemia

Chebsko region
(part of the Holy Roman Empire;
long-term lien)

The net of so called „Bohemian fiefs"
located inside the Empire but belonged
to the Bohemian Crown

CHAPTER 6

BOHEMIAN PARTICIPATION IN THE SCHMALKALDIC WAR, AND THE ESTATES REVOLT (1546–1547)

As a result of the offensive Imperial policy of his elder brother Charles V., King Ferdinand found himself in a very complex and unenviable situation in autumn 1546. After the declaration of the Imperial anathema and the mobilization of the army, it was to clear to everyone involved that the diplomatic phase of the talks would turn into a gauging of military power. Bohemian society was informed of events in the Empire both indirectly, in the form of newspaper reporting, and through personal experience, as a number of domestic nobles had worked in both the Habsburgs' courts, whether in clerical or military functions. Also, the most eminent domestic magnates had close (in some cases even family) contacts with the main representatives of the Schmalkaldic League. However, none of the Bohemian leaders interfered with the active Diet policy in the Empire; de jure it would not even have been possible.

From a legal perspective, Imperial Diet talks did not relate to the Bohemian lands at all. This situation did not change even after the election of Ferdinand I. as King of Bohemia in 1526, or after Ferdinand I. became King of Rome (1531). However, from a social perspective, the Imperial Diets acquired a new context for the Bohemian environment after 1526, as it was customary for representatives of the countries which the monarch ruled to accompany him on various journeys. So the Bohemian nobility gradually also began to get used to being able to set off for the Imperial Diet in Germany in the King's company from time to time. The Bohemian nobles' presence at the Diet did not have any formal political or diplomatic significance (Bohemian representatives did not participate in any Diet talks Curiae), which was not perceived as any great loss by the Bohemian side. At the

Diet, they appeared in a position similar to parts of delegations from other countries outside the Empire. It was merely a social and representational affair where participants could get to know one another, although the Diet's unofficial guests could obviously also have met one another while it was in progress.[1]

Apart from the King's immediate courtiers or employees (who travelled with the King as part of their duties), Bohemian nobles' participation in the royal entourage was voluntary, and financed from their own resources. That is why we see the Bohemian nobles' physical presence in the royal entourage mainly in the case of Diets that were held close to the Bohemian borders (Regensburg, Augsburg, Nuremberg), while journeys from Bohemia to more remote places (Speyer, Worms) were not very common. But, for example, at the Imperial Diet in Augsburg in the year 1530, when King Ferdinand needed to show himself as a mighty and influential monarch before the Imperial nobility, he was accompanied from Bohemia by a relatively impressive delegation, which included influential members of the State government: Supreme Justice Zdislav Berka of Dubá, Supreme Chancellor Adam of Hradec, and others.[2]

So far, we do not have direct sources at our disposal which would document a more significant participation by the Bohemian nobility at the Imperial Diet in Regensburg in 1546, but given the important role which King Ferdinand and his family played here (he married two of his daughters off here), we can assume that Bohemian nobles were present among the members of the Royal Court. But even if no important member of the Bohemian nobility was present in Regensburg at the time (which is highly unlikely) then, thanks to the well-developed contemporary intelligence network, the fact that military conflict was brewing in the Empire could still not have escaped the Bohemian environment. Not only because news of the greater concentration of troops in southern Germany was spreading quickly, but also because the Elector of Saxony was also mobilizing an army close by, in the Bohemian neighbourhood.

---

1 Petr Vorel, Říšské sněmy a jejich vliv na vývoj zemí Koruny české v letech 1526–1618 (Pardubice, 2005), 88–107.

2 Franz Bernhard Bucholz, Geschichte der Regierung Ferdinand des Ersten, Bd. III. (Wien, 1832), 661–662; Friedrich Roth, ed., Die Chroniken des schwäbische Städte – Augsburg, IV. Band (Leipzig, 1894), 268–269, 294.

However, in the 1540s, war was almost constantly being waged in one part of the Empire or another, regardless of the participants' confessional affiliation. So, in Bohemia in the summer of 1546, few could probably have anticipated that some military unrest in the neighbouring Empire could directly affect the Kingdom of Bohemia. No such fact even emerged from the Imperial Diet's resolution of the 20th of July 1546, which declared an Imperial anathema against the leaders of the Schmalkaldic League, and which authorized King Ferdinand and Moritz of Saxony to impose this anathema.

But even at the Bohemian Land Diet, which commenced in Prague on the 26th of July 1546, the royal instructions (i.e. for the proposed Diet talks) included two important requirements, which may not have appeared in any way "suspicious" in formal diplomatic language, but which in fact reflected the actual dramatic situation in the Imperial power scene: the renewal of the old alliance treaty with neighbouring Saxony from 1459, and the convening of the Land military forces.

The first of these requirements was the King's request to update the friendly agreements with the Saxon Wettins, which had been concluded almost one hundred years ago (in 1459)[3] by George of Poděbrady, King of Bohemia, with Frederick, Elector of Saxony (1428–1464), great-grandfather of former Elector John Frederick (1532–1547). These agreements also included the dynastic linking of both families, as the Elector's younger son Albert (born 1443, † 1500) was married to Zdeňka, daughter of George, King of Bohemia. Duke Albert of Saxony and Zdeňka of Poděbrady were the grandparents of Duke Moritz of Saxony. That is why King Ferdinand requested that the alliance treaty from 1459 be renewed only with Moritz of Saxony, who had one quarter royal Bohemian blood in his veins. The Land Diet did not explicitly refuse this proposal, but it argued that the agreement from 1459 related to all descendants of Elector Frederick, and that the main representative of the Saxon Wettins in 1546 was Elector John Frederick. That is why the updating of the old alliance treaty (whose validity the Bohe-

---

3   André Thieme, and Uwe Tresp, eds. Eger 1459 – Fürstentreffen zwischen Sachsen, Böhmen und ihrer Nachbarn: Dynastische Politik, fürstliche Repräsentation und kulturelle Verflechtung / Cheb 1459 – Setkání panovníků Saska, Čech a jejich sousedů: Dynastická politika, panovnická reprezentace a kulturní vazby. Saxonia. Schriften des Vereins für sächsische Landesgeschichte e. V., Bd. 13 (Wettin-Löbejün 2011).

mian Land Diet recognized), was to relate to both Elector John Frederick, and to his second cousin Moritz of Saxony, in equal measure.

Of course, such an interpretation did not suit the King. Therefore, this issue was not concluded at the Diet; it merely appointed a commission composed of members of the lordly and knightly Estates, which was to prepare the text of the potential alliance treaty with Moritz of Saxony. It's not clear whether all the members of this "Saxon committee" were Habsburg policy sympathizers in this phase, but they all soon became supporters (and were rewarded by the King after suppressing the revolt). They quickly agreed on the wording of an alliance treaty (whose text had already been prepared) with Moritz of Saxony's representatives, and concluded it without discussing it at the Land Diet. After all, the royal side had interpreted the wording of the Diet resolution in such a way that the Diet-appointed representatives were authorized not only to prepare its draft text, but also to conclude the new alliance treaty on the Bohemian Estates behalf. So, the dispute about this legal interpretation only arose at the very end of the Diet, when the Diet resolution of the 14th of August 1546 was to be approved and subsequently entered in the Land tables, whereby it would have attained the weight of State law.

Representatives of the urban estate protested against the thus-created alliance treaty because they had not had a chance to influence the preparation of the text (they did not have their representatives in the committee, and the text was not discussed at the Diet), and therefore refused to fulfil any potential obligations arising from this treaty. This complaint was interpreted in the King's presence on the urban estate's behalf by the Chancellor of the Old Town of Prague, Sixt of Ottersdorf. The King formally accommodated this complaint (he promised that this issue would be discussed again at a later time, and that the urban estate's rights would not be affected by this omission of them) but, with the support of the noble Estates' (lords and knights) representatives who were present, he succeeded in approving this alliance treaty whose content few were privy to. Minor changes in the wording, by which the royal side amended the text of the Diet resolution before entering it in the Land tables, later enabled its broader legal interpretation.[4]

---

4   Zdeněk Beneš, Historický text a historická skutečnost - Studie o principech českého humanistického dějepisectví (Praha, 1993), 79.

The King's second requirement was the convening of the Land military forces, whose purpose was to defend the country's territorial integrity. Such requests had also been regularly discussed at previous Diets, during talks on defence against the Turkish danger, but this time the purpose of the convening of the Land forces was not precisely specified. At that time, complicated military manoeuvres by large armies (the Habsburgs' and the Schmalkaldic League's) were already taking place in southern Germany, and it was generally known that the Emperor was preparing for a military confrontation with the Elector of Saxony. That is why the Bohemian Estates at the Diet refused to approve the convening of the Land forces for the King, unless their purpose was precisely specified. At first, the draft Diet resolution included the wording that the Land forces would be convened as defence against the Turkish danger. However, no such danger actually existed at that time, which is why the final decision was changed to a more general wording about any enemy endangering the integrity of the lands of the Bohemian Crown.

In this situation, the King used an older property-legal dispute, relating to the territory of the Cistercian monastery of Dobroluk in Lower Lusatia, as a pretext.[5] This territory, in the complicatedly-defined Saxony-Lower Lusatia borderland, actually formally belonged to the lands of the Bohemian Crowns, and was occupied in the year 1546 by the Elector of Saxony's military garrison, but there was no imminent military threat. The Saxon dukes had already held the Dobroluk Monastery territory for quite a long time. After all, King Ferdinand had secured Maximilian I.'s old promissory note, issued to Frederick II., Elector of Saxony (1486–1525), with this property shortly after his accession to the Bohemian throne. This obligation was transferred to Ferdinand of Habsburg, who temporarily (until the debt was paid) transferred the Dobroluk monastic property to the Saxon side. By 1546, the monastery itself in its original form no longer existed. Its territory (just like the extensive surroundings) had already been Lutheranized in the 1530s, and the remaining members of the local Cistercian community had left the monastery building.

5   Dennis Majewski, "Die territorile Politik der Zisterzienserabtei Dobrilugk (Die Herrschaft des Lausitzklosters in Zeit und Raum)", in Die Nieder- und Oberlausitz – Konturen einer Integrationslandschaft, Band I, Mittelaler (Studien zur branderbungischen und vergleichenden Geschichten, Band 11), eds. Heinz-Dieter Heimann, Klaus Neitmann and Uwe Tresp (Berlin, 2013), 177–188.

King Ferdinand and the Elector of Saxony had engaged in a diplomatic dispute about this Dobroluk territory for a long time, at the same time as the dispute about the settlement of an old claim made by the Elector on a small territory in northern Bohemia (the so-called "Grünhain Estates"). These were ten villages located between the north Bohemian towns of Kadaň and Žatec, to which the Cistercian monastery in Grünhain in Saxony had property rights in the Middle Ages. After the Lutheranization of the Grünhain monastery (1533) and the physical demise of the abbey (1536) the Elector of Saxony, as the landed nobility of the former monastery, requested a property settlement, as the former monastery villages were held under lien by Albert Slik of Pasoun who had ceased to pay Saxony the revenue from these villages, which had previously been paid to the abbot of Grünhain. In 1540, as payback, the Elector of Saxony confiscated the revenue from the dominions of the former Dobroluk Monastery in Lower Lusatia. In 1541, local noble Mikuláš of Minkvice, with the knowledge of his uncle John of Minkvice (who had been the royal governor of Lower Lusatia) tried to use military force to occupy the monastic dominion in the name of King Ferdinand. However, the Elector of Saxony prevented him from doing this. After that, a permanent Saxon military garrison was stationed in Dobroluk, and the Elector and King Ferdinand discussed the settlement of the dispute; from the very start, they also discussed compensation for the Bohemian Grünhain monastery property.

An agreement about this north Bohemian property was drawn up in the year 1544 in favour of the Elector (his assets here were calculated to be worth 13,300 Rhenish guilders),[6] who as a result was more helpful on the issue of Dobroluk in Lusatia. Both sides agreed on the formation of a bipartite commission chaired by the Supreme Chancellor of the Kingdom of Bohemia, Henry of Plauen.[7] This commission calculated the Saxon claim to the Dobroluk dominion to be 30 thousand Rhenish guilders. In the given context, it was a relatively small nominal sum; however, the total sum was increased by the conversion of the exchange rate between the "old coin"

6   Emil Herzog, "Geschichte des Klosters Grünhain", Archiv für die sächsische Geschichte 7 (1869), 60–96; Rudolf Lehmann, Die älteste Geschichte des Klosters Dobrilug in der Lausitz (Kirchhain, 1917); Rudolf Lehmann, ed., Urkundenbuch des Klosters Dobrilugk und seiner Besitzungen (Dresden and Leipzig, 1941).
7   Buchholz, Geschichte, 265.

(i.e. the currency in which the original claim was secured) and the current Imperial currency, as well as possible interest, which significantly increased the original claim. Logically, the Bohemian side refused to pay interest for the period during which the Elector collected the revenue generated by this property. Thus, the two sides never managed to agree on the resulting sum. Afterwards, King Ferdinand requested that the dominion be released to him, while the Elector of Saxony refused to withdraw his soldiers from Dobroluk until he was actually paid this nominal debt (recognized by King Ferdinand), plus another sum (not accepted by the Bohemian side) arising from the offsetting of interest against loss caused by the change in the exchange rate.

The declaration of the Imperial anathema (20th of June 1546) freed King Ferdinand from any former obligations towards the anathema-affected Elector John Frederick. Although, at the time, the Elector's former claim to the Dobroluk Monastery property was recognized by King Ferdinand as being at least partly legitimate, after the 20th of June 1546 this no longer applied. So the presence of the Saxon garrison, which had been residing peacefully in the old Dobroluk Monastery since the year 1541, was meant to be the said imminent threat to the territorial integrity of the Bohemian multi-state coalition?

Ferdinand's argument about an invasion by enemies into the Crown lands territory in connection with the Dobroluk dispute truly lacked factual justification, and this was universally known in Bohemia.[8] The old disputes about the Dobroluk Monastery property were merely used by the King as a formal pretext so that the Bohemian Estates could meet their King halfway (if they wanted to) without violating Land laws or estate freedoms. However, the Bohemian Estates' reaction was similarly half-hearted.

The Land Diet formally met the King halfway, but in such a way that it accommodated the monarch on the one hand, while making sure this helpful step could not be effectively used against the Elector of Saxony on the other. At the time, a significant part of the Estates expressed its consent to this solution. Only a part of the nobility protested against the convening of these Land forces in principle, just like some royal towns (Hradec Králové,

---

8   Tieftrunk, Odpor stavův českých, 33–39.

Chrudim, Čáslav, Kouřim and others). The main area of direct protests was the eastern part of the country, where the Unity of the Brethren held relatively important positions.

However, in the decision on where the Diet-approved Land army would march, the King was dependent not only on the opinion of the supreme Land military commander, but also the independent regional commanders who comprised his advisory committee. The Land Diet stipulated a decisive role for itself in the occupation of these positions, as the Diet directly nominated the commanders of the individual regions' military contingents; in the case of the main Land commander, the King could choose only from candidates proposed to him by the Diet.

The Land army was to be financed only for a period of two months, i.e. from the time of the planned concentration of the soldiers at individual regional marshalling areas (the 13th of September 1546) to the 12th of November 1546. This financing was arranged proportionately, with regard to the amount of property. The basis for stipulating the mandatory number of soldiers, financed by individual nobles, was the so-called tax register (statement of the declared value of landed property) from the year 1544.[9] For every 2,000 three-scores of Bohemian groschen of tax-declared landed property value (which in contemporary Imperial currency corresponded to a sum of 5,000 Rhenish guilders), four infantrymen and one cavalryman were to be armed, paid and sent into the field. Less affluent nobles, whose property value did not reach 2,000 three-scores of Bohemian groschen, were to formally unite into larger groups, whose combined property value reached the afore-mentioned threshold value, within the relevant region.

The Land army convening system still formally presumed that the nobles would personally participate in the military campaign with their King, as was customary in the Middle Ages (In Bohemia, this system still worked well under the reign of George of Poděbrady); i.e. an experienced noble was to ride his horse into the field, accompanied by four infantry armour-bearers from the ranks of his garrison. However, by the mid-16th century, this system was an anachronism and was not even physically feasible. By the mid-16th century, there were not even that many fighting fit

---

9   Václav Pešák, ed., Berní rejstříky z roku 1544 a 1620 (Praha, 1953).

nobles living in Bohemia. In the late 15th century, membership of privileged nobility was limited to only the two highest classes of the aristocratic structure (the lordly and knightly Estates, which usurped political rights for themselves), which had also been legally secured in the year 1500. The lowest (third) class of minor servile and rural gentry, from which most of the systematically-trained soldiers (the so-called squires) came in the 15th century, had practically ceased to exist by the mid-16th century. Within two generations, the descendants of these squires had either been promoted to the knightly estate, or fell to the level of rural stewards, whether they had become serfs to wealthier nobles or remained so-called "freemen".

Understandably, this structural demographic change reduced the Land army's readiness for action, constructed on the basis of military experience which had proved itself in the mid-15th century, but which was no longer usable a hundred years later. In reality, in the mid-16th century, even the Bohemian Land army was organized using a mercenary system, which the Land Diet resolution had also taken into account. The nobles' personal participation in the army was not strictly required. If, for some objective reasons, one of the lords or knights could not go into battle himself (subjective health reasons, which were difficult to verify, were generally acceptable), he could send one of their relatives or anyone from the higher Estates instead, so that for every eight cavalrymen there was at least one person from the higher Estates (a lord or a knight), who simultaneously held the lowest commanding function within the cavalry's organization. Nobles' representation among the infantry was not expected.

If someone did not have the ability to provide the appropriate number of soldiers directly from their dominion, they could pay money in lieu of a physically dispatched contingent instead, being 12 Rhenish guilders to finance a cavalryman (i.e., with this sum, the relevant noble could "buy himself out" from his obligation to physically participate in the military campaign), or 3 three-scores of Meissen groschen for an infantryman.[10]

---

10   1 Rhenish guilder = 60 kreutzer = 24 Bohemian groschen in 1546. In the Bohemian currency system, Meissen groschen were merely a numerical monetary unit, created at the time of the currency reform in 1469 and converted at a rate of 1 Bohemian groschen = 7 white pennies = 2 Meissen groschen. Therefore, it was physically possible to pay a sum of 3 three-scores of Meissen groschen (i.e. 180 Meissen groschen = 90 Bohemian groschen) in the coins in circulation - 70 pieces of silver Prague groschen, because 1 silver coin Prague groschen paid 9 white pennies. See Vorel, Monetary Circulation, 88–104.

This money was then used to hire mercenaries. Therefore, if someone completely "bought themselves out" of their personal obligation to participate in the military campaign, and did not send any soldiers, they paid a sum corresponding to 0.54% of the value of their landed property, which was quite a lot.[11]

If someone failed to supply the soldiers or the assessed pecuniary sum instead of them on time, they were threatened with a property sanction of triple the originally-assessed obligation. These fines could even be demanded by appointed officials (so-called regional tax collectors) in the form of seizure of landed property.

In theory, landowners were to pay most of this money from the revenue generated by their dominions. However, the Land Diet allowed them to request "participation" from their serfs, to an amount of almost 1.5% of the value of their rustic properties: for every 60 groschen of land value, the nobles were to contribute as much as 6/7 groschen. Given the fact that the prices of large rural plots of land at that time were usually in the order of several hundred three-scores of Bohemian groschen, most of the landed nobility could easily transfer their Diet-approved financial burden to their serfs. The Diet also approved the organizational structure which was to procure the troops (i.e. estimates of property values, collection of money, etc.) in individual regions. This wasn't anything difficult; the Bohemian Land army had been organized in a similar manner in previous years, in the case of the march to the Turkish border in Hungary. In every region, troops were to gather at the pre-determined marshalling area (usually near the relevant regional town) on the 13th of September 1546; every region's military forces were then commanded by an Diet-appointed regional military commander (hetman) who was to lead the troops to the main provincial marshalling area and subsequently also command these units in battle. Prague organized its own army outside the regional marshalling area system; Prague inhabitants also had the right to nominate their own commander.

In the given context, the main army commander was obviously a very important person. The Land Diet proposed four possible candidates to the

---

11   1 cavalryman (12 Rhenish guilders = 288 Bohemian groschen) and 4 infantrymen (12 three-scores of Meissen groschen = 360 Bohemian groschen) = 10 three-scores and 48 Bohemian groschen (i.e. 0.54% of a value of 2,000 three-scores of Bohemian groschen).

King: two from the lordly estate (Adam of Šternberk and Sebastian of Weitmille) and two from the knightly estate (Otík of Buben and Wenceslas Pětipeský of Krásný Dvůr). From these, the King chose "his man", Sebastian of Weitmille, who belonged to the pro-Habsburg minority among the wealthy Bohemian nobility.[12] The Land army's main commander was due a monthly salary of 400 three-scores of Bohemian groschen (i.e. 1,000 Rhenish guilders); the regional army commanders received 40 three-scores of Bohemian groschen (i.e. 100 Rhenish guilders).

Immediately after the end of the Land Diet in Prague, the King commenced talks with specific Bohemian aristocratic leaders in order to verify their willingness to participate in the campaign in Saxony. In this phase, a core of "loyal men" was forming among the Bohemian nobility, who made their services fully available to the King, regardless of their confessional orientation (similarly to the case of the German Lutherans' services for Emperor Charles V.). For the king, the most important nobles were the ones who had military command experience and a good knowledge of the territory where the military campaign was to take place. Most importantly, this group included three men:

Thus, the main advocate of King Ferdinand's interests became the ardent Lutheran Henry of Plauen,[13] then Supreme Chancellor of the Kingdom of Bohemia, whose main property interests were in the Bohemia-Saxony border area (the Vogtland). The Bohemia-Saxony borderland is birthplace of the main commander of the Bohemian Land army whom the King appointed, Sebastian of Weitmille, as well as the meritorious commander from the Turkish wars, Bohuslav Felix Hasištejnský of Lobkovice. We later meet these three experienced officers at the head of the King of Bohemia's army, throughout the entire conflict in the Empire (1546–1555).

The King also found political support with a minority of the Land government members. Supreme Justice Jan Popel of Lobkovice, Supreme Hofmeister Zdislav Berka of Dubá, Volf of Vřesovice and royal Vice-Chamberlain George of Gerštorf all joined the royal side. Significant support was also offered to him by the Supreme Royal Governor in Jáchymov, Christo-

---

12 Pešák, Berní rejstříky, 31.

13 Berthold Schmidt, Burggraf Heinrich IV. zu Meißen, Oberstkanzler der Krone Böhmen, und seine Regierung im Vogtland (Gera, 1888).

pher Gendorf of Gendorf, as well as the south Bohemian Rosenberg dominions. Brothers William and Peter Wok of Rosenberg may still have been minors in the year 1546, but their guardians (led by Albert of Gutstein) fulfilled the King's requests for military participation. Given the extent of the Rosenbergs' south Bohemian dominions, this participation was significant.

The monarch also managed to bring some members of the traditionally pro-Saxon, and by that time exclusively Lutheran, Slik of Pasoun family, former miners and also founders and long-time operators of the Jáchymov mint, over to the royal side. Of this extended family (most of which was very actively involved in the opposition, as they hoped for a possible return of their influence in Jáchymov silver mining), it was mainly Albert Slik of Pasoun, who had engaged in the afore-mentioned dispute about the defunct Saxon Grünhain monastery village with John Frederick, Elector of Saxony, since the start of the forties, who placed his fate in the services of King Ferdinand.

At the start of September 1546, King Ferdinand convened a conference of the Land army commanding staff in Prague, attended by Sebastian of Weitmille as well as all the regional commanders. He discussed the plan for his participation against John Frederick, Elector of Saxony, with them. The reason was to be the defence of both the Dobroluk dominion and other territories of the Bohemian Crown. These were the Bohemian fiefdoms in the Empire which had previously been held by the Elector of Saxony. After the proclamation of the Imperial anathema, the Elector's property - and therefore also feudal rights - were taken away. King Ferdinand (as the feudal lord of a significant part of the Saxon territory) wanted to transfer these Bohemian fiefdoms under his own control; this was understandably also interesting for his circle of supporters, who may have been set to acquire extensive property in the event of a Habsburg victory. However, most of the Bohemian Land army's regional commanders did not let themselves be enticed by the King's promises or scared by his threats, and expressed themselves clearly: their regional military forces would not move outside the territory of the Kingdom of Bohemia.

The afore-mentioned requirement was based on the old medieval rule which the kings had granted to the domestic nobility since the end of the Přemyslid period: the country's internal resources could be mobilized for military purposes only for the defence of own territory, not for campaigns in foreign countries. This principle was not the manifestation of some late medieval Bohemian pacifism. Bohemian lords and knights, and their squires, were happy to march with their king and occupy foreign countries or defend their monarch's foreign interests, but the King had to pay them well for it.

On the 10th of September 1546, despite this apparent complication, King Ferdinand issued a notice in which he announced that the former Elector of Saxony John Frederick, who lost all his rights on the basis of the Imperial anathema, was an enemy of the Kingdom of Bohemia. The former Elector was supposedly preparing to invade Bohemia and occupy the silver mines in Jáchymov. That is why the King ordered the Diet-approved Land army to set off from its regional marshalling areas towards the town of Kadaň (lying in the foothills of the Ore Mountains), located only about 35 km from Jáchymov and from the Saxon border. They were all to reach Kadaň by the 28th of September 1546. In order to increase the Bohemian Estates' willingness to go to war, the King also promised that he would support the power of the Land army (financed by the Estates) with his own units, which he would fund himself, consisting of 2,000 cavalrymen, 4,000 infantrymen and his own artillery.

In the given context, the Jáchymov silver mines really represented an object of great interest for both competing sides, as they held metallurgical silver reserves and were also a mining location that generated significant income for the monarchal treasury. At the time, older Bohemian literature estimated Ferdinand I.'s annual income from the Jáchymov mint around the year 1546 to be 320 thousand tolars[14] (i.e. 384 thousand Rhenish guilders, when converted to Imperial currency).[15] More recent research has not confirmed such large sums, but trustworthy data on the amount of mined silver confirms that the monarchal chamber's profit in the mid-forties may well have been that high. Preserved evidence documents the officially recorded quantity of pure silver processed in the smelting plants in the years 1546–1550 to be 22.5 tonnes in weight, whereby just the profit of the miners working in the Jáchymov ore district in 1544–1546 was slightly over 100 thousand tolars per year.[16]

---

14 Tieftrunk, Odpor stavův českých, 41.
15 Vorel, From the Silver Czech Tolar, 60–67.
16 Lubomír Nemeškal, Jáchymovská mincovna v první polovině 16. století (Praha 1964), 74–75, 91.

Therefore, it's no surprise that, at this dangerous time, the King sent experienced military commander Bohuslav Felix Hasištejnský of Lobkovice, a wealthy Bohemian lord from the Žatecký region,[17] to assist Christopher Gendorf who, as Supreme Governor, had looked after the King's material interests in Jáchymov since the sentencing of the Sliks in 1545. He was to very quickly recruit sufficient soldiers in the vicinity and, if necessary, command the mining district's defence.

Gendorf and Hasištejnský began preparing the royal army by extensively recruiting conscripts in the vicinity of Jáchymov at the start of September. However, the town's surroundings were mostly Lutheran, and although the royal commissioners had sufficient cash at their disposal at the time, by the 10th of September 1546 they had only managed to hire very unreliable and untrained units numbering around 3,000 men. This recruitment campaign (which was probably also of a violent nature) was in its own way even counterproductive, as masses of potential conscripts began to flee from the populous mining area to the Saxon side and let themselves be recruited into the Elector's army, which was being formed just a few kilometres further north, near present-day Boží Dar (Gottesgab).

The Jáchymov town council was opposed to military activities for any purpose other than the town's defence, so royal commissioners Gendorf and Hasištejnský had little opportunity to contribute to the Saxon campaign from Jáchymov. The partial assault by which the Jáchymov army attacked and occupied the weakly-defended Boží Dar in mid-October 1546 made no sense; on the contrary, it contributed to criticism of the royal commissioners' overall actions in Jáchymov itself. Boží Dar and its immediate surroundings may have belonged to the Schwarzenberg Electoral dominion, but they were located on the Bohemian side of the border. Gendorf and Hasištejnský, who did not have any specific instructions from the King or from Sebastian of Weitmille, did not dare to go any further than the State border with the unreliable Jáchymov army, especially when its dubious military quality "showed itself" during a vain attempt to occupy a nearby mining district in Horní Blatná which was (just like Boží Dar), part of a small Saxon property enclave in the Bohemian border area. Frequent escapes by

---

17   Pešák, Berní rejstříky, 32.

soldiers, fleeing to the Saxon side, constantly reduced the numbers of the recruited royal army, which remained in uncertain positions in the vicinity of Jáchymov until the end of October 1546 without engaging in any significant military activity.

In the meantime, it was a question of what to do with the Land army, which had been organized within individual regions of Bohemia. According to the King's orders it was to gradually gather at the town of Kadaň, in order to be prepared for a parade on the 28th of September 1546 but, at the same time, it was not to cross the State borders. However, in the end, even the Estates which had originally agreed to the convening of the Land army delayed the dispatch of the troops, so at Kadaň at the end of September 1546 there were no Bohemian troops to be found. Individual, not very numerous and badly-armed forces, lacking a united command, gradually gathered only at the start of October.

Some of the Diet-appointed regional governors explicitly refused to bring their armies from the regional marshalling areas to Kadaň, as the legal conditions for their use had not been fulfilled: there was no reason to march with the Land army to the Saxon border, where the country was not being attacked, when the main reason for organizing the army was defence against the Turkish danger. Thus, six regional governors (mainly from the eastern part of the country) flatly refused to march towards the Saxon border with their regional forces; eight governors arrived at Kadaň, but with significantly smaller divisions than the King had expected. The Prague Towns (whose military forces were organized outside the regional army system) also refused to send soldiers to Kadaň (the Prague army only set off for Kadaň, at the King's insistence, in mid-October). Some forces, sent by the few exponents of the Habsburg side among the Bohemian nobility, which had gathered at Kadaň, were prepared to march into battle in Saxony, but most of the lower commanders refused to cross the State borders.

Thus, in the upcoming campaign, King Ferdinand stayed reliant on his own resources. These comprised around three battalions (1,500 soldiers) of mercenaries, whom he had recruited in Lower Austria during the summer, and who had been sent from Vienna to Bohemia. These infantry forces set off on the 9th of October 1546 from Prague in the direction of Kadaň. Several days later, they were followed by a strong cavalry unit (about 1,200

Hussars) sent from Hungary to help the King. In the end, this was the main military force that King Ferdinand had at his disposal in late 1546.

The actual postponement of the starting date of the Habsburg allied invasion of Saxony was related not only to the primary military unpreparedness, but also to the fact that, at the end of September, Ferdinand of Habsburg and Moritz of Saxony had still not agreed on how to divide Elector John Frederick's territory, which they were to conquer together. These talks, which took place in Prague Castle, lasted the entire first half of October, i.e. from Moritz's arrival in Prague (the 30th of September 1546) to the conclusion of a secret bilateral treaty dated the 14th of October 1546 which, apart from its signatories, nobody knew about, (King Ferdinand did not even include its text in his "Acts", and Sixt of Ottersdorf was not privy to it either).[18]

Although both sides were already dividing a territory which was not yet under their control, these talks were complicated. In the end, they agreed as follows: King Ferdinand would acquire all of Elector John Frederick's territories in Saxony that were part of the Bohemian Crown and which the Elector held as fiefdoms from the King of Bohemia. Moritz of Saxony would then acquire all of Elector John Frederick's territories that were part of the Empire (including secularized Church Estates). Moritz renounced Saxon claims to the Dobroluk Monastery property, which he was to hand over to King Ferdinand. They divided the border Schwarzenberg dominion in such a way that Moritz would keep the territory on the Saxon side and Ferdinand would take over the Bohemian side (including Boží Dar). Furthermore, Moritz of Saxony was to pay King Ferdinand material compensation for the Bohemian fiefdoms located in Moritz's existing territory (the dominions of Eulenburg, Koldice and Lesnice). Ferdinand even agreed to the possible exchange of these fiefdoms for other territories in Saxony; however, in future, these territories (either the original dominion, or another dominion provided as a replacement) were to remain part of the Bohemian Crown, and Moritz of Saxony was to accept them from Ferdinand of Habsburg in the form of a feudal commitment.

Only after the conclusion of these treaties (on the 14th of October 1546) did the military machinery begin to move. Ferdinand's Hungarian Hussars

---

18   Winter, "Prag 1546", 371–380.

set off from Prague in the direction of Kadaň and Moritz of Saxony set off towards his army in Saxony, so that a joint attack could commence on the 30th of October 1546.

At the end of October, King Ferdinand had three parts of the army at his disposal: 1) his own hired troops in the vicinity of Jáchymov, which was commanded by Bohuslav Felix Hasištejnský of Lobkovice and which had remained encamped in the vicinity of Jáchymov since September; 2) Austrian infantry and Hungarian cavalry, which moved from Prague to Kadaň in the second half of October; 3) the symbolic remainder of the Bohemian Land army, commanded by Sebastian of Weitmille.

There was a serious problem with the Land army; when, on the 29h of October 1546, Supreme Commander Sebastian of Weitmille ordered it to start marching in the direction of Saxony, most soldiers refused to carry out this order, arguing that they were not allowed to march across the country's borders. Thus, around 3,000 soldiers remained idle in the military encampment at Kadaň. Similarly strong divisions pulled out from Kadaň, but they only reached the State border, around 35 km away. There the soldiers stopped, and refused to continue further. Thus, only a very small number of Bohemian Land army soldiers actually entered Saxon territory; the Prague army (its activity was influenced by the personal presence of the Old Town Mayor and Court Hofrichter Jacob Fikar of Vrat, who had had to set off for the field camp on the King's orders), as well as the nobles present in the encampment, whose enthusiasm for the military campaign was to be influenced by the personal presence of Lutheran leader and Supreme Chancellor of the Kingdom of Bohemia, Henry of Plauen.

However, Elector John Frederick and his army were in southern Germany, in the Danube, from whence he only departed for Saxony on the 16th of November 1546, and it took two to three weeks for his army (composed mainly of infantry Landsknechts) to cover the distance of around four hundred kilometres. That is why, at the start of November 1546, the Habsburg army did not have any significant adversary in Saxony, so there was actually no need for any effective help from Bohemian Land army. Ferdinand of Habsburg had his Austrian soldiers and a strong cavalry division of Hungarian Hussars at his disposal, which was sufficient for an occupation of Vogtland (part of the Bohemian Crown, held by Elector John Frederick as a fiefdom) and other "Bohemian fiefdoms" on Saxon territory, defended only by local militias. Waging war against the Saxon peasants was great!

Together with Duke Moritz of Saxony, King Ferdinand occupied the Elector's Saxon territory with only slight resistance by local garrisons (they did not dare attack the large fortifications); their main interest was understandably in the mining regions near the Bohemian border, where the main Saxon sources of silver were found (Schneeberg, Annaberg etc.). The only significant military operation which could be called a battle took place between the two opposing sides in the Vogtland, on a plateau near the small town of Adorf.[19] King Ferdinand and Moritz of Saxony boasted of a joint victory in Saxony on the 9th of November 1546.

By now, however, the time period for which the Bohemian Land army was to be at the King's disposal (until St. Martin's Day, i.e. the 11th of November 1546) was coming to an end. Thus, the King asked the Bohemian Estates to extend the financing of the Land army by at least one month, but to no avail. Even the remaining soldiers, who had marched with Sebastian of Weitmille to Vogtland, or who camped disorganizedly in various places around Kadaň (merely to formally fulfil their obligation to remain in the field until the 11th of November; the time period for which they had been paid), left for their respective homes. Moritz of Saxony's garrisons stayed in Saxon towns, while the Bohemian fiefdom area was to be controlled by small divisions of the royal army under the command of Bohuslav Felix Hasištejnský of Lobkovice and Melichar Hoburk, who were to gradually transfer all these territories under royal control.

The King had been accommodated, the Land Diet's resolution had been fulfilled, and the Bohemian army had not harmed anyone. But the King was of different opinion.

At the very start of December, the King began to prepare a court process against royal towns, including the Prague Towns, that had not demonstrated sufficient willingness at the time of the march to Saxony in 1546. Here, however, he encountered a legal problem. The supreme judicial (and appeal) authority for the urban Estates in the Kingdom of Bohemia was

---

19 Siegfried Thomä, Der Schmalkaldische Krieg 1546/47 im Vogtland – Adorf unter der Geißel der Hussauer, (Aalen, 1992), 3, the Map: "Lageskizze zu den Ereignissen des Schmalkaldischen Krieges 1546/47 im Vogtland".

represented by the Town Councillor's Office of the Old Town of Prague. Thus, potential disputes between the King and the royal towns were to be discussed before this office (or before the Land Diet). Any other procedure (for example the appointment of a special judicial tribunal by the King) was regarded as a breach of the royal towns' estate rights.

Therefore, on the 1st of December 1546, King Ferdinand had the representatives of the town council of the Old Town of Prague (Chancellor Sixt of Ottersdorf, town councillors Jacob Fikar of Vrat, Master Thomas of Javořice and council scribe Matthias of Paumberg) called before the Chamber Court. Before them, charges were brought against the Old Town of Prague, as a legal entity. If the Old Town officials believed that the charges brought against them by the King should not be discussed before the Chamber Court, but before another legal institution, they were to submit the city privileges, or other legal documents which would demonstrate this fact, by the following day (the 2nd of December 1546). However, by the following day, the town council of the Old Town of Prague had merely submitted a long-winded explanatory response stating that procuring all the required information would take a long time (around two or three years).

The King was satisfied with that for the time being; he left the towns alone and turned his attention to the nobility, as he expected specific nobles' culpability to be easier to prove than the guilt of royal towns as legal entities.

So, on the 22nd of December 1546, nobles who had flatly refused to send provincial troops from their dominions were called before the court. They were accused of failing to fulfil a Land Diet resolution. These were mainly noble members of the Unity of the Brethren from the Boleslavský region, including the main Brethren leader, Ernest Krajíř of Krajk (6 lords and 14 knights in total).[20] However, they drew up and submitted a written protest against the King's accusations, and requested that the issue of their possible guilt be judged by the Land Diet, which had convened the troops, and not the King.

---

20 Fridrich of Donín, Jan senior Křinecký of Ronov, Karel Křinecký of Ronov, Jan of Bibrštejn, Adam of Vartmberk from the lordly estate and Jan Špetle of Janovice, Jiřík Vančura of Řehnice, Jan Hrzáň of Harasov, Tobiáš Hrzáň of Harasova, Markvart Stranovský of Sovojovice, Václav Sokol of Leskovec, Jiřík Dešenský of Dešenice, Jan Malobratřický of Řehec, Adam Budovec of Budov, Václav Klusák of Kostelec, Jan Habartický of Habartice, Václav Močidlanský of Močidlany, Mikuláš Netonický of Nebílovy and Václav Hrušovský of Hrušov from the knightly Estates stood beside Ernest Krajíř before the court at the end of the year 1546.

Thus, in this phase, we already find a relatively advanced form of joint action by the aristocratic oppositions, which King Ferdinand could not have underestimated. He adjourned this group of nobles' judicial hearing indefinitely, and the summoned persons pledged to attend the court in person. The date would be set four weeks beforehand. The King had not succeeded here so far, just like in the case of the urban estate.

The last group of accused persons consisted of regional army commanders who had marched with their regional armies to Kadaň but refused to follow Supreme Commander Sebastian of Weitmille's orders when they got there. They were charged with military revolt and sentenced by the royal tribunal (whose members were loyal Moravian nobles appointed by the King) to death. Preserved records differ in terms of who was accused and punished in this group, and how; apparently, however, nobody was executed. The King did not treat other nobles, who had not demonstrated sufficient loyalty, any more severely; he merely summoned for questioning some lower commanders who, during the entire event, mockingly commented on the King's authority and the purpose of the whole campaign.[21]

So, despite all the pronounced sentences, the judicial processes from the turn of the years 1546 / 1547 did not result in any specific punishment. However, they certainly stimulated the Estates opposition, which was now more clearly aware of the danger from the royal side, and who had also verified that the only option for an effective defence lay in a common approach and insisting that the supreme authority in decisions on military issues in the Kingdom of Bohemia is the Land Diet, not the King.

The development on the Saxon battlefield changed fundamentally after the Elector's main army arrived in Saxony from the Danube during December 1546. This quickly drove out the weak garrisons that the "victorious" Habsburg side had left behind in November from the occupied territories. Moritz of Saxony soon lost the easily-acquired territories, and was unable to confront the might of the Elector's army. Thus, Elector John Frederick not only liberated his own territories, but also began a counter-attack and occupied his second cousin Moritz's Saxon territories. Moritz of Saxony kept retreating until he fortified himself in Leipzig, whose siege Elector John

---

21 Tieftrunk, Odpor stavův českých, 57, 175.

Frederick commenced on the 6th of January 1547. During this time, Moritz of Saxony repeatedly officially asked King Ferdinand for military assistance on the basis of the alliance treaty of the 14th of October 1546, which they had jointly concluded in Prague. Elector John Frederick had not yet entered Bohemian territory at that time, but on the 10th of January 1547 he again occupied Dobroluk in Lower Lusatia, which had been the original pretext for Ferdinand's autumn campaign.

In this phase of the military clash, King Ferdinand badly needed to mobilize resources in the immediate surroundings as, during the winter months, he could not count on the supply of new mercenary regiments recruited in more remote regions. That is why he also began to issue specific orders relating to recruitment districts. In Bohemia and Lusatia, recruitment of soldiers by anybody other than King Ferdinand's or Moritz of Saxony's recruiters was strictly forbidden and threatened with punishment. Despite this, however, there was a serious danger that King Ferdinand and Moritz of Saxony would not be able to effectively confront the Saxon winter offensive.

At the very beginning of January, King Ferdinand turned to some of the wealthiest Bohemian nobles and royal towns with a request for military assistance against John Fredrick of Saxony in the form of a personal letter dated the 5th of January 1547. He asked the Bohemian aristocratic leaders to dispatch a force numbering 2,250 men, or money which would allow him to hire the same number of mercenaries for a period of two months. The reasons for sending such a request are not completely clear. The King could quite realistically assume that the vast majority of the addressed persons would refuse to give such a "voluntary" gift, as the recipients (apparently selected according to a property criterion) also included clear opponents of the Habsburg campaign in Saxony.

So, within a few days, the King changed his decision, and one week later (on the 12th of January 1547) he issued a royal decree (a so-called mandate), by which he ordered all the Kingdom of Bohemia Estates to dispatch troops.[22] These were to gather at the town of Litoměřice, according to individual regions, either on the 24th of January 1547 (neighbouring regions) or

---

22 SČ II, 44–51.

on the 2nd of February 1547 (more remote regions). The pretext for convening the Land army allegedly became the acute danger to the country's security, which had already been attacked by enemy troops; by this he meant the repeated occupation of the Dobroluk Monastery dominion in Lower Lusatia, and the adjacent areas of Lower Lusatia, on the 10th of January 1547.[23]

The State laws had counted on the possibility of such a situation (i.e. a rapid military mobilization, announced by a monarchal mandate), if there was a danger in case of a delay, and if the timely convention of a Land Diet, which would be the main decision-making authority in this matter, was not possible. In such a case, if the security of the attacked country had to be ensured immediately, the King or the State government, according to the valid law (repeatedly confirmed in the so-called Vladislav Land Constitution of 1500)[24] could order the extraordinary convening of the army without discussion at the Land Diet. For disobeying such a crisis mobilization notice, every citizen was threatened with loss of honour and property, and capital punishment.[25]

Thus, King Ferdinand had used an exceptionally powerful legal instrument. The content of the mandate provoked resistance in the vast majority of the nobles and towns to which it related. It was perceived a clear breach of estate freedoms, and a great danger in the future. The meaning of one of the most important State laws, adherence to which the Estates held particularly important, was deliberately interpreted by the King completely differently to the Estates. The King had changed the meaning of this "safeguard" in such a way that, with its help, he could force the Bohemian Estates to finance his Habsburg power policy against its will. This is what the Estates leaders viewed as the greatest danger in future development. If they submitted to the King without resistance now, the King could use a similar (because for him it was the most effective) approach any time in the future.

---

23 Eberhard, Monarchie und Widerstand, 410–453.

24 Jaroslav Pánek, "Zemská zřízení v kontextu ústavních proměn ve střední Evropě v 16. a na počátku 17. století – Die Landesordnungen im Kontext der Verfassungsrechtlichem Veränderungen in Mitteleuropaim 16. und zu Beginn des 17. Jahrhunderts – Ustawy krajowe w kontekście zmian konstytucyjnych w Europie Środkowej w XVI i na początku XVII wieku", in Vladislavské zřízení zemské a počátky ústavního zřízení v českých zemích (1500–1619), Sborník příspěvků z mezinárodní konference konané ve dnech 7.–8. prosince 2000 v Praze, eds. Karel Malý and Jaroslav Pánek, 403–441 (Praha, 2001), 403–441.

25 SČ II, 194.

The January royal mandate was a surprise for the Bohemian environ-ment, and appeared to be a complete absurdity; especially in a situation when one Land Diet had recently finished (in autumn 1546), another was to be held in the spring (1547), and there was no military threat by anybody against the Kingdom of Bohemia.[26] According to the January mandate, roughly the same army was to have been dispatched from Bohemian sources this time as in autumn 1546, but with a particular emphasis on cavalry divi-sions, whose usefulness (in comparison with infantry battalions) was proven in the Saxon battlefield at the end of the year 1546. For every thou-sand three-scores Bohemian groschen of tax-declared property, one cavalry-man or three infantrymen were to be dispatched into the field; or a pecuni-ary equivalent of 12 Rhenish guilders was to be paid; i.e. the monthly cost of 1 cavalryman (12 Rhenish guilders) or 3 infantrymen (4 Rhenish guil-ders each). Thus, in comparison with the year 1546, the pecuniary equiva-lent per cavalryman had been left at the same level, while in the case of infantrymen it had been increased, from 3 three-scores Meissen groschen (=3 Rhenish guilders 45 kreuzer) in September 1546 to 4 Rhenish guilders in January 1547. Thus, the expected cost of maintaining Bohemian merce-naries was now in line with the standard common in the Imperial territory at that time.

By the first stipulated date (the 24th of January), no troops had gathered at Litoměřice; not even the King's ardent supporters were able to recruit, equip and transport the required number of soldiers to the border marshalling area that quickly (in 12 days) in the depth of winter. However, a number of nobles who were willing to negotiate at least responded in writing and asked for an extension of the deadline. Thus, King Ferdinand repeated his mandate of the 12th of January with an order on the 28th of January 1547 that had a similar content, and confirmed the validity of the second deadline, originally intended only for more remote areas (the 2nd of February 1547).

The domestic Estates quickly began to recover from its initial surprise at the vigour of the royal orders and threats which could arise from a failure to obey the mandate. The first evidence of the gradual emergence of an orga-nizational base of anti-Habsburg revolt in Bohemia has been documented

---

26 Vorel, "Politická komunikace", 57–59.

since the start of February 1547, i.e. after the issue of the second (repeated) mobilization mandate. Even when using fast mounted messengers, it always took several days before the verified reports reached the appropriate places; it also always took a few days before interested nobles were able to travel to regional meeting places dozens of kilometres away, or even in Prague, in the middle of winter. Given the contemporary context, the Bohemian Estates actually reacted immediately, which is definitely associated with a certain alertness caused by the King's December attempt to punish nobles and towns for their unwillingness to wage war in Saxony.

For the Estates opposition, the situation at the start of 1547 was made even more complicated by the fact that the regional level of political life had not functioned for two decades. Regional Assemblies, which represented a very important element of the organization of social life during the Jagiellonian period, had been significantly restricted by King Ferdinand shortly after his accession to the throne or, rather, he made their possible organization contingent on his consent. These Regional Assemblies, at which the rural nobility could comment on matters of national importance and send their representatives to the subsequent Land Diet in Prague, had been always held in regional towns prior to the year 1526, which were easily accessible for the local nobility in terms of communication and finances (low accommodation costs). Thus, they also represented an important platform for bringing together the political standpoints of the nobility and the royal towns in the relevant regions, especially if they were connected by common religious interests. This was primarily the case in eastern Bohemia, where the main Unity of the Brethren centres (Litomyšl and Mladá Boleslav) were located.

At the start of February 1547 King Ferdinand moved from Prague to Litoměřice, where some of the domestic nobles and town representatives had begun to gather at the end of January. Some had actually brought the required military divisions with them (this was mainly how nobles from the vicinity of Litoměřice responded, i.e. from the Litoměřický, Žatecký and Slánský regions; others, including those who pledged allegiance to the Unity of the Brethren, merely came to negotiate with the King. The strange atmosphere at these talks was to a large extent influenced by the fact that, on the 27th of January 1547, the King's wife, Anna Jagiellon, had died in Prague during the birth of her last daughter. The day after the Queen's death (the 28th of January 1547), the King confirmed the validity of his mandate but, due to the expected date of the Queen's funeral (the 30th of January 1547), he postponed his departure for the army marshalling area at Litoměřice to the 4th of February 1547.

The Queen's death was strongly perceived as a definite sign in Bohemia, but nobody was certain whether this warning by a "higher power" was intended for the King (who had lived with Anna Jagiellon for 27 years, truly humanely loved his wife and was not interested in any other woman, neither during his marriage nor later as a widower) or to the opposition Estates (which had had an important intercessor in Queen Anne; she had managed to moderate disputes between the Estates opposition and King Ferdinand). The Estates certainly took the Queen's sudden death, which had significantly influenced Ferdinand's mental state, into consideration from a social point of view, but it was not reason for them to step back from their requirements for the preservation of Estates freedoms.

However, certain room for negotiation was provided by the temporary peace on the Saxon battlefield, caused by winter weather which was unsuitable for war. After the unsuccessful siege of Leipzig, Elector John Frederick began to gather forces at the start of January for a spring military campaign. The Vogtland was occupied by the Bohemian army, commanded since the start of January by Supreme Hofmeister Zdislav Berka of Dubá (former field hetman of the Kingdom of Bohemia from the time of the Hungarian front military campaign at the start of the thirties);[27] administration of the occupied territory was entrusted to royal commissioners Bohuslav Felix Hasištejnský of Lobkovice and Melichar of Hoberg, who settled in Zwickau, and coordinated the deployment of the garrisons together with Berka.[28]

At that time, the King's commanders in Vogtland were mostly sending him repeated requests for money. From these, it transpires that they had still not been paid for certain units which the King had ordered brought from Vienna in autumn 1546 (they were hired on the King's behalf by Austrian noble John of Lodron). A unit of fifty cavalrymen, sent to the battlefield from Świdnica in Silesia, had also gone without pay. In their case in

---

27 Rg, Book No. 169, 211.
28 ČDKM I, Case Nr. 17, fasc. I – 1547 – January; writing of Bohuslav Felix Hasištejnský of Lobkovice and Melichar of Hoberk dated 27th January 1547 in Zwickau.

particular, the commissioners warned the King that if these Silesians were not paid on time, they could become more dangerous than the Elector's soldiers. The commanding corps, including Zdislav Berka of Dubá, had not received the pay they had been promised either. He had assumed supreme command of the troops in Vogtland at the start of January 1547, but had still not been paid. Thus, he himself drew up a proposal for the King of how he was to be paid (he considered the originally proposed monthly pay of 250 three-scores Bohemian groschen to be insufficient). He also requested the allocation of an experienced secretary (scribe) to handle correspondence; for this position he proposed George of Jeleč, who had a good command of both Czech and German. In addition, he made staying in his function contingent on the provision of funds for an intelligence network ("...*good spies, upon which the war affair depends greatly...*") and for technical support, especially for the transport of artillery.[29]

From these somewhat confused and disparate reports, it's evident that the Bohemian administration of occupied Vogtland was accompanied by considerable improvisation, was not properly militarily secured, and reports about the preparation of a possible counter-attack by the Elector caused great fears. One such incentive was a letter of apology by George of Gera, sent on the 25th of January 1547 to the royal commissioners in Zwickau. The writer wanted to create an "alibi", so as not to be later accused of cooperating with the Elector (he was still under Imperial anathema, and any assistance to the Elector could be subject to criminal prosecution in the future). He informed the commissioners that John Frederick of Saxony had arrived at his dominion near the town of Weida with a division of 500 horses, for which George of Gera was forced to supply feed.

Understandably, these warning rumours forced the King to speed up the negotiations about military assistance from Bohemia. The movement of such large units by the Elector in the direction of the Vogtland borders during the winter months hinted at the preparation of an imminent attack.

The monarch commenced talks with the representatives of Bohemian Estates immediately after his arrival in Litoměřice on the 6th of February 1547. King Ferdinand still could not speak Czech well, so the talks were

---

29 ČDKM I, Case Nr. 17, fasc. I – 1547 – February; writing of Zdislav Berka of Dubá dated 1st February 1547 in Zwickau.

conducted with the help of intermediaries appointed by both sides. Supreme Burgrave of the Kingdom of Bohemia, Volf Krajíř of Krajk, spoke on behalf of the King; Gabriel Klenovský of Ptení spoke on behalf of the Estates opposition. After complicated negotiations, King Ferdinand accepted some of the Bohemian Estates' objections and, on the 9th of February 1547, he explicitly declared that the January mobilization mandate was revoked.[30]

However, the King balanced this formal concession to the Bohemian side with a repeated request for voluntary participation by all the Estates in the military campaign in Saxony, whose purpose was to be the defence of the Bohemian Crown territory. This meant primarily the territory of Lower Lusatia, including the Dobroluk Monastery and the Bohemian fiefdoms which had been held by John Frederick but which, due to the forfeiture of his property on the basis of the Imperial anathema, were transferred back to the King of Bohemia.[31] The Bohemian Estates did not have to participate in this campaign compulsorily on the basis of a royal order (the January mandate had been revoked); instead, participation in the military campaign outside the Kingdom of Bohemia would be a private affair for each participant, carried out at their own expense. If someone was to march into the field with the King in this manner, it would not be viewed as fulfilment of the alliance treaty with Moritz of Saxony (by which the Estates did not feel bound); instead, their participation would be regarded as part of the personal and voluntary defence of the King, who had found himself in difficulty. This would violate neither the Estates freedoms, nor the legal code of the Kingdom of Bohemia.

The extent of this "voluntariness" was then specified by the King in his request to the nobles and royal town representatives who were present to immediately draw up two written lists in Litoměřice: one would list the people who were willing to march into war with the King voluntarily, and the other would list those who refused (and who, after the King won the war, would bear the consequences).[32] The Bohemian Estates refused to do this, and insisted that further talks be conducted only within the frame-

---

30 Teige, Sixt z Ottresdorfu - Knihy památné, I, 76; Josef Janáček, ed., Sixt z Ottersdorfu - O pokoření stavu městského (Praha, 1950), 20.
31 HNL, sign. L 92/1/13.
32 Teige, Sixt z Ottresdorfu - Knihy památné, I, 78.

work of the Land Diet. With this decision, on the 10th of February 1547, most of the people present then abandoned the King.

A day later, King Ferdinand and the remainder of the nobles who were present (who were willing to support the King) agreed that, instead of personal participation in the war, he would accept their voluntary financial assistance in the form of a special one-off tax at the amount stipulated by the January mandate (i.e. a contribution of 12 Rhenish guilders for every 1,000 three-scores groschen of tax-declared Bohemian property, which was a property tax of 0.48%).

We do not know the specific names of these "King's loyal men" but, according to the testimony of Sixt of Ottersdorf, it was around ten persons from whom the King received a one-off contribution of 16 thousand tolars, i.e. 18.6 or 19.2 thousand Rhenish guilders (depending on whether the author was referring to contemporary Bohemian or Imperial tolars).[33] This was quite a large sum of money; it corresponds to a tax base of 1.52 million three-scores Bohemian groschen (in 1544, the tax base of the entire Kingdom of Bohemia only slightly exceeded a value of 7.8 million three-scores Bohemian groschen).[34] So, these persons had to have included the Rosenbergs' guardians (where it can be expected), but also other important magnates, even from the ranks of non-Catholics. They quite demonstrably also included John of Pernštejn, who may not have been present in Litoměřice in person (he stayed in his Moravian Estates), but he sent his diplomat, Christopher Skuhrovský of Skuhrov,[35] to see the King. On a general level, he was then instrumental in ensuring that the King did not insist on his "loyal men" participating in the campaign personally, but instead "merely" accepted a financial contribution.

An important role in this phase of the negotiations began to be played by Volf Krajíř senior of Krajk, then (since the year 1542) Supreme Burgrave of Prague. He was a close relative (first cousin) of Mladá Boleslav Bohemian Brethren leader Ernest Krajíř of Krajk, which is why the King was

---

33 Petr Vorel, "Směnné kursy jako nástroj mocenské politiky v Římsko-německé říši počátkem čtyřicátých let 16. století", Český časopis historický 112 (2014), 379 – 401.

34 Petr Vorel, "Frühkapitalismus und Steuerwesen in Böhmen (1526–1648)", Anzeiger der philosophisch - historischen Klasse, Österreichische Akademie der Wissenschaften 137 (2002), 167–182.

35 Petr Vorel, "Pernštejnská diplomacie v době stavovského povstání roku 1547 (edice listů Jaroslava z Pernštejna z února a ž června 1547)", Východočeský sborník historický 3 (1993), 236–237.

particularly interested in an alliance with Volf. At that time (start of January 1547) Volf of Krajk paid the soldiers wages amounting to 3,000 tolars on the King's behalf; the King reimbursed him this sum in the form of ponds and vineyards in the vicinity of Waidhofen an der Thaya in Lower Austria.[36] Despite Volf's relatively old age (he was already over sixty), the King was negotiating conditions with him in February 1547 under which he could accept the function of Supreme Commander (Field Marshal) of the Habsburg army. He was offered a personal monthly pay of 1,000 Rhenish guilders, as well as maintenance of 16 members of a personal guard with a monthly pay of 8 Rhenish guilders, and other staff servants (6 buglers, 1 hornist, chaplain, barber etc.); in total, 1,236 Rhenish guilders per month.[37] Volf of Krajk did not accept this offer (apparently due to his old age); or at least the sources don't mention him in the position of Supreme Field Marshal. However, he served the King loyally until his death [† 7th of January 1552].

While part of the nobility and the towns gathered in Litoměřice to negotiate with the King, others began preparing joint action in the form of political meetings, which were forbidden at that time. All of the below-mentioned talks (in Litoměřice, in Pardubice and in Prague) took place concurrently during the first ten days of February 1547. Participants in one event did not know what had been agreed elsewhere; given the fact that communication took place using conventional intelligence resources (i.e. mounted messengers), it was necessary to allow several days for the delivery of every report over such a great distance (and in the middle of winter). Given the necessary conspiracy, we do not have the names of specific participants precisely documented; however, we can guess them with a certain degree of probability on the basis of subsequent royal sanctions.

The first source-documented event that was already clearly an organized preparation of joint action against the King took place in the east Bohemian castle of Pardubice, in the main headquarters of John of Pernštejn, former leader of the Bohemian Neo-Utraquist opposition. This convention, involving an unspecified number of nobles, was diplomatically masked as participation at the then popular aristocratic winter entertainment, which

---

36 ČDKM I, Case Nr. 17, fasc. I – 1547 – January, draft of King's writing dated 3th January 1547.
37 ČDKM I, Case Nr. 17, fasc. I – 1547 – February, draft of King's writing dated 21th February 1547.

was cock-fighting (even back then, bets on winning cocks were operated as gambling), organized in Pardubice Castle on the 7th of February 1547.

Given the previous role John of Pernštejn had played in Bohemian Estates society, participants in this meeting logically assumed that he would become the leading personality of the resistance against the royal mandate.[38] Not only did John of Pernštejn not participate in this meeting, held in his own castle headquarters (his eldest son Jaroslav, then nineteen, was to look after the guests), he pretty much distanced himself from it. He agreed with the proposed convening of the extraordinary Land Diet in March that year (if the King allowed it) but, other than that, he did not intend to become actively involved in the resistance against the royal mandates. But Pernštejn's hesitant approach was logical. He could not openly oppose the King, as Ferdinand had ensured his neutrality well; in the Habsburg army's military staff, one of the formal command functions had been entrusted to seventeen-year-old Vratislav of Pernštejn, Pernštejn's other son, who was part of Archduke Maximilian's "Bohemian company".[39] The aristocratic segment of the anti-royal camp was surprised by Pernštejn's hesitance and unwillingness to lead the revolt, and could not find a sufficiently authoritative and influential personality that would stand at the head of the revolt against the King. However, even this problem was eventually solved.

At the same time as the nobles' negotiations in Pardubice Castle, talks among Prague town councillors were taking place in Prague (the 7th to the 9th of February 1547). The holding of joint meetings by Prague Town representatives was forbidden, which is why the dispatched Old Town and New Town councillors met away from the town hall, and held talks in the main university lecture theatre (in the Karolinum). Other royal towns asked Prague politicians for clear standpoints on how to proceed further. After all, only three urban municipalities had explicitly obeyed the royal mandate: the Catholic towns of Plzeň and České Budějovice, and the Utraquist Ústí nad Labem. Initially, the Prague Towns councillors tried to avoid any decision that could be ex post considered to be an anti-royal standpoint.

---

38 Vorel, "Pernštejnská diplomacie", 231 – 272.
39 Nicolao Mamerano Lucemburgo, Catalogvs Omnivm Generalivm, Tribvnorvm, Dvcum, Primorumq[ue], totius Exercitus Caroli V. Imp. Aug. & Ferdinandi Regis Roman. Super Rebelleis & inobedienteis Germ. quosdam Principes ac Ciuitates conscripti, Anno 1546. (Colonia, 1550), 7–8.

They had been warned by King Ferdinand, who had sent George Gerštorf of Gerštorf, royal Vice-Chamberlain, and Volf of Vřesovice, governor of Prague Castle, as his authorized negotiators on military assistance to the Prague urban municipalities at the start of February.

However, the aggravated political situation led to a power coup in the Prague Towns. Under pressure by the Prague craftsman's guilds, the King convened a forbidden gathering of the so-called large municipalities (i.e. all fully-fledged citizens). As a result of talks by these "large municipalities", more radical politicians were appointed to Prague town hall, who were aware of both the danger of royal towns taking a stance against the King in the future, and of course the need to discuss joint action with their current opponent, i.e. the aristocratic Estates, which also felt threatened by the royal mandate.

The aristocratic opposition quickly reached the same conclusion and decided, from that point on, to coordinate its resistance against the King with the royal towns, which it had previously clearly regarded as its political adversary (regardless of confessional affiliation). However, this political "marriage of convenience" between the Bohemian nobility and the royal towns lasted less than three months, and failed to remove the deep-rooted antagonisms between these two important segments of contemporary Bohemian society. On the contrary; King Ferdinand later wanted to cleverly use this fact to dissolve this shaky alliance, but few people in Bohemia thought about this danger at the start of February.

Thanks to the afore-mentioned two preliminary meetings, a joint convention involving both parts of the Estates opposition (aristocratic and urban) commenced on the 12th of February 1547, convened in the University of Prague lecture theatre. Participants in the talks expressed their disappointment at John of Pernštejn's stance but, at the given time, nobody sufficiently authoritative (and also wealthy) was found among the nobility that could replace him as revolt leader. As the upper nobility's main representative, it was mainly William Křinecký of Ronov (impoverished member of an old lordly family) that dealt with the Prague Towns in this phase; in addition, the main initiative was taken by wealthy east Bohemian magnate Bohuš Kostka of Postupice, in whose house in Prague's Old Town (Celetná street) the opposition aristocratic segment's main conference had been held on the 14th of February 1547 (after he returned from Litoměřice).

The first important result of these joint negotiations was primarily the agreement to announce an extraordinary Land Diet, which was to convene in Prague in the second half of March. The monarch was formally asked to announce the Diet, but the Estates had already agreed that it would be held even if the monarch refused to convene it.

The second result was the compilation of a public notice in which the participating estate representatives rejected the King's January mandate as a violation of Estates freedoms, and asked others to join this manifesto by adding their seal to the afore-mentioned text.

In my opinion, we can assume that the idea of compiling a list of opposition Estates only came about in connection with the afore-mentioned February talks in Litoměřice, at which King Ferdinand I. himself expressed his wish for a written record of who would voluntarily accommodate the King in his request for the dispatch of troops, and who had decided not to oblige him voluntarily. It was a clear threat, regardless of the fact that the January mandate had been formally revoked.

Bohemian Brethren magnate Bohuš Kostka of Postupice, a direct participant in the Litoměřice talks, arrived in Prague on the 13th of February 1547, and thus could immediately interpret the result of the negotiations with the King. Therefore, we can assume that Kostka's standpoint directly influenced the wording of the text of the Estates declaration of the 15th of February 1547. In it, representatives of the Bohemian regions (ten of fourteen regions; the Litoměřický, Žatecký, Rakovnický and Plzeňský regions are not mentioned here) and the Prague Towns contractually undertook that they would provide mutual protection to one another, if any of them were affected by their decision not to respect the January mandate's provisions. At the same time they sent the text of this agreement to their regions with an invitation to other nobles, who could not be personally present at the February talks in Prague, to join the thus-created association, bound to mutual protection.

The text of the Estates declaration of the 15th of February 1547[40] was quickly reproduced in print under the title "The Bohemian Estates' Friendly Resolution" in several textually identical printed versions and in two lan-

---

40 SČ II, 120–121.

guage variants (Czech and German) and distributed around the Bohemian regions with an invitation to other nobles and towns to register by making two parchment copies of the document with a seal attached (a sample form text of the anticipated signatory deed was attached to the printed matter). In it, the signatories undertook to provide protection to one another in the event that any of them faced future sanctions from the King for disobeying the January mandate. The participants in the February meeting in Prague subsequently distributed this declaration around the various regions. We assume that these were the afore-mentioned printed versions in Czech or German language, distributed with regard to the prevailing linguistic situation in the relevant regions.

However, we do not know whether, at this time (i.e. between mid-February and mid-March 1547) this invitation to the mass "registration" for the Estates' challenge received any extensive response. Obviously we cannot rule it out, but in mid-February there was still no organizational staff, nobody was directing the Estates Revolt, and nobody in Bohemia knew much about developments on the battlefield in the Empire. In fact, we still do not know today which specific nobles added their names to the February memorandum of the 15th of February 1547, or rather to what extent the proclaimed February "reconciliation" of the royal towns and the nobility (celebrated in the urban environment – but, as far as we know, nowhere else – even in song) was a reflection of actual political reality.

In mid-February 1547, most important and wealthy Bohemian nobles were still in Litoměřice, or on their way home from Litoměřice, rather than in Prague. After all, from the diction of the February memorandum, it's evident that its main initiators were the urban politicians of Prague, who had conducted a written diplomatic dialogue with King Ferdinand for several weeks, and not the nobility. This fact is also documented by a detail (apparently inadvertent) in the wording of the conclusion of the February memorandum. It states that one of the originals of the registration deeds was to be given to the "lordly and knightly state" (but it does not state specifically to whom, or where) while the other original is to be handed over to "...us, Prague citizens and towns...".[41]

---

41 Vorel, "Politická komunikace," 68–69.

Even from a purely technical perspective (if we strip away the former long-term generally hostile relations between the upper Estates and the royal towns in Bohemia, still clearly visible at the highest level of politics at the end of the year 1546), it's difficult to imagine that, in the middle of a deep winter (in mid-February) Bohemian rural nobles bought parchments, paid scribes and created such a serious referential piece of evidence against their own persons en masse, on the basis of a printed tract which some lords or knights had brought from Prague, when the actual February memorandum contained no deadline or possible sanction. For a common rural noble, who did not actively participate in political life, there was no reason for a hasty reaction in this initial phase of the revolt.

All the same, this February memorandum already gave King Ferdinand a clear signal that he could not count on the Bohemian Land army for his campaign in Saxony. After his experiences in autumn 1546, he no longer relied on the Bohemian Estates army (or on its "volunteer forces") and began to intensively raise money so that he could hire his own royal army. He expected to quickly form a contingent of approximately 1,300 cavalrymen and 22 battalions of infantrymen (around 11 thousand soldiers). This army was to be commanded by Margrave Albert Alcibiades of Brandenburg.

Several main sources were to be used in the hiring of this army.

One of them was the afore-mentioned contribution of 16 thousand tolars, provided to the King by Bohemian magnates, and a so-called "barrel levy" (a tax on beer production) which was to be collected for the year 1546 both in Lusatia and also in the immediate princedoms (ruled by the King directly) in Silesia.

Another source was money which Church institutions in Silesia were to lend the King.

Bohemian vice-Chancellor George Žabka of Limberg travelled around Silesian monasteries, and collected their disposable cash and jewellery reserves for the monarch's needs.

The fourth source, whose use attested to the King's truly desperate situation, was the remaining real estate belonging to the at least formally surviving Catholic Church institutions in Silesia and in Lusatia, which King Ferdinand confiscated despite the affected institutions' protests and used as reimbursement for direct financial loans which he had received from certain Silesian nobles.

It was mostly this source that provided the King with funds in the order of several tens of thousands of Rhenish guilders during his most difficult moments (in February and March 1547), which could be used to hire a decent army (the monthly cost of a thousand-man cavalry regiment was 24 thousand Rhenish guilders).

In terms of financial volume, the largest sum was represented by 40 thousand tolars from Margrave John of Brandenburg, in return for which the King ceded him the Mariazell Monastery property in Lower Lusatia. Also, some of the Silesian nobles found significant cash sums in their coffers, in return for which they received lien rights over Church property. Brothers Fabian and Sebastian Šejnoch provided the King with more than twenty thousand tolars; Ferdinand received other large sums from several members of the Goč family of Chojnik, and others. These sums, secured with Church property in Silesia, were significantly larger in this phase than what the King had managed to obtain in the form of loans from the citizens of Nuremberg.[42]

Even with the enforced financial assistance which gradually gathered in Silesia (especially in March 1547), King Ferdinand did not have sufficient money available in February 1547 to hire an army of the size he had originally intended. He had enough resources to hire 1,200 cavalrymen, but the infantry forces were significantly weaker; instead of the originally planned 11 battalions, they numbered approximately half of this. However, Emperor Charles V. had already promised to provide assistance in the form of four battalions of infantry mercenaries.

So, this joint army, which was led by Margrave Albert Alcibiades of Brandenburg, contained almost the number of troops that King Ferdinand

---

42 An overview of royal loans from this period, published by Janáček, České dějiny, I/2, 346, includes only the sums recorded in the Viennese Court treasury ledgers (i.e. money which was received in physical form). These records completely omitted large sums which creditors paid out directly in lieu of the King (i.e. mostly soldiers' wages in cash, which had to be paid as soon as possible). While the afore-mentioned Viennese accounting chamber records income of around 70 thousand Rhenish guilders from cash loans during February 1547, King Ferdinand obtained at least 120 thousand Rhenish guilders during the same period by placing Church goods under lien. However, these sums are only recorded in the accounting documentation of the Court Chamber's Bohemian division, ČDKM I, Case Nr. č. 17, fasc. I – 1547 – February.

had originally expected to be deployed when he requested Bohemian military assistance. At the end of February 1547, this army began marching from Ústí nad Labem in the direction of Saxony. It headed through the Elbe valley towards Dresden and from there, in an outflanking manoeuvre from the north, towards Chemnitz in Saxony, where Moritz of Saxony was entrenched. Both armies were to merge at Chemnitz in Saxony, and jointly attack John Frederick of Saxony.

However, all of Ferdinand's efforts came to naught, as his army was annihilated by Elector John Frederick 30 km before reaching Chemnitz in Saxony on the 2nd of March 1547, after a brief night-time attack against the encamped army in the Battle of Rochlice. The Imperial mercenaries (mostly Spaniards) were killed or captured; the King's soldiers (mostly ethnic Germans) were released after laying down their weapons, and a significant number of them agreed to be hired into the Elector's army. Margrave Albert Alcibiades himself, who had surrendered to the Elector, ended up spending some time in a comfortable "honourable prison".

The Habsburgs suffered this embarrassing defeat two weeks before the commencement of the March Assembly in Prague. The reaction to the Elector's victory, which was spread rapidly by the Lutheran side in contemporary newspaper reports (printers in Wittenberg and elsewhere were working at full capacity)[43] was very well known in Bohemia.

By the start of March, the King had no other significant resources at his disposal; he had used all his "reserves" to dispatch the army at the end of February, and these investments had come to naught. The rest of the promised financial loans during March (after the Habsburg troops' defeat) were being provided only reluctantly.

Ferdinand of Habsburg (who had not marched on Rochlice personally, instead staying in well-fortified Dresden) and Moritz of Saxony desperately awaited the assistance the Emperor had promised, while Elector John Frederick seized control of the Saxon territory and began preparing a counter-offensive. One of the possible tactical variants was also the Elector's coun-

---

43 Von Marggraf Albrecht von Brandenburg Whrhafftige Zeitung, Der sich unbedacht seiner Ehren und Pflicht, Under Erdichtem Schein, mutwilliglich und freuenlich. Wider den Churfürsten zu Sachsen und Burggraffen zu Magdeburg, zuuerdrückung Warer Christlichen Religion, als eyn Feind, eingelassen, durch Gottes gnedige schickung, sampe dem Lantgrauen von Leuchtenburg, mit allem irem Kriegsvolck, zu Roß und fuß, um bund bei Rochlitz erlegt, und gefangen worden seind. 1547.

ter-offensive on Bohemian territory, which is why John Frederick of Saxony began to negotiate directly with the Bohemian Estates opposition about the conclusion of a new alliance treaty.

Therefore, King Ferdinand sent a somewhat confused open letter (dated the 8th of March 1547) from Dresden to the Bohemian regions, in which he ordered the Bohemian Estates to mobilize the Land army under the command of Sebastian of Weitmille (who had been appointed Supreme Commander of the Bohemian Land army in the year 1546, but whose term of commission by the Land Diet had long since expired) as defence against the imminent invasion of Bohemia by the Elector's army. This was another important impetus for the Estates opposition, which was preparing for Diet talks, convened unilaterally (despite King Ferdinand's explicit disagreement) in Prague.

Some time around the 10th of March, the Elector's army, which faced no military obstacle on the Bohemian side, actually crossed the Bohemian border in the Ore Mountains. Their formal objective was primarily the Elector's Estates in Bohemian territory, which had been previously occupied by royal soldiers during the retreat from Jáchymov (i.e. Boží Dar and Horní Blatná). The main Saxon commander, William Thumshirn, also demanded protection for his small estate which he owned on the Bohemian side of the border in the Loket region. However, it was nearby Jáchymov which was the real objective. "At stake" was not only control of an important mining area; at the start of March 1547, a significant amount of newly-mined metallurgical silver had been found in local storehouses. In his request for reinforcements, the local military commander, Bohuslav Hasištejnský of Lobkovice, estimated the amount of the stored silver at 4 thousand pounds. This was surprising news for the King, as such an amount of silver corresponded to a sum of 33 thousand Bohemian tolars, i.e. 39,600 Rhenish guilders. With this sum, he could hire almost twenty battalions of infantry Landsknechts for one month. Thus, Sebastian of Weitmille received an order to recruit as many soldiers as possible in the immediate surroundings, and use them to defend Jáchymov. There was plenty of silver in Jáchymov, but there weren't enough human resources. As a result of the repeated recruitment of troops at the Bohemian-Saxon border by both sides in the conflict, there were no longer any men that could be dressed in a uniform and quickly trained to use weapons.

On the basis of the King's order on the 8th of March 1547, the afore-mentioned Sebastian of Weitmille issued a special circular three days later (on the 11th of March 1547), in which he invited the Bohemian Estates to send military reinforcements from the interior as soon as possible on the basis of their voluntary promise; they were to gather near Jáchymov (at the town of Ostrov on Ohře) to defend the land against the Elector's army. This time, soldiers were only sent by the King's "loyal" towns of Plzeň, České Budějovice and Ústí nad Labem; to the surprise of the others, these were also joined by Kutná Hora.

However, this symbolic military assistance by a few of the King's "loyal" towns was not sufficient for an effective defence against the Elector's army (whose "Bohemian" contingent numbered around 400 cavalrymen, 6 infantry battalions and two siege cannons). The royal side did not manage to organize an effective defence of Jáchymov, and the town and adjacent mining area were occupied by the Saxon army in mid-March 1547 (no later than the 20th of March 1547), and practically without a fight. A certain part in this affair was obviously also played by the fact that the immediate environs of Jáchymov were predominantly Lutheran, just like the town council, so the Saxon army was welcomed in the region as a friendly power rather than an enemy.

In such a hectic atmosphere, an informal Diet took place in Prague from the 17th to the 22nd of March 1547. From the monarch's perspective this was an illegal event, as the King had explicitly rejected the Estates' request to announce the March Land Diet (in a letter dated the 19th of February 1547, sent from Ústí nad Labem) and set the date of the regular Diet's commencement as the 19th of April 1547. He expressly forbade any other political talks (at a regional or nationwide level). Thus, only active members of the Estates opposition participated in the March Estates' Assembly. This Assembly brought about three significant changes in the revolt's organizational base.

The first of these was the establishment of a twelve-member steering committee (titled "...authorized persons..."), comprising four members from each estate. However, we still do not have trustworthy sources documenting the first twelve members' names from March 1547, as the management staff worked within a conspiracy. We only discover the main protagonists' identities from the subsequent investigation after the revolt was suppressed, but it's likely that the management staff of the revolt changed, and apparently not even the number of twelve persons and the individual Estates' parity representation was strictly adhered to. The Old Town of Prague Chancellor Sixt of Ottersdorf, who left behind him the most important source of the Estates Revolt's history, named the following noble committee members: Ernest Krajíř of Krajek, William Křinecký of Ronov, Diviš Slavata of Chlum and Košumberk and Bořivoj of Donín on behalf of the lordly estate; Zdislav Tluxa Vrábský of Vrábí, Melichar Ror of Rorov, Bernard Barchanec of Baršov and Hynek Krabice of Weitmille on behalf of the knightly estate. From the preserved imprints of seals on one of the letters, sent to John Frederick, Elector of Saxony, in late March, two other committee members were identified in addition to those named above – Wenceslas Valkoun of Adlar and Wenceslas Pětipeský of Krásný Dvůr.[44]

Official documents sent by the committee used the term *"authorized persons from the Estates of the Kingdom of Bohemia and citizens of all three Prague Towns"*. This was diplomatically more suitable, as specific persons were not named (and therefore exposed to potential danger from the royal side) and also the relevant documents, sent on behalf of the steering committee, could create an impression of greater political support than that which they actually had. From the committee's composition, it's evident that its main aristocratic activists were members of the Unity of the Brethren.

The other important conclusion of the March Assembly talks was the decision to convene a Land army, which if necessary was to be used as defence against their own monarch, if King Ferdinand became dangerous from the perspective of the preservation of estate privileges and freedoms. The size of this army was the same as in the case of the Diet resolution of 1546, i.e. for every two thousand three-scores Bohemian groschen of tax-declared property there was an obligation to dispatch one cavalryman and four infantrymen (alternatively two cavalrymen or eight infantrymen) into the field.[45]

In terms of military history research, this resolution is more important than regular Diet materials, as it also specifies other technical circumstances of the Estates army's functioning: for every twenty cavalrymen, one

---

44 Teige, Sixt z Ottersdorfu - Knihy památné, I, 137–138.
45 SČ II, 170.

vehicle with a crew of two was to be dispatched; or three such vehicles for every hundred infantrymen. These vehicles were to be used not only to transport weaponry while moving; they also carried smaller calibre fire-arms (harquebuses) and engineering equipment. In addition to physically dispatching Land army soldiers, every person was also to hand over a finan-cial sum corresponding to 0.1% of tax-declared property. This money was to be used to cover the army's ordinary needs, as well as the commanding corps' salaries. Each region was to appoint its own supreme regional com-mander, as well as a lower officers' corps (Staff Sergeants).

After a certain initial reluctance, the function of Estates army com-mander was accepted by Kašpar Pluh of Rabštejn,[46] who was allegedly cho-sen from twelve proposed persons by drawing lots.[47] However, appointing Kašpar Pluh Supreme Commander of the Estates army had a certain logic: the west Bohemian magnate was expected to be very active within the framework of the Estates opposition, because he himself had engaged in a dispute lasting several years with King Ferdinand over the dominion of Bečov, or rather about the profitable mining rights to his west Bohemian dominions. In this respect, Kašpar Pluh had a common interest with the Sliks of Jáchymov and the Saxon Elector's court.

The third important step implemented at the March Assembly was the formulation of a joint programme declaration. This was an extensive docu-ment, divided into several dozen points of diverse content.[48] From the het-erogeneous structure of its content, it's evident that it was compiled gradu-ally and quickly, without the opportunity to repeatedly discuss and precisely formulate its final wording, as was the norm in Diet talks. Besides funda-mental issues such as the definition of the estate and monarchal share of power, and protection of religious confession, the text also contains indi-vidual towns' specific requirements objections against certain monarchal exponents. Apparently, the main authors of this text were Bohemian Breth-ren leader Bohuš Kostka of Postupice and Old Town of Prague Chancellor Sixt of Ottersdorf. However, the only version of this text that has been pre-

---

46 Václav Bůžek, "Mezi Bečovem, Wildbergem a Norimberkem (Příspěvek ke komunikaci českých stavů se zahraničím ve čtyřicátých letech 16. století)", in Stavovský odboj roku 1547 - První krize habsburské monarchie, ed. Petr Vorel (Pardubice and Praha, 1999), 65 – 80.

47 Tieftrunk, Odpor stavův českých, 124.

48 Tiefrunk, Odpor stavův českých, 364 – 384; Janáček, České dějiny I/2, 250–257.

served is in Sixt of Ottersdorf's handwriting, written only after the revolt was defeated, so the individual phases of preparation, or even the actual material accuracy of Sixt's secondary transcription of this text cannot be distinguished.[49]

But the main significance of this text, which was formally declared as the Estates' proposal for talks at the upcoming April Land Diet (permitted by the monarch), was not in the small details of its content. It was also titled *"The Bohemian Estates' Friendly Resolution"*,[50] just like the February memorandum, which caused problems in older historical interpretations, as the relationship between these two texts was not clear.[51]

The text of the memorandum of the 15th of February 1547 rejected only the King's January mobilization mandate, and simultaneously stated that acceptance of this mandate would mean the loss of all the Bohemian Estates' freedoms. However, by mid-March, it was generally known that the King had revoked his January mandate. Ferdinand I. himself explicitly confirmed this in an open letter dated the 19th of February, addressed to the Prague Towns. So the Estates committee had to specify a new joint programme base, or rather specify which other traditional estate freedoms (aside from the already-revoked January mandate) were being violated by the King. That was the new meaning and content of the second "Friendly Resolution" whose members on the 22nd of March 1547 were demonstrably considered to be a total of 33 Bohemian lords and 103 knights who had stamped their seals on the letter, sent directly from the convention talks to John Frederick, Elector of Saxony. Apparently these men comprised the core of the "Friendly Resolution" signatories; by the 25th of April 1547 their number had increased to the so far more or less precisely identified 1,749 Bohemian nobles (168 lords and 1,581 knights).[52]

This quick (and mostly positive) response to the March convention talks was also due to the better thought out logistical arrangement of the entire petition action. The revolt's organizers had learned from the tactical mistake they had made in the February memorandum (it did not contain

---

49 Tieftrunk, Odpor stavův českých, 110, 364–384.

50 Petr Vorel, "Přátelské snešení stavův českých" z března 1547 a jeho signatáři", in Stavovský odboj roku 1547 - První krize habsburské monarchie, ed. Petr Vorel (Pardubice and Praha, 1999), 81–124.

51 Eberhard, Monarchie und Widerstand, 425; Vorel, "Politická komunikace," 66.

52 Vorel, "Přátelské snešení stavův českých", 97–120.

any deadline or potential sanctions) and, in mid-March 1547, they approached the formation of the Estates association's signatory base completely differently. The March text also served as a symbolic joint declaration of anti-royal opposition, but every Estates member had to assume a positive or negative standpoint towards it by a certain deadline; join it, or reject it.

The Estates committee actually dealt with the "Friendly Resolution" text in this simple manner in the following weeks. The addressed nobles and royal towns then expressed their standpoint in relation to the revolt via this text. If they expressed agreement with it, they simultaneously undertook to contribute to the dispatch of the Land army, organized by the opposition committee, which was even willing to defend the country against its own king if need be. Agreement could be expressed by specifically affixing their own seal to two copies of the special registration letter; one copy was archived by the inhabitants of Prague (they were lodged with the Old Town Chancellor Sixt of Ottersdorf), and the other copy was filed with the Land tables office (i.e. under the nobility's control).

Whoever did not agree with the text of the "Friendly Resolution" and refused to affix their seal to it, simultaneously refused to participate in the mobilization of the State army in a crisis situation. However, for such a refusal, they could be punished with confiscation of property and expulsion from the country in accordance with the wording of the State laws: "...*so that the property would be confiscated by the state and used for the public good, while the former owner would be expelled from the land...*".[53]

So, the "Friendly Resolution" of March 1547 intentionally divided the Bohemian Estates into two camps. That is why many nobles were hesitant to express a clear standpoint, and tried to avoid this by referring to the need to discuss these matters at the regular Land Diet (whose date was set as the 19th of April 1547). One of the main persons to remain undecided until the last minute was John of Pernštejn, whose own military forces (the largest in the country) would comprise a significant part of the Land army's Estates troops if he were to engage in opposition activity. It was mainly because of John of Pernštejn that the Estates committee repeatedly extended the dead-

---

53   SČ II, 173.

line by which the circle of the "Friendly Resolution's" signatories was to be definitively closed.

While the Estates negotiated in Prague and neared the end of their Assembly talks (the Assembly ended on the 22nd of March 1547), the situation in north-western Bohemia changed again. The Saxon (pro-Habsburg) army, led by Duke Augustus, Moritz of Saxony's younger brother, began to march from Dresden towards the Jáchymov area which had been taken without a fight by Elector John Frederick's army. Around the 21st of March, Moritz's army crossed the Bohemian border and occupied the town of Most and its environs. King Ferdinand and Moritz of Saxony reached the occupied town a few days later.

In late March, the opposition Estates faced a difficult dilemma. Two foreign armies had entered the country, both Saxon, both led by Lutheran princes, and mutually hostile. One (the Elector's) had occupied Jáchymov without a fight, the other (Moritz of Saxony's) had settled around Most and was getting ready for a battle over the Jáchymov mining area. At the same time, two "domestic" armies were forming in Bohemia. One was being convened by Sebastian of Weitmille: soldiers provided voluntarily to the King by the Bohemian nobility and towns were to gather near Ostrov on Ohře. The other Bohemian army, i.e. the Land army, of which Kašpar Pluh of Rabštejn was appointed leader on the basis of the March Estates convention's decision, was to be formed on the basis of a mobilization notice dated the 23rd of March 1547.[54] This mobilization notice was reproduced in print and distributed around the regions, together with the text of the letter dated the 21st of March 1547, in which the Estates committee notified Sebastian of Weitmille that his appointment as captain of the State army (approved at the Land Diet in the year 1546) had expired, so he no longer commanded the State army and anything he undertook would be at his own risk.

In the event of an actual launching of a military conflict in the given situation, the Estates opposition side could rely on the military might of the Saxon army, deployed on the Bohemian side of the Ore Mountains, but only the most radical (the Lutheran, and in the given situation apparently

---

54 SČ II, 168–174.

also the Bohemian Brethren) section of the opposition, which at that time commanded both the revolt's political control centre and its potential army, which was still to convene, was willing to do this. However, this would mean dragging the Bohemian state into the war in the Empire (in the form of a military clash between two Saxon armies on Bohemian territory), which the Bohemian political representation had wanted to avoid from the very beginning. So, despite the opposition side's apparent superiority, the largest magnates (who were actually meant to finance the Estates army's troops) hesitated in clearly supporting the opposition committee's side. Apart from this, it was already known that Emperor Charles V.'s large military forces were heading towards the Bohemian borders, with the clear objective of supporting Moritz of Saxony's weak army, in which even King Ferdinand had found "refuge" (at the time he was lacking his own army, lost in the Battle of Rochlice in early March 1547), in the anticipated military clash.

Thus, intensive negotiations began in Bohemia between the King and the Estates opposition.

The King offered the following interpretation: the Elector of Saxony's troops have attacked the country and occupied Jáchymov. Therefore, it is necessary to mobilize all military power and liberate the Bohemian territory from the foreign aggression. For this purpose he asked Moritz of Saxony, who was obliged to provide the King with military assistance on the basis of the October 1546 alliance treaty, for help.

The Estates committee contradicted this with the following explanation: John Frederick of Saxony's troops are not actually in Bohemia, and military control of Jáchymov has been taken over by the Estates army under the command of Kašpar Pluh of Rabštejn. Therefore, the Estates are asking King Ferdinand to negotiate with Moritz of Saxony on the rapid departure of his troops from Bohemia, or his actions will be interpreted as an attack on the country by a foreign power (the Estates did not recognize the alliance treaty between Ferdinand I. and Moritz of Saxony dated the 14th of October 1546). If Moritz of Saxony attacked Jáchymov, the Estates army would defend it. Jáchymov and its resources (the silver reserves, and the precious metal which was still regularly mined) would be used "for the good of the land", i.e. to hire troops to potentially defend it against Moritz of Saxony.

However, at the time, Kašpar Pluh did not actually have any Bohemian Estates army troops at his disposal yet; these were only supposed to convene on the 5th of April 1547 on the basis of the mobilization notice dated the 23rd of March. But at Bečov, where Kašpar Pluh resided, a larger unit gradually formed at the turn of March and April, financed by the resources of local Lutheran nobles; by the start of April 1547, Pluh's Bohemian Estates army numbered around 2 thousand men. In Jáchymov itself, part of Thumshirn's original army, which had settled in the town around the 15th of March, also remained at Pluh's disposal. This is also evidenced by the fact that, later, Kašpar Pluh was still in constant contact with Henry Reuss of Plauen, commander of the Elector's army, and William Thumshirn; they had de facto military control not just of Přísečnice, but also of Jáchymov.

The Estates committee's claim that none of the Elector's troops were in Jáchymov sounded illogical, but formally this was apparently the case. If the Estates made arguments with references to State laws, then they could not afford to state facts in their response to the King that the King could easily dispute. The Elector of Saxony's troops may have been deployed in Jáchymov and its environs, but formal command over them had, for the afore-mentioned reasons, apparently been transferred to Kašpar Pluh. Given the contemporary context, we can quite logically assume that, in return for this "military assistance", the Elector kept the afore-mentioned four thousand pounds of metallurgical silver which lay in the Jáchymov storehouse in early March. In this way, the Saxon soldiers could have been formally hired by Kašpar Pluh for a certain period using the Jáchymov silver (just like Pluh's Bohemian army, formed at Bečov). Such an agreement most likely did not constitute a major problem for any of the participants. Kašpar Pluh himself had been a close relative and ally of the Jáchymov Sliks and the Elector of Saxony in previous years, and had also maintained very friendly relations with William Thumshirn, Supreme Commander of the Saxon army which was deployed in Bohemia. It was only on the 18th of April 1547 that the Estates committee in Prague explicitly approved Kašpar Pluh's use of the metallurgical silver reserves stored in the Jáchymov mint to pay the soldiers' wages, but from the context I believe that this was merely a retrospective approval of a financial transaction that had taken place long before then.

Given this situation, the Habsburg side withdrew from its plan to strive for the military control of Jáchymov and, in early April, the army divisions of Ferdinand Habsburg and the Saxon brothers Moritz and Augustus began to march from Most in the direction of Cheb, where they were to merge with the Imperial army. This army reached Cheb on the 5th of April, and the Imperial army arrived the very next day (on the 6th of April), without any military clash (the march through the Bohemian regions was accompanied only by the customary pillaging of rural settlements and towns).

The town of Cheb (Eger) and its environs were not just chosen as a military marshalling area for Imperial, royal and allied Saxon armies because the town lay close to the border. The Chebsko region's constitutional law character was also important in the given situation. This small territory on the western periphery of the Bohemian multi-state coalition was still formally part of the Holy Roman Empire, and it had only belonged to the King of Bohemia since the 14th century as a long-term lien. Thus, in the event of a dispute with the Estates opposition, the King could argue that the Imperial (i.e. foreign) army had not crossed the Bohemian State borders, but was merely moving across Imperial territory (albeit belonging to the King of Bohemia in the form of a long-term lien). This was a situation opposite to that of the so-called "Bohemian fiefdoms" in the Empire. They were regarded as the direct territorial possession of the King of Bohemia, and had merely been transferred under the feudal tenure of specific Imperial nobles or towns.

For such a large concentration of troops around Cheb, a sufficient amount of rations had to be procured in advance. The preferential right to purchase meat, flour, corn, butter and also alcohol (beer and wine) at discounted prices was awarded to Jakub Hruška of Březno, a wealthy knight from the region of Žatec.[55] He was appointed the Habsburg army's main supplier. The gathered supplies were to be deposited in the main food storehouse behind the ramparts of the town of Cheb.

Thus, at the start of April 1547, the distribution of power on both sides briefly stabilized in anticipation of the great spring offensive, which in Bohemia was expected to be a war over the Jáchymov silver mines.

---

55 Pešák, Berní rejstříky, 35.

In the meantime, the Habsburg camp's great allied army was resting after the march, and increasing its numbers in the Cheb area. In total, these allied armies were to number 10 thousand cavalrymen and 17 thousand infantrymen.

The Elector of Saxony had divided the army into two parts: a significant part was deployed at the Bohemian-Saxon border (around Jáchymov and Přísečnice in Bohemia, with a part on the Saxon side of the border), where it operated with the Bohemian opposition Estates' approval (it numbered around 12 thousand men), while the other part of the Elector's army was concentrated in Meissen in Saxony. The core of this army was a powerful cavalry (around 2,000 horses) complemented by eight infantry battalions (around 4,000 Landsknechts).

In mid-April, the Bohemian Estates army, under the command of Kašpar Pluh of Rabštejn, which was gathering around Bečov, numbered around 5 thousand men. However, a separate great Prague Towns army numbering several thousand men and commanded by Wenceslas Pětipeský of Krásný Dvůr was forming around Prague.

Via messengers, both feuding sides formally declared an effort to negotiate some peaceful solution, but the situation was very confusing. It was hard to guess what Emperor Charles V. was actually intending to do with the allied, and relatively powerful, army.

The first signal of any major military activity was the military invasion of the Kynžvart dominion, belonging to Kašpar Pluh of Rabštejn, by small Imperial divisions on the 12th of April 1547. The systematic burning and destruction of his own property was intended to divert the attention of the Bohemian Estates army's Supreme Commander and the allied Saxon units. After all, this initial military activity by the allied Habsburg army indicated that the Imperial army would continue to march into the Bohemian interior to help King Ferdinand suppress the Estates Revolt.

Such a fundamental change in the conduct of the war by the Habsburgs also suited Elector John Frederick because, in this "scenario", a part of the Habsburg army would be tied up in Bohemia, and the Bohemian Estates opposition would be forced to take actual military action against the Habsburgs. Thus, the Elector's commanders Thumshirn and Reuss began occupying other areas in western Bohemia (Loket, Karlovy Vary), and prepared for a clash with the garrisons that had been left behind by Sebastian of Weitmille and Moritz of Saxony in Most, Chomutov and elsewhere. This significantly restricted the operational capabilities of the part of the Elector's army which was deployed at the Bohemian-Saxon border, and Elector John Frederick lost several days before he could decide on a different tactical approach. This was to prove fatal for him at the town of Mühlberg, during his retreat from Meissen.

The main Imperial army had already left the environs of Cheb on the 13th of April 1547, and it now quickly marched along the German side of the border, through Adorf and Altenburg, in the direction of Meissen where Elector John Frederick dwelt at the time. Reports on the troops' movement only arrived in Meissen after several days' delay; that is why the Elector only began to gradually withdraw his troops from the Bohemian-Saxon border back into Saxony on the 16th and 17th of April, in order to merge his armies and thus be better able to confront the Imperial attack. Given the fact that the Imperial army had several days' head start, he did not wait for the Emperor in Meissen, but instead set out in a north-easterly direction along the Elbe to the better-fortified fortress of Torgau, about 60 km from Meissen, so that he could buy more time to merge his armies. The other part of the Elector's army set off from the Bohemian border directly for Torgau. The Habsburg side took advantage of the Saxon army's withdrawal from the Bohemian border; on the 16th of April 1547, it took Jáchymov back for King Ferdinand without any great effort.

However, reports of events on the battlefield only reached Prague after a significant delay, and they were often confused. It was only Kašpar Pluh that regularly supplied the Estates committee with requests for money, which he needed to pay the troops (from his correspondence it transpires that, by then, he was paying the Estates army at least partly from his own money), and with instructions on how to actually proceed. However, in fundamental political matters, the Estates committee awaited the decision of the Land Diet, which had yet to commence in Prague. Thus, Kašpar Pluh, as Supreme Commander of the Estates army, never actually received clear political instructions on whether to fight with the Habsburgs or against them. He had to make important decisions by himself (and he also bore the responsibility for them afterwards).

Thus, the April Land Diet convened in a situation that was significantly different to that of the March Estate (opposition) Assembly a month earlier. It commenced on the 18ᵗʰ of April, i.e. at a time when military tension in the Empire was at its peak and it was still not clear how the war between the Habsburgs and the Elector would end. However, by then, an imminent danger of war no longer threatened the Kingdom of Bohemia itself. At the time of the commencement of the Land Diet (the 18ᵗʰ of April 1547), the huge Habsburg army had already left the Bohemian area (on the 13ᵗʰ of April), and was marching to Saxony. Similarly, Elector John Frederick's troops, who were marching strenuously to try to make up the delay and merge with the Elector's main army in Saxony, had also left Bohemian territory. Thus, it was evident that the military clash would take place outside the Bohemian territory, but there was no way of knowing how the conflict between the Emperor and Elector John Frederick would turn out. The forces were balanced, and the Elector had the advantage of a "domestic" environment (he could even use his well-secured fortresses for defence).

The political polarization of contemporary Bohemian estate society was also clearly evident from the fact that the Land Diet talks which had commenced on the 18ᵗʰ of April 1547 were held, unconventionally, in two locations in Prague. The opposition grouping, i.e. the signatories of the "Friendly Resolution" conducted their talks at the university (in the Karolinum). The King's supporters, and others who were still undecided and had not yet affixed their seal to the "Friendly Resolution", were gathered in Prague Castle. Both gatherings sent written messages to one another, and express messengers travelled across Charles Bridge with them. King Ferdinand did not participate in this Diet personally (albeit he had still expected to at the start of April), but he sent a group of authorized representatives in his place and supplied them with detailed instructions on how to negotiate with the Bohemian Estates on his behalf. In addition to these written instructions, whose text we are familiar with, some of the King's trusted diplomats were also supplied with a special verbal authorization on how to conduct talks at the Diet in the event of some unexpected development in the situation on the Imperial battlefield.[56]

---

56 Vorel, "Politická komunikace", 81.

In the end Ferdinand I. himself, as an experienced politician, had to take the alternative of the Emperor's possible defeat in Germany into consideration. Why should he completely burn his bridges to a possible future agreement with the opposition in Bohemia, if he found himself on the defeated side in the war in the Empire? So, in the last phase of the closing of the estate programme's circle of signatories, i.e. those who "...*are lovers of the freedom of the Kingdom of Bohemia and the public good, or those who are true Bohemians...*", not only the still-hesitating John of Pernštejn, but also evident exponents of pro-royal policy, such as for example Vice-Chamberlain George Gerštorf of Gerštorf, deputy scribe Ulrich Humpolec of Prostiboř and Christopher Skuhrovský of Skuhrov, could become members of the opposition association.

To a certain extent, we can assume that some of the Bohemian nobles acceded to the Estates association after a previous secret agreement with the King, in order to hinder potential radical tendencies and thereby neutralize Bohemian military potential in the dispute in the Empire. This is also indicated by the rather excited discussion on the theme of whether members of State governments, who had previously clearly stood on the King's side, should accept the "Friendly Resolution".

The question is to what extent this step was previously agreed with King Ferdinand, who shortly before the Diet's official commencement still warned the hesitant Bohemian politicians against joining the Estates association. At that time, the situation on the Imperial battlefield was very uncertain, and although Ferdinand Habsburg could not outwardly express doubt about the Habsburg armies' final victory, as a pragmatic politician he surely would have also thought over the situation in which he would find himself in Bohemia if his campaign in Saxony was not successful. Similarly, the domestic Bohemian nobles, unless they adhered to one of the two extreme political standpoints and explicitly tied their future to the victory of one of the sides on the Imperial battlefield, looked for a solution that would not personally threaten them, no matter what the outcome of the war in the Empire was.

Thus, at the start of the second half of April, the situation in Bohemia was such that the hesitant segment of the Bohemian nobility, which so far did not want to explicitly act against the King's interests, began to count on the Imperial opposition's victory and tried to join the Estates camp. The reasons may have included fears of potential sanctions from the side of the rebel camp (for those who had not joined the "Friendly Resolution") but also the monarch's interest. After all, it was only in the case of a formal registration as signatories of the "Friendly Resolution" that these men could effectively participate in the subsequent negotiation of political conditions under which the opposition Estates (even after the Habsburgs' potential failure on the battlefield in the Empire) would be willing to accept Ferdinand I. as their king in the future. Thanks to this very clever diplomatic move by the King (if it was actually agreed with the King, which we don't know), supporters of Habsburg policy could also join the "Friendly Resolution", and thereby influence the opposition camp's talks "from the inside", without any fear.

Surprisingly enough we found the town of Plzeň, which until then had belonged among decisive monarchal policy supporters, and had asked the King for military protection against the Bohemian opposition Estates as late as the start of April 1547, among "Friendly Resolution" members. But it's in the very case of Plzeň that preserved sources indicate that accession by the King's followers who were in Bohemia at the time of the April Diet (and not in the field campaign in Saxony with the King) took place with the King's knowledge; or rather it was one of the possible solutions which was only verbally (in conflict with the King's previous written instructions) interpreted by his agents, which in the given case was apparently George Žabka of Limberg. That is also apparently why, in the final phase of the April part of the Diet, the Supreme Burgrave of Prague, Volf of Vřesovice, suddenly began persuading other Land officials and royal councils (who until that time had only the King's written instructions forbidding them to join the Estates association) that it was now desirable to join it. Finally, by the 25th of April 1547, everyone came to an agreement on this, and talks commenced aimed at the adoption of the Diet resolution which defended the Estates' existing approach. This was still the case on the 27th of April 1547.

Estates who were formally part of the opposition (among whom, however, apparent Habsburg policy supporters, as "Friendly Resolution" signatories, had also found themselves) wanted to wait and see how the war in Saxony would turn out before deciding how to negotiate with the King in the future. This diplomatic room for manoeuvre proved to be an advantage primarily for the revolt's aristocratic segment. The expansion of the opposition Estates association to include John of Pernštejn and his diplomats, who simultaneously also maintained contacts with the pro-royal camp, moved the focus of the entire revolt away from the original idea of some radical military action (promoted by the revolt's contemporary leadership, with Kašpar Pluh or Rabštejn at the helm) and back to a diplomatic level, i.e. a position which could theoretically be defended within the framework of the dualistic monarchy's existing legal system.

The participants in the Land Diet belonged to all parts of the contemporary political spectrum. Nevertheless, they managed to find a suitable form of communication (even though, initially, they could not even meet in the same place) and agree on a temporary solution that would not be destructive for any of them, no matter how the war in the Empire turned out. Why should someone in Bohemia risk everything, including their life and property accumulated over generations, just because the Imperial princes could not come to an agreement? The primary issue was not religion, even though this argument was commonly used in the Schmalkaldic League's and Papal Curia's propaganda leaflets.

Such campaigning could not work in Bohemia if it did not even bring about the anticipated response in Germany. If the Elector could not get effective assistance from the German Lutheran princes (of whom many worked in the Imperial army for good pay), he could hardly expect that, with an appeal for the defence of a shared religion (which in the case of Bohemia was not even completely true), the Bohemian nobility would risk their lives and property to reverse the balance of power in the Empire. In April 1547, radicals from the ranks of the Estates committee did not manage to convince the others that it was the right time to overthrow the King and join the war in Germany on the Lutheran opposition's side. The Bohemian opposition did not actually cross this imaginary Rubicon, so it assumed that talks with the King would continue on a diplomatic level, no matter how the war in the Empire turned out.

Talks at the April Diet in Prague continued for several more days after the opposition programme signatories' circle was closed, i.e. at a time when the Habsburg army defeated the Schmalkaldic League at the Battle of Mühlberg (on the 24th of April 1547) and captured Elector John Frederick.

A verified report of the victory of Emperor Charles V. and his allies in Saxony reached Prague after several days' delay (on the 28th of April 1547), and caused considerable concern among the Diet participants. Although King Ferdinand himself did not actually have a large military force at his disposal, a quite realistic idea emerged of a victorious royal army marching into Bohemia, accompanied by Imperial forces and the army of Moritz of Saxony, whose military support King Ferdinand explicitly requested for the purpose of controlling rebellious Bohemia.

The report on the downfall of John Frederick, Elector of Saxony, who would represent the primary potential ally in the event of a military clash between the Bohemian opposition and King Ferdinand, caused the almost instantaneous collapse of the Estates opposition's former leadership. The Bohemian opposition's radical leaders remained isolated; the Schmalkaldic League was defeated, and its leaders captured or persecuted. They had not even received support from Estates in the neighbouring lands of the Bohemian Crown in March, when the situation looked more positive, so they could not expect anyone who had so far remained neutral to now risk showing support for the Bohemian opposition, which had found itself on the defeated side.

Thus, the Land Diet, after confirming the information from the Saxon battlefield, merely adopted a provisional resolution and its participants left for their respective homes, to secure their dominions and headquarters in anticipation of the imminent conflict. In this phase, previously hesitant experienced politicians such as John of Pernštejn took over the deserted leading positions in the Estates committee. Thanks to this group of nobles, who were able to foresee the danger associated with the opposition's complete capitulation, an appearance of unity among the Estates was at least outwardly maintained. This provided limited, but at least some, room for manoeuvre when negotiating with King Ferdinand. Therefore, the hasty departure by most of the Diet participants from Prague on the 28th of April 1547 was declared to be merely a temporary interruption of the Diet, whose talks were to continue three weeks later (on the 20th of May), when the situation became clearer.

The Land Diet's April resolution may have been formally dated the day of commencement of the Diet, on the 18th of April 1547, but in reality this record only came into existence on the 28th of April 1547. [57] In addition to information about the suspension of Diet talks until the 20th of May, this text mainly contains a verification of the Estates association's procedure when convening the Land army via a mobilization notice dated the 23rd of March. In the preserved version of the Diet resolution, the Estates agreed on an unusual wording relating to the Land army. The April Diet formally announced a convening of the Land army to defend the country, or rather the collection of a tax for the financing of this army, at 0.1% of property. At the same time, this army, convened "legally" on the basis of an official Land Diet resolution, was to replace the existing Estates army, established on the basis of the Estates committee's previous decision in March and operating under the command of Kašpar Pluh of Rabštejn. This "old army" was to be immediately dissolved ("...*and the people who have been dispatched into the field should immediately withdraw from the field and return home...*") and replaced by the new Estates army. From the ranks of the Estates, representatives of both the Estates and the Habsburg side were dispatched together as messengers to bring this resolution to the King; at the time, they were all members and signatories of the "Friendly Resolution".

However, not even King Ferdinand was interested in a military solution. For now, he was in no hurry to travel to Bohemia, as at the turn of April and May he could still expect armed resistance. From his reporters, he knew that the Estates committee still had its own army at its disposal, and he did not underestimate the economic potential that the Bohemian royal towns and some aristocratic leaders could mobilize for further defence. It was a very complicated situation for King Ferdinand (despite all the advantages arising from the victory at the Battle of Mühlberg). Emperor Charles V. may have publicly declared and promised him potential military assistance in Bohemia but, even so, such an open conflict would be dangerous for him. The Emperor's promises could not be completely relied on (between them, both of the Habsburg brothers were involved in a number of contentious issues); after all, even after the victory over Elector John Frederick, Emperor Charles V. did not have the entire Empire under control. At the time, the Schmalkaldic League's northern army still successfully resisted

---

57   SČ II, 239–241.

the Habsburgs, just like some important Imperial towns such as, for example, Konstanz, Magdeburg and Bremen.

Nevertheless, even the military assistance promised by Charles V. was not a clearly positive solution for King Ferdinand in this phase. He himself considered it more advantageous to offer the defiant Bohemian nobility some compromise solution, rather than let a land that was to represent an important source of his monarchal income in the future be pillaged and robbed by his brother Charles V.'s Italian and Spanish mercenaries. The example of the German areas, through which these Spanish and Italian troops had marched during the previous months, was a deterrent for him. Thus, he waited and negotiated.

Before taking further action, it was important to see how the talks in the second part of the Bohemian Land Diet, which resumed in Prague on the 20th of May 1547, would turn out. Here, the Estates confirmed their common standpoint, according to which the formation of the Estates association was a legitimate step.[58] They made further negotiations with the King contingent on the monarch coming to Bohemia, and his repeated confirmation of Estates freedoms (mentioned in the Estates' March programme), which were to be legally assured by a new entry in the Land tables (the old records had burned during the Prague Castle fire in 1541). Actually, it was as if nothing had happened; after all, no war had broken out – the Bohemian Estates merely showed its King that there are things that it wouldn't put up with, and that it was ready for armed resistance if necessary.

In late May, Diet participants could still depart from Prague for home with feelings of a restored and publicly proclaimed Estates unity among the Bohemian nobility and towns, united in a supra-confessionally formed anti-royal opposition. For now, in this form, it could truly be a considerable force that the King did not want to confront in open battle.

The King's reaction to the Bohemian Land Diet's May resolution was surprising. Even before leaving Dresden, he sent personal letters to a large group of Bohemian nobles, whom he asked to come to Litoměřice immediately after receiving the letter.[59] Shortly after he himself crossed the country's border and arrived in Litoměřice with his army in June 1547, he issued

---

58   W. Eberhard, Monarchie und Widerstand, 457–640.
59   Vorel, "Pernštejnská diplomacie", 244–245.

a monarchal decree dated the 3ʳᵈ of June 1547.[60] In it, he offered mercy and immunity from prosecution to all nobles who had become members of the opposition Estates association (i.e. affixed their seal to the "Friendly Resolution"), but did so only due to a misunderstanding and now regretted their actions. They were to express their effective regret by immediately coming to Litoměřice to see the King, and personally apologizing to their King for this mistake. Any of the Estates' programme's signatories who failed to do so would be exposed to royal wrath and punishment.

This June mandate represents one of the prime manifestations of King Ferdinand's diplomatic skills. He deliberately only issued his decree several days after the end of the Land Diet, so that its participants would not have time to discuss it with one another. He gave the Bohemian nobility no time to think it over; everyone had to quickly decide for themselves whether to travel to Litoměřice to see the King, with a vision of easily reversing potential sanctions, or continue to adhere to the opposition standpoint and be exposed to the danger of isolation and exemplary punishment. Some of the less decisive lords and knights, who had registered for the "Friendly Resolution" out of a sense of belonging to the Estates rather than due to active anti-royal attitudes, did not hesitate for a moment and saddled their horses for the trip to Litoměřice. Others quickly followed their example, so, at the start of June 1547, domestic nobility from all corners of the country was heading for Litoměřice.

During the mutual negotiations, the King looked for – and finally found – a way to reach an agreement with the nobility, and offered it a compromise solution. He even accepted that the establishment of an opposition Estates association could be accepted as legitimate, but only under the assumption that the Estates would abolish this association themselves at the next Land Diet. The King would not punish anyone who was merely a member of this association, and otherwise did not take any action against the King.

For the nobility, this was a very important moment which decided on the definitive collapse of the active opposition. The King had promised the nobility de facto immunity from prosecution, obviously with the exception of several persons whom he had designated as the revolt's main architects

---

60   SČ II, 291–297.

and agents of the captured Elector of Saxony. This was mainly a group of Bohemian politicians who had had common interests with the Elector of Saxony's court before the year 1547, and several wealthy and influential nobles from the ranks of the Unity of the Brethren. They later had a significant part of their property confiscated as part of the punishment stipulated by the King, and they were prevented from actively participating in public life in the future. But, even, in their case, the King did not resort to capital punishment or the complete loss of rights and social degradation.

The price of this obligingness was an agreement under which the upper Estates would not prevent the King in his decisive reckoning with the royal towns. For the domestic nobility, this perspective was acceptable, and even the sacrifice of a temporary political ally (the urban estate) was not too great a price to pay for rectifying relations with the King and averting the danger of an internal war. On the contrary; the prospect of a significant weakening of the royal towns' influence suited the domestic magnates, as the royal intervention would suddenly solve old disputes relating to agricultural business which had been a bone of contention between the nobility and the towns for the entire first half of the 16th century.

We do not have any direct source at our disposal that would document who, from the Estates opposition, negotiated the conditions of an amicable settlement of the dispute with the King, but from the context we can assume that the main activity in this regard was undertaken by a circle of diplomats linked in some way to John of Pernštejn. This is indicated by the subsequent contradictory stances by King Ferdinand towards John of Pernštejn and his sons – the former Estates leader surrendered to the King's mercy, but negotiated conditions under which the Estates would be willing to come to an agreement.[61] As an experienced politician, King Ferdinand could appreciate this, but not forgive it.

At the start of the second half of June 1547, there were two more large gatherings of opposition nobility that still refused to submit to the King – one in Prague, and another simultaneously in Pardubice. King Ferdinand asked John of Pernštejn to explain the monarch's standpoint to the participants in these talks, and not to allow any armed unrest. Under the influ-

---

61 Vorel, Páni z Pernštejna, 172–174.

ence of the monarchal declaration's helpful tone, even the most radical part of the opposition allowed itself to be convinced that, in the given situation, open resistance towards the King was unnecessary, and that they would achieve better results through negotiations.

The royal towns were still in danger. Their representatives also set out for Litoměřice in early June 1547 to ask for forgiveness, but the King did not grant them an audience (unlike the nobles). By this, he made it clear that he intended to settle accounts with the towns in a different manner, but at the time nobody knew how. Thus, the royal towns, and particularly the Prague Towns, remained a key anti-royal opposition segment.

Even at this time, there was still a significant and well-organized opposition military force in Bohemia – i.e. the Prague municipal army, led by experienced military commander Wenceslas Pětipeský of Krásný Dvůr (one of the four men proposed to the King by the Land Diet in autumn 1546 as the potential Supreme Commander of the Bohemian Estates army).

CHAPTER 7

LONG-TERM CONSEQUENCES OF THE CHANGES IN THE POWER AND ECONOMIC STRUCTURE OF BOHEMIAN SOCIETY AFTER THE YEAR 1547

When King Ferdinand managed to dismantle the aristocratic-urban alliance inside the opposition camp in Bohemia during June, he set off from Litoměřice to Prague in early July 1547. It was only the inhabitants of Prague, whose relatively powerful municipal army was prepared for defence, who anticipated the King's arrival in a state of combat readiness. In the end, it was also in Prague that the only significant direct clash between royal and Estates troops took place.

Prague Castle remained under monarchal officials' control, and the royal army occupied this main monarchal seat in Bohemia, lying on a hill above the left bank of the river Vltava, without a fight. The Prague Towns themselves (i.e. the united Prague Old Town and Prague New Town) lay on the opposite river bank. At the time, easy crossing between the two banks was only possible across the stone Charles Bridge. That is why there were several smaller incidents at the very start of July, when royal troops tried to penetrate the part of the city in the lower Prague Castle (the so-called Lesser Town) to gain safe access to Charles Bridge. The royal army's efforts to fortify the Lesser Town side of the bridge caused a reaction by the Prague Towns allied army, and the defence of the Charles Bridge foreland on the left bank on the 2nd of July 1547 became the first direct military clash. The Prague municipal army showed its superiority in this confrontation, and the royal divisions had to retreat from the Lesser Town back to the safety of Prague Castle.

This, and some other minor armed clashes, did not have any fundamental strategic significance, but they later became an important argument that King Ferdinand used to justify property and political sanctions against Prague. A ceasefire, and the peaceful return of the Prague municipal army to the right bank of the Vltava, was only negotiated by Moravian provincial governor Wenceslas of Ludanice, who came from Litoměřice to Prague together with the King and gradually assumed the position of the most important advocate of royal policy among the domestic nobility.

For King Ferdinand, Ludanice's loyal service in this phase of the conflict was very important, as the Moravian provincial governor was blood-related to most of the important Bohemian magnate families, and therefore offered the Bohemian nobility a certain guarantee of a possible agreement with the King. But the King did not negotiate with the towns. On the 3rd of July 1547, the Prague Town councillors received a charge sheet and summons to court proceedings which were to commence on the 6th of July 1547. Without the nobility's support, further armed resistance by the royal towns had no hope of success, and in an atmosphere of universal hope for an amicable agreement with the King, members of town councils also favoured laying down weapons and disbanding their armies.

However, not everybody was prepared to accept the danger that resulted from complete capitulation. During a short time, the commanders of the existing Prague municipal army managed to significantly strengthen the military potential of Prague, regularly armed from the town armoury. The organizer of this mobilization was most likely the existing commander of the Prague army, knight Wenceslas Pětipeský of Krásný Dvůr. He was an experienced military commander. As early as 1541, the urban estate in Bohemia appointed him lifelong Supreme Commander of the municipal armies, and awarded him an adequate annuity.[1] He was also one of the four men whom the Land Diet of 1546 proposed as the Supreme Commander of the entire Bohemian Estates army. The large municipal army, supplied with sufficient ammunition, was able to defend the part of the Prague Towns on the right bank, and if necessary even attack the Lesser Town and Prague Castle as, after all, was demonstrated on the 2nd of July.

With the approaching court date (the 6th of July) tension in Prague peaked, but in the end did not spill over into a more extensive battle between the two sides. The conflict stayed limited to mutual shelling between the two banks of the Vltava, and a few skirmishes at the access gates near

---

1   Tieftrunk, Odpor stavův českých, 139.

Charles Bridge. During the few days when it wasn't clear whether the tension in Prague would finally spill over into regular military conflict between the King and the municipal army (between the 2nd and 6th of July 1547), the inhabitants of Prague tried to organize the supply of military reinforcements from the countryside.[2] However, the King's supporters managed to thwart even this potential support. During the first week of July, the King obtained assurances from most eminent domestic magnates (most of them still formally members of the Estates association) that they will suppress potential unrest in individual Bohemian regions and prevent the armed hordes marching towards Prague, if anybody tried anything of that sort. Ernest Krajíř of Krajk, George Vchynský of Vchynice, John Čejka of Olbramovice and apparently also some other nobles were to march with their divisions to assist Prague; some royal towns were also preparing operative military aid. However, reports from this period are very vague.

The complicated diplomatic negotiations, about the conditions under which the inhabitants of Prague would surrender and accept the royal verdict, took several days. While they were in progress, the King admitted a representative of the Prague Towns into the negotiations; the Old Town Chancellor Sixt of Ottersdorf spoke with the King personally. The monarch also sent his diplomats to the talks of the "large municipalities" of Prague. i.e. meetings of all fully-fledged citizens. Bohemian Vice-Chancellor George Žabka of Limberg, and Moravian Vice-Chamberlain Přemek Prusínovský of Víckov, negotiated with the inhabitants of Prague on behalf of the King.

It was not intended to be a "court" in the true sense of the word, as by the end of the year 1546 it was evident (both in the case of the nobles, and the royal towns) that it actually wasn't clear what level such a matter should be dealt with on, in legal terms. The King intentionally wanted to avoid court proceedings which would try to prove the degree of guilt, or whether a violation of some laws even took place. He offered the Estates opposition an amicable solution: if the opposition itself recognized that it had committed an offence against the King, surrendered to the King's mercy and left the decision on guilt and punishment to the King, then the King would be lenient.

---

2   Janáček, České dějiny, I/2, 296–297

In general, the King promised the Prague town councillors that, in his decision "*...he does not want to commit any injustice or violence against any of them..*". For the councillors, this was apparently a sign of the King's amicable standpoint, as the individual councillors really did not have to feel personal responsibility for the Prague Towns' collective participation in the Estates Revolt.

The King's threats could not be taken lightly, but the aristocratic opposition leaders who had been personally involved in the revolt were also forgiven, if they demonstrated effective remorse.

The possibility of an analogous solution to the crisis was also foisted on the royal towns by the King's diplomats, who conveyed to the citizens the King's alleged words that if the inhabitants of Prague lay down their weapons and surrender, he, in return "*...will be their King and gracious lord, but also wants to forgive the guilty because of the innocent...*". In this phase of the talks, the most important role was played by experienced lawyer and long-time deputy scribe of the Kingdom of Bohemia, Ulrich Humpolec of Prostiboř, who personally wrote the court summons to the Prague town councillors. It was he who aroused the greatest hope at the Prague municipalities' talks with his words that the King would also forgive the rebellious towns, if they surrendered voluntarily.[3]

Apparently these arguments were considered by the Prague municipalities, which had to decide whether to continue in their armed resistance or capitulate. At the given time, the Prague armies were more powerful than the royal garrison and its auxiliary Imperial divisions, but what next? Thus, after a mutual agreement, the Prague municipalities themselves decided that their municipal army will be dissolved, and that the addressed town councillors will appear before the royal tribunal in accordance with the wording of the summons and await the monarch's mercy.

The court case involving the Prague Towns commenced on the 8th of July 1547. It was not only the town councillors themselves that were called before the monarchal tribunal, but also all the representatives of all three Prague Towns' local governments; 240 persons in total. Some of them had nothing personally in common with the resistance, and many had spent

---

3   Tieftrunk, Odpor stavův českých, 253.

recent days actively promoting a calming of the tense military situation and a restraining of radical officers. However, in the given context, this was not important at all.

The tribunal was chaired by King Ferdinand and his second-born son, Archduke Ferdinand. The rest of the committee was formed exclusively of representatives from other lands of the Bohemian Crown (not the Bohemian nobility). The King appointed a large number of non-Catholics among the tribunal members, to make it clear that the trial of the offenders did not have a confessional subtext.[4] In addition to both bishops whose dioceses were spread over the lands of the Bohemian Crown (i.e. the Bishops of Olomouc and Wrocław), half of the members of the Moravian provincial government also sat on the tribunal. Supreme Governor Vavřinec Drahotušský of Drahotuš, Supreme Chamberlain John Senior of Vrbno and Supreme Justice John Planknar all sat on the tribunal on behalf of the Princedom of Opava (which at the time was still considered a part of Moravia, albeit with its own estate structure). The Silesian princes were represented by prince Wenceslas Těšínský. Some other nobles who worked in the King's services in individual adjacent princedoms also came from Silesia; nobles from both Lusatian magraveships were also well represented. These were mostly nobles who had shown their loyalty during the war and either personally participated in the King's campaign in Saxony, or at least provided the King with money.

However, none of the estate tribunal members decided on the defendants' guilt or the imposed punishments; their role was only of a symbolic and political nature. This point was also underlined by King Ferdinand when he officially published the list of names of all the tribunal members in print in the year 1547. None of the Bohemian Estates were represented among the observers, even though the King had loyal and deserving supporters among them. He rewarded them in a different way.

The court case involving the citizens of Prague was staged in accordance with the script that had already been used in late 1546 by Emperor Charles V. in his cases involving the Imperial towns. There was no investigation, and no trial. The Prague Towns were to surrender to the King's mercy.

---

4   Josef Kořán, Antonín Rezek, Josef Svátek and Justin Václav Prášek, Dějiny Čech a Moravy nové doby, I. 1526–1609 (Praha, 1939),112; Janáček, České dějiny, I/2, 300.

Thus, it was only the King's unilateral decision on the form and extent of the punishment that was expected, not the demonstration of guilt or innocence.

Even on the first day of the proceedings,[5] 240 representatives of the Prague Towns came to listen to the King announce his punishment in the Vladislav Hall in Prague Castle (where, on other occasions, Land Diet talks were held).[6] The citizens heard the King's allegation, and through the Old Town Chancellor Sixt of Ottersdorf they admitted their guilt and undertook to unreservedly accept the royal verdict, as had been agreed in advance.

All of those present really were pardoned and, except for isolated cases stipulated by the King (one of these being Sixt of Ottersdorf), none of them was actually subjected to any further personal sanction, as long as they paid the pecuniary fine which the King had assessed in cash. This was stipulated individually as a sum of between 10 and 4,000 tolars, based on the specific citizen's amount of property and not at all related in their participation in the revolt. However, all of them were imprisoned, until the Prague Towns (as legal persons) fulfilled what the verdict had ordered them to do. And therein lay the main point of the monarchal sanctions – i.e. the punishment of the towns as legal persons, rather than individual citizens. In addition to a large pecuniary fine, the King ordered the Prague Towns to hand over all municipal privileges, weapons, all landed property and municipal income, and imposed a permanent tax on the production and sale of beer; a so-called hereditary barrel tax.[7]

The announcement of the sanctions against the Prague Towns interrupted the tribunal's activity for almost two weeks. In the subsequent round of trials involving individual nobles and royal towns, which commenced on the 20th of July 1547, the monarch acted differently towards the aristocratic and urban part of the rebel camp.

The aristocratic municipality was only relatively little, and highly selectively, affected by the King's disfavour. Of almost two thousand signatories of the opposition nobility's programme ("The Bohemian Estates' Friendly

---

5   Janáček, České dějiny, I/2, 300–304.
6   Eberhard, Monarchie und Widerstand, 481–484.
7   Alois Míka, Stoletý zápas o charakter českého státu 1526–1627 (Praha, 1974), 76–77; Vorel, "Frühkapitalismus und Steuerwesen", 170–177.

Resolution") only 35 persons were charged (16 lords and 19 knights). Of the thirty five charged some had emigrated; they were tried in absentia. These were some of the main activists of the rebel committee, politically linked to the Court of John Frederick of Saxony; primarily William Křinecký of Ronov and Melichar Ror of Rorov. The King was strict on them. They lost all their property and privileges, and were sentenced to capital punishment. However, this action did not have any immediate significant results, as these nobles were either poor or had only a small amount of landed property. Those who did not leave the country and surrendered to the King's mercy were punished by having a part of their property seized, or having it changed from free tenure to a dominion. Thus, none of the convicted wealthy nobles who remained in the country were thrown into desperate poverty, or lost their social status, as a result of the material punishment. However, they had provide the King with a so-called capital punishment undertaking, in which they bound themselves not to engage in any future opposition activity against the King under threat of loss of the remainder of their property, privileges or death. In 1548, the remainder of Petr Malovec of Malovice's property (of the Březnice dominion) was seized from him as punishment for breaching this undertaking.

In this way, however, King Ferdinand unilaterally removed the Unity of the Brethren from the highest level of political life. A large number of the punished nobles belonged among the political leaders or at least members of the Unity of the Brethren (for example Ernest Krajíř of Krajk and Bohuš Kostka of Postupice).[8] In the given situation, the King could not directly punish them for their religious conviction, as this would have resulted in radical resistance by all the nobles, regardless of their confessional affiliation. However, the convicted nobles lost their right to participate in the Land Diet as fully-fledged members of their estate, as immediately after the year 1547 they did not hold any free landed property registered in the Land tables (they had to accept the property that the King had left them in the form of fiefdoms). Even though, soon after the year 1547, some of the punished nobles expanded their landed property again to include other free dominions (for example Sigismund Anděl of Ronovec), they were prevented

---

8   Rezek, "Statky zkonfiskované r. 1547", 451 – 482.

from engaging in long-term political activity by being confined to house arrest. Therefore, they had to remain only in the territory of their own dominion, and every journey anywhere else (for example even to family celebrations held in a neighbouring stronghold) had to be permitted by a special letter issued by the King.[9] In this way, the King gained firm control over the former opposition leaders, and an unauthorized journey by any of them to political talks in a neighbouring noble's castle, or to the Diet in Prague, could become a pretext for further sanctions. In the subsequent years, the affected nobles really did have to regularly ask the monarch directly for his consent, even for short-term journeys such as a visit to relatives or a trip to a rehabilitative stay in a spa. These measures, humiliating for the contemporary nobles, were only abolished by the monarch for those of the convicted who were still alive in the year 1556 (except Brethren's Bishop John Augusta).[10]

Part of the theatrical trial of the year 1547 was also the imposition of capital punishment. However, this did not affect the main members of the Estates committee's aristocratic segment. They had either gone abroad immediately after the revolt's collapse and found themselves outside the reach of royal power, or they were punished with a partial confiscation of property, or more precisely an imposition of feudal dependence.

In the end, four men who had participated in the revolt but had not played a leading role in its organization were executed as a warning. At the public execution, held the day before the August Land Diet in Prague, two knightly estate members (Bernard Barchanec of Baršov and Wenceslas Pětipeský of Krásný Dvůr) and two Prague citizens (Jacob Fikar of Vrat and Wenceslas Hrubý of Jelení) were beheaded. Of the four who were executed, the most eminent personality was Wenceslas Pětipeský of Krásný Dvůr, an experienced soldier from the Hungarian battlefield who had served as commander of the Prague Towns army, and commanded military operations during clashes with royal divisions in the Lesser Town in early

---

9   Petr Vorel, "Majetko-právní důsledky panovnických sankcí roku 1547 pro pozemkový majetek rodu Tluksů Vrábských z Vrábí," Folia Historica Bohemica 29 (2014), 201–255.

10 František Bednář, ed. Jan Augusta v letech samoty 1548–1564, Sloupové pamětní, Kniha III. (Praha 1942); Jiří Just, "Internace Jana Augusty na Křivoklátu jako příklad konfesijního násilí a problém její interpretace," Folia Historica Bohemica 30 (2015), 33–46.

July 1547. In his case, the King really could prove that the accused had taken up arms against his own king.

However, these executions were mainly deterrent in nature. It's typical that the executed did not include any members of the lordly estate. Thus, the monarch symbolically concluded his "settling of accounts" with the Bohemian nobility, and turned his attention to the royal towns.

In the case of the "rural" royal towns, the King proceeded similarly as in the case of the Prague Towns. Firstly, a direct financial fine in the order of tens of thousands of three-scores groschen was imposed on the accused towns, which the citizens had to pay immediately and in cash themselves. The King forced the individual towns to fulfil this requirement by imprisoning all members of the town councils who had to compulsorily attend the hearing of the verdict. They stayed in prison until the assessed fine was paid. The King responded to frequent objections by other citizens that the municipal coffers did not have such sums in cash with a curt message that they could take out loans if they wanted, or collect the money among themselves. The King was very well informed of the individual towns' actual financial capabilities so, despite the high nominal values of the assessed fines, the citizens managed to procure these sums quickly in order to secure the release of their councillors from prison.

However, confiscations of property, by which the royal towns lost all landed property which they had laboriously acquired in the previous decades, brought greater economic consequences than the one-off emptying of municipal and private coffers. These were mostly the compact territories of dozens of villages, surrounding the relevant towns.[11] But only a small part of this confiscated property became a permanent part of the monarch's chamber assets. The vast majority of the municipal confiscated property, divided into small Estates or individual villages, was offered by the Royal Chamber for direct sale to interested nobles. A significant part of this confiscated property, mostly the assets of wealthy east Bohemian royal dowry towns, was exchanged by King Ferdinand shortly after its confiscation with John of Pernštejn for the dominions of Nový Bydžov and Chlumec nad Cidlinou. This transaction, disadvantageous for Pernštejn, signifi-

---

11 Eva Semotanová, Jiří Cajthaml and others, eds. Akademický atlas českých dějin (Praha 2014), 174–176.

cantly expanded the monarch's compact block of landed property in the Elbe region.[12]

Furthermore, the towns had to hand over all their privileges, and all the weapons from their municipal armouries, to the King. That is why one significant collection of early modern weapons from former municipal military store equipment is still preserved today, and that it the Plzeň armoury (currently in the collections of the Museum of West Bohemia in Plzeň) as Plzeň, which demonstrated loyalty to the King, was not affected by the confiscation of the weapons.

There was also a temporary abolition of municipal craft guilds.[13] The King burdened the municipal economies with so-called "perpetual barrel tax," which was a permanent tax on beer production, i.e. on a highly profitable business activity. The monarch secured control over the future administration of royal towns by appointing new royal officials who were superior to town councils.[14] The new function of royal governors was established for the Prague Towns, to which members of the higher estate were appointed. In other royal towns, the new officials were called royal magistrates. Loyal persons were appointed to these functions, who were to ensure municipal local government organs made decisions in accordance with the monarchal policy.[15]

28 Bohemian royal towns were punished for their participation in the Estates Revolt, i.e. the vast majority of the municipal estate in Bohemia. Thus, royal sanctions were even directed against towns that had tried to remain neutral and avoid supporting the revolt directly, such as for example Kutná Hora. The only exception were three Bohemian royal towns, which had explicitly stood on the royal side during the revolt, and which had provided the monarch with the military contingent required by the royal mandate: Plzeň, České Budějovice and Ústí nad Labem.

12 Eduard Maur, "Vznik a územní proměny majetkového komplexu českých panovníků ve středních Čechách v 16. a 17. století", Středočeský sborník historický 11 (1976), 53–63; Vorel, "Vývoj pozemkové držby pánů z Pernštejna", 11–76.

13 Josef Janáček, "Zrušení cechů roku 1547", Československý časopis historický 7 (1959), 231–242.

14 David Novotný, Královští rychtáři ve východočeských zemepanských městech v době předbělohorské (Olomouc, 2012), 139–144.

15 Vladimír Bystrický, "Osoba prvního královského rychtáře ve Stříbře po roce 1547", in Stavovský odboj roku 1547 - První krize habsburské monarchie, ed. Petr Vorel (Pardubice and Praha, 1999), 125–134.

The former extraordinary political significance of the Bohemian royal towns, which until the year 1547 had formed a separate and de facto independent Land Diet Curia, was completely equalized. According to the King's new decision, the punished provincial royal towns kept their vote at the Land Diet, but only within the monarch's will.[16] With this measure, King Ferdinand completely controlled the Land Diet Curia that had formerly been the most radically anti-royal. After all, if the punished majority of the royal towns at the Land Diet was not willing to support the royal demands, then their vote could simply be cancelled, and the right to make decisions in the Municipal Curia would be held only by the afore-mentioned trio of towns loyal to the King. In terms of formal ceremony, this change was expressed by an amendment to the seating arrangement at the Land Diet. The Prague Towns' representatives still sat at the helm, but these were now immediately followed by the trio of towns loyal to the King, which had priority over the others.[17]

Thus, the King did not have to agree to the complete abolition of the royal towns' participation at the Land Diet; quite the opposite. The royal towns, controlled by loyal town councillors and controlled by royal magistrates or governors, stopped playing an opposition role in Estates society in the mid-16th century. The political radicalization of the municipal estate only came about again after the generational change half a century later, when the political scene was divided differently than according to the estate principle. The royal towns never again achieved the importance they had in Bohemia before the year 1547. They also never rid themselves of their financial problems, or the drawn-out indebtedness of royal towns as legal persons.

The monarchal sanctions, aimed at the royal towns, definitively solved the dispute about the economic control of the country in favour of the nobility. The development of the large self-sufficient aristocratic Estates, which was rapid and unrestricted by municipal demands, became the decisive economic trend of the second half of the 16th century. After, all the royal towns

---

16 Jaroslav Pánek, "Města v politickém systému předbělohorského českého státu", in Česká města v 16.-18. století (Sborník příspěvků z konference v Pardubicích 14. a 15. listopadu 1990), ed. Jaroslav Pánek (Praha, 1991), 15–39.

17 Jiří Pešek, "Political Culture of the Burghers in Bohemia and Central Europe during the Pre-White Mountain Period." in Political Culture in Central Europe (10th – 20th Century), eds. Halina Manikowska and Jaroslav Pánek (Prague, 2005), 203–214.

were so economically weakened and rid of political influence as a result of the punishment imposed on them after the Estates Revolt of 1547 that they ceased to be serious competition for the large aristocratic Estates.

The tribunal's proceedings commenced on the 8th of July 1547 with the theatrical pronouncement of a verdict against the Prague Towns, and ended on the 22nd of August 1547 with the execution of four victims. A day later, on the 23rd of August 1547, when the official Bohemian Land Diet commenced, the participants no longer had to worry about also being accused and punished by the monarch. Thus, the August Land Diet took place in a conciliatory atmosphere. The persecuted nobles were not allowed to take part in it, and although the others outwardly expressed regret about the royal oppression and the fate of the former political allies, they were mostly glad that they had emerged from the complex conflict relatively unscathed and without direct danger to life and property.

Nobody spoke publicly about the revolt against the King any more. Participants in the Land Diet, which took place from the 23rd of August to the 3rd of September 1547, accepted a resolution according to which the Estates association, established between February and April the same year, was abolished.[18] Deeds with the text of the "Friendly Resolution", which specific nobles and towns used to register for the association by affixing their seals to it, were destroyed by a commission, just like the vast majority of written documents created by the steering committee's activity.

Thus, the Estates Revolt formally ended. Its winner was clearly the monarch, but he was not in the position of absolute victor. He only achieved a victory without a fight thanks to the compromise agreement with Bohemian aristocratic leaders, and this also required certain concessions by the royal side. However, King Ferdinand apparently made the most of the situation that emerged at the time. During the year 1547, King Ferdinand managed (primarily from the economic potential of Bohemian royal towns) to obtain operative financial resources (mostly cash) in excess of 1 million Rhenish guilders, i.e. roughly twice the sum spent from his own resources while waging the Schmalkaldic War. In addition to this he gained landed property, which he used in part to expand the complex of direct royal assets

---

18   SČ II, 472–479.

(and thereby also the amount of money flowing from their revenue into the monarchal coffers). He gradually sold off the rest of the confiscated property at its full market value. After the year 1547, the King also fully controlled the mining and distribution of Jáchymov silver, which until the mid-forties was de facto controlled by foreign investors and their domestic partners (all predominantly from the Lutheran environment). The sources of monarchal income after the year 1547 were also significantly expanded by newly-established export and import duties, collected at the country's borders, as well as a single significant food tax, which was paid by beer producers (both municipal and aristocratic). Its rate was derived from volume of production, regardless of the quality of the product.

The main change in the country's political system was brought about in the year 1547 by the submission of formerly autonomous royal towns to direct monarchal control. It was not just about creating a dependency at an Diet level (in this way, the King practically controlled the Land Diet's Municipal Curia); this change also had long-term economic consequences. Since the mid-16th century, Bohemian royal towns were forced to provide loans to the monarch according to his needs, or even directly pay some of the King's expenses on his orders. Thus, after the year 1547, Bohemian royal towns as legal persons lost their position as important centres of domestic finance, and suffered long-term indebtedness.

The punishment of the Estates opposition in the Roman-German Empire in the years 1546–1547 was declared by the Habsburgs as a matter of a criminal law nature, which had nothing in common with the confessional issue. King Ferdinand also maintained this basic idea during sanctions in the Bohemian lands; within the scope of decisions on punishments, the issue of the confessional affiliation of the affected does not appear as a material argument at all. In the previous years of his rule, King Ferdinand applied confessionally-defined oppression in the year 1528 against the Anabaptists, who had taken shelter in the Bohemian lands before persecution on German territory (most of them settled in Moravia after the year 1528), and in the year 1541 against the Jews, who had resided in small enclaves in the Bohemian lands since the Middle Ages (the prohibition on their residence in Bohemia was restricted after the year 1543). Both of these waves of confessional oppression enforced by the King only brought economic damage to the Kingdom of Bohemia. This could also be expected of oppression against the Unity of the Brethren, whose members comprised the base of the Estates Revolt's organizational staff among the aristocrats. This well-organized domestic church, which was very widespread in Bohemia, was regarded by King Ferdinand as highly dangerous for his monarchal plans. However, the King did not have to engage in any special negotiations on sanctions against the Unity of the Brethren, as the so-called St. Jacob's Mandate of 1508, which forbade the Unity of the Brethren's activity in Bohemia, was still a valid part of State law.[19]

Nevertheless, the King waited with the sanctions against the Unity of the Brethren until other court proceedings were finished. Only on the 5th of October 1547 did he remark on the validity of St. Jacob's Mandate of 1508, and began asking the Bohemian Estates to apply it consistently. At the same time, he logically argued that during his election promise in the year 1526 he undertook to comply with all State laws, which included St. Jacob's Mandate. He himself began to apply it in late 1547 in his chamber dominions and in confiscated Estates, which also included the main existing power centres of the Unity of the Brethren in Bohemia, i.e. Mladá Boleslav and Litomyšl.

The Litomyšl dominion, seized from Unity of the Brethren leader Bohuš Kostka of Postupice, represented the Unity of the Brethren's main centre in Bohemia at the time before the Estate Revolt, with its own printer, archive and power base, which is why the wave of religious emigration after the year 1547 is mainly associated with Litomyšl and its environs. Even the former main church representative of the Unity of the Brethren, bishop John Augusta, whom King Ferdinand was searching for, was hiding in the forests around Litomyšl. After being captured, Augusta was imprisoned by King Ferdinand and held for several years in a jail in Křivoklát Castle as one of the first explicitly political prisoners in early modern Bohemia. The King accused him of dealing directly with John Frederick of Saxony, and of the organizational preparation of the entire Bohemian revolt.[20]

---

19 J. T. Müller, Dějiny Jednoty bratrské, I., 224–236.
20 Ferdinand Hrejsa, Dějiny křesťanství v Československu V. Za krále Ferdinanda I. 1526–1564, Spisy Husovy československé evangelické fakulty bohoslovecké, řada A, Sv. IX. (Praha, 1948), 155–158; Just, "Internace Jana Augusty", 33–46.

In the rest of the territory, which belonged mainly to domestic Utraquist nobility, every noble could decide the extent to which they were willing to participate in religious oppression. If someone did not agree with the sanctions against the Unity of the Brethren, or did not want to lose their subjects, they had to at least ensure the abolition of Brethren bodies and officially claim that they did not have any members of the forbidden church in their dominions. Regular Unity of the Brethren members from the ranks of citizens and subjects could either join one of the legal confessions (a conversion to Utraquism was expected) or leave Bohemia.[21] The Brethren who were not willing to convert really did leave the Kingdom of Bohemia en masse during the year 1548. These were hundreds of Bohemian Brethren families, most of which set off from eastern Bohemia, through Silesia and Poland, into Prussia.[22]

However, even at the time of the temporary persecution of the Unity of the Brethren immediately after the year 1547, the main tenet of political culture remained the estate principle, in which the Royal Court shared power with the nobility regardless of religious affiliation. That is why the main supporters of monarchal power from the ranks of the contemporary Bohemian nobility also included influential magnates and politicians who pledged allegiance to the Reformation. After all, one of the main supports for King Ferdinand I. in Bohemia at the time of the Estates Revolt in the year 1547 was the Lutheran Henry of Plauen [† 13/05/1554], Supreme Chancellor of the Kingdom of Bohemia in the years 1542–1554. However, the long-term power concept, based on a restoration of the influence of the Catholic Church, was taken into consideration by King Ferdinand during the formation of a new circle of "court" nobility, formed by subsequent generations inside individual magnate families. In the end, this aspect played an important role during the power clash within the Bohemian Estates, during which the young William of Rosenberg, a Catholic nobleman who was entering politics at the time, defended his priority position in the Bohemian Estates against Henry of Plauen, one of the main figures in the existing "royal" side in Bohemia.[23]

---

21 Hrejsa, Dějiny křesťanství V., 139–142.
22 Henryk Gmiterek, Bracia czescy a kalwini w Rzeczypospolitej (Połowa XVI – połowa XVII wieku) - Studium porównawcze (Lublin, 1987).
23 Jaroslav Pánek, "Bohemia and the Empire: Acceptance and Rejection", in The Holy Roman Empire 1495–1806. A European Perspective, ed. R. J. W. Evans, and P. H. Wilson (Leiden 2012), 121–141.

The conflict, which seemingly originated as a personal dispute about a priority position in the seating arrangement at the Land Diet and the Land Court, developed into a drawn-out dispute that divided Bohemian society into two camps. Henry of Plauen, and his supporters among the domestic nobility, defended his priority position before the old Bohemian lordly families (including the Rosenbergs), as he was an Imperial prince and his formal superiority was (against the Bohemian Estates will) formally enshrined in the printed version of the State laws, compiled by deputy scribe of the Kingdom of Bohemia Ulrich Humpolec of Prostiboř and printed in the year 1550. William of Rosenberg (and most domestic lords and knights who formed the temporary "Rosenberg side" on the political scene) defended the "ancient" domestic customs, according to which Imperial or Silesian princes, seated in Bohemian and Moravia, could at most join the lordly estate; otherwise they could not be in any way prioritized before the domestic lords. In the end, the monarch used his authority to support the Rosenberg standpoint. Thus, key positions at the helm of the Estates were occupied soon after the mid-16th century by representatives of the upcoming generation of old lordly families, pledging allegiance to the Catholic faith (William of Rosenberg, Vratislav of Pernštejn, the lords of Hradec) whose authority was naturally respected even by Protestant adherents of other faiths on the basis of the estate principle.[24]

One measure to which the King rightly attributed extraordinary political significance became the temporary establishment of print censorship.[25] The only printing company that was to operate in Bohemia after the year 1547 became the Prague workshop of Bartholomew Netolický.[26] Even at the time of the revolt, Vice-Chancellor Žabka commissioned Bartholomew Netolický to reproduce Czech and German language versions of royal decrees, which could then be quickly disseminated (in the form of news leaflets or brochures). The printer Netolický reliably fulfilled the assigned tasks during this restless period. That is why, after the end of the revolt, the King

24 Jaroslav Pánek, "Zápas o vedení české stavovské obce v polovině 16. století (Knížata z Plavna a Vilém z Rožmberka)", Československý časopis historický 31 (1983), 855–884.

25 APK, sign. 1448 XLV-21 (1549); Petr Voit, "K dějinám cenzury v předbělohorské době (Některé problémy období 1547 - 1567)", Folia Historica Bohemica 11 (1987), 305–320.

26 Petr Mašek, Význam Bartoloměje Netolického pro český knihtisk 16. století, Příspěvky ke knihopisu 4 (Praha, 1987).

not only granted him a monopoly on printing in Bohemia, but also commissioned Netolický in the year 1547 to print an extensive biased work containing texts of written documents that were the compromise of the leaders of the Estates Revolt and clearly demonstrate their guilt in it.[27] The response to the governmental printed matter became an extensive manuscript of Sixt of Ottersdorf, who worked as Chancellor of the Estates committee at the time of the revolt. By transcribing contemporary written documents and adding his own extensive commentary, he wanted to preserve evidence about what, in his opinion, was the actual course of these events, and the great inequity that royal oppression was causing the urban estate.[28]

A monarchal reform with long-term effect, which was also a consequence of the collapse of the Estates Revolt, became the establishment of a new central judicial institution, a so-called appeals court, on the 20th of January 1548.[29] The King originally intended it to be a supreme appeals authority for courts of all categories; i.e. including the Land court. However, this plan constantly failed, and the appeals court functioned primarily as an institution superior to the municipal courts. This step was a significant shift in the centralization of the municipal judicature, which in the first half of the 16th century was still fragmented and organized according to medieval municipal legal circles.

In the neighbouring so-called lands of the Bohemian Crown, the Schmalkaldic War had different consequences than in Bohemia. It was only the situation in Upper Lusatia,[30] whose strongest power grouping was

---

27 Akta všech těch věcí, které sou se mezi nejjasnějším knížetem a pánem, panem Ferdinandem, římským, uherským, českým etc. králem etc. a některými osobami z stavu panského, rytířského a městského Království českého léta tohoto etc. XLVII zběhly, Praha 1547.

28 Zdeněk Beneš, "Akta aneb Knihy památné čili historie Sixta z Ottersdorfu (Studie o genezi jednoho historického textu)", Český časopis historický 90 (1992), 188 – 203.

29 Karolina Adamová, "Apelační soud v Českém království v letech 1548 – 1651", in Pocta akademiku Václavu Vaněčkovi k 70. narozeninám (Praha, 1975), 101 – 112.

30 Joachim Bahlcke, "Einen gar considerablen Platz in denen merkwürdigen Geschichten Teutschlandes und des Königreiches Böhmen" (Die Stellung der Oberlausitz im politischen Systém der Böhmischen Krone)", in Welt – Macht – Geist (Das Haus Habsburg und die Oberlausitz 1526 – 1635, eds. Joachim Bahlcke and Volker Dudeck (Görlitz and Zittau, 2002), 73 – 88; Lenka Bobková, "Zemská zřízení a zemské stavy v Horní a Dolní Lužici v 16. století." In Vladislavské zřízení zemské a počátky ústavního zřízení v českých zemích (1500–1619), eds. Karel Malý and Jaroslav Pánek (Praha, 2001), 165–179; Norbert Kersken, "Die Oberlausitz von der Gründung des Sechsstädtebundes bis zum Übergang an das Kurfürstentum Sachsen (1346–1635)", in Geschichte der Oberlausitz (Herrschaft, Gesellschaft und Kultur vom Mittelalter bis zum Ende des 20. Jahrhunderts), ed. Joachim Bahlcke (Leipzig, 2003), 99–142.

the so-called "Six Towns," i.e. six Upper Lusatian towns (Budyszyn, Zgor-zelec, Zittau, Kamenec, Löbau and Lubań) which practically controlled this small margraveship. Thus, the main punishment primarily befell the Upper Lusatian towns, according to the same model as the Bohemian royal towns: a large financial fine, loss of all property and rights, and subordination to the royal administration.[31]

The King did not have to take any mass action against the Lower Lusatian Estates. By then, the territory of Lower Lusatia was relatively small; furthermore, it was affected by old medieval liens on parts of this margraveship which were still formally parts of it but de facto lay outside the Lower Lusatian governor's administration. This applied primarily to the dominion of Chotěbuz, the geographic and economic centre of Lower Lusatia, held in the form of a long-term lien by the Brandenburg Hohenzollerns since the mid-15th century.[32] Thus, the remaining "Bohemian" part of Lower Lusatia geographically formed a kind of horseshoe, formed only of rural dominions which were mostly the secularized property of two large Lower Lusatian monasteries (Dobroluk and Mariazell). King Ferdinand used these monasteries' assets to pay his financial obligations from the Schmalkaldic War.

Just like the Bohemians, the Moravian political representation assumed serious reservations against Habsburg policy in their country. Nevertheless, a suggestive written invitation to Estates in other Crown lands, in which the Bohemian leaders requested the dispatch of a Land army to Prague or to Bečov, sent from Prague to Moravia on the 20th of March 1547, did not receive any official response. Of course, from the Moravians' perspective, there was no reason to assume any standpoint in relation to the situation in Bohemia, as the royal mandates of January 1547 did not relate to Moravia. The context used by King Ferdinand in Bohemia (i.e. the Dobroluk Monastery property and the defence of Bohemian fiefdoms in the Empire) could not be used in Moravia. The Moravian provincial governor, Wenceslas

31 Neumann, Theodor. Beiträge zur Geschichte des Schmalkaldischen Krieges, der Böhmischen Empörung von 1547, sovie des Pönfalles der Oberlausitzischen Sechsstädte in demselben Jahre (Görlitz, 1848); Lenka Bobková, "Pönfall neboli Šestiměstí v protihabsburském odboji roku 1547", in Stavovský odboj roku 1547 – První krize habsburské monarchie (Sborník příspěvků z vědecké konference konané v Pardubicích 29.- 30. 9. 1997), ed. Petr Vorel (Pardubice and Praha, 1999), 41–64.

32 Rudolf Lehmann, Geschichte der Niederlausitz (Berlin, 1963).

Chropyňský of Ludanice, accepted the Bohemian opposition Estates' request, but took no further official steps in his capacity, and did not inform the monarch of the Bohemian invitation. No legal instrument existed on the basis of which, for example, Moravian provincial officials could convene a Land army and march with it into Bohemia. De facto, no motive existed that was sufficiently strong to prompt them to do this.[33]

The Moravian Estates played an important role only after the suppression of the Bohemian Estates Revolt; mainly when the monarchal tribunal was formed from their ranks. However, the Moravian Estates were only ostensibly passive; just a few prominent personalities in Moravian political life belonged among royal advocates (Wenceslas of Ludanice, the brothers of Lipá). As soon as the King tried to restrict estate freedoms in Moravia at the start of the 1550s, (at the time of Habsburg superiority in the Empire), he encountered relatively effective resistance here. Also, the prohibition on the Unity of the Brethren did not apply in Moravia. Taking previous development also into account (when, in the 1520s, the Margraveship of Moravia provided refuge to the Anabaptists, expelled by the Habsburgs both from the Roman-German Empire and from the Kingdom of Bohemia), Moravia at the start of the 1550s became the most confessionally varied and free territory in all of contemporary Europe.

Despite calls for a joint resistance against royal decrees that violated Estates freedoms, the rebel committee failed to gain evident political support in Moravia or Silesia, even though some Silesian Lutheran princes openly sympathized with the anti-Habsburg opposition in the Empire.

Silesia represented a significant anomaly within Central Europe in the late Middle Ages and at the start of the early modern times. It was an integral part of the Lands of the Bohemian Crown supra-state structure, created during the 14th century by the Luxembourgs. However, in terms of constitutional law, it created quite a diverse mix of sub-territories belonging directly to the monarch (the King of Bohemia) or individual territorial princes (including some Imperial princes) who were the King of Bohemia's vassals. Part of the Silesian territory also had a different legal status (free

---

33   Josef Válka, "Morava a porážky českých stavovských povstání", In Stavovský odboj roku 1547 – První krize habsburské monarchie (Sborník příspěvků z vědecké konference konané v Pardubicích 29.- 30. 9. 1997), ed. Petr Vorel (Pardubice and Praha, 1999), 29–40.

estate dominions, liens etc.). This persevering territorial fragmentation (which was a remnant of the gradual medieval division of the Silesian territory among secondary branches of the Polish monarchal Piast family) resulted in the ruling families of all the surrounding lands showing an extraordinary interest in Silesia. After all, Silesia represented one of the few options in Central Europe for members of ruling families, who for some reason had not attained the monarchal sceptre in their own country, to acquire their own "land". Thus, Silesian territorial princedoms at the start of the 16th century were ruled not only by the descendants of the secondary branches of the Polish Piasts, the Bohemian Minsterbergs, the Saxon Wettins and the Prussian Hohenzollerns, but also Jagiellonian princes who, it was originally presumed, would not be able to rule directly in the Polish state.[34]

As a result of the afore-mentioned territorial fragmentation, individual Silesian territorial princes had their own political interests. The conditions for the emergence of some larger Estates opposition (such as in Bohemia) did not exist, just like there was no need to weaken the economic and political influence of royal towns in Silesia (like in Lusatia and in Bohemia). No such urban network of politically-significant towns existed here. The most important Silesian town, i.e. Vratislav (Breslau, now Polish Wrocław) was by itself a legal entity in the role of a territorial prince (it owned one of the princedoms in the form of a lien tenure) and entered politics as a separate entity, just like the influential Wrocław Bishopric.

The most significant Silesian political figure at the time of the Schmalkaldic War was prince Frederick of Lehnice. In the 1540s, he represented the main supporter of the Lutheran Reformation in Silesia, and an important political ally for the Brandenburg Hohenzollerns.[35] He played a large part in promoting the Lutheran faith in Silesia, across whose borders this religion had spread (just like from Brandenburg and Prussia) to the Polish territory.[36] However, by the time of the Schmalkaldic War, prince Freder-

---

34 Radek Fukala, Slezsko – Neznámá země Koruny české. Knížecí a stavovské Slezsko do roku 1740 (Hradec Králové 2007), 146–149, 174.

35 Christel Krämer, Beziehungen zwischen Albrecht von Brandenburg-Ansbach und Friedrich II. von Liegnitz (Ein Fürstenbriefwechsel 1514–1547 – Darstellungen und Quellen), Veröffentlichungen aus den Archiven Preussischer Kulturbesitz, Band 8 (Köln and Berlin, 1977).

36 R. Fukala, Slezsko, 150–151.

ick of Lehnice found himself in poor health, and he died in the year 1547. Nevertheless, before his death, he leaned towards King Ferdinand, and even supported his campaign in Saxony with a small military force. King Ferdinand also managed to gain the support of the most eminent Lutheran princes in Silesia by appointing Frederick's eldest son and heir (Frederick II. of Lehnice) as military commander of the Habsburg army in the war in Saxony.

Thus, in the critical moments of the war with the Elector of Saxony in early 1547, it was Silesia that served as King Ferdinand's main operative source for acquiring more money and soldiers. However, even this fact did not prevent King Ferdinand using his temporary power superiority to significantly heighten his influence in Silesia, and increase the financial income which this land was to generate for the Habsburgs; nevertheless, this process took place somewhat later here than in Bohemia and Lusatia.

The Habsburg victory in the Schmalkaldic War had a huge effect on King Ferdinand's relationship with some Silesian princedoms. Firstly, the long-standing disputes about the Princedom of Opole-Racibórz were simplified; after the extinction of the Opole branch of the Piasts (1532), it was held under lien by Brandenburg Duke George of Ansbach, who also ruled the Silesian Krnov (Jägerndorf) princedom. Even in the early forties, while George of Ansbach (†1543)[37] was still alive, complex property disputes relating to financial claims by Cieszyn princes, Lehnice princes and King Ferdinand I., were conducted about Opole-Racibórz. In this respect, the war in the Empire simplified the situation for the Habsburgs. After the Battle of Mühlberg in the year 1547, King Ferdinand took over the guardianship administration of Opole and Racibórz (which until then had belonged to Brandenburg Margrave Albert Alcibiades) and compensated the Brandenburg Hohenzollerns for their financial claims.[38]

Another issue was the princedom of Żagań, which had been held since the year 1541 by the young Duke Moritz of Saxony. After the Battle of

37 Radim Jež, "Jan z Pernštejna ve sporu o Opolsko-Ratibořsko ve třicátých a čtyřicátých letech 16. století", Východočeský sborník historický 14 (2007), 69–85; Petr Vorel, "Problemy rodzinne i finansowe Piastów Ciesińskich w połowie XVI wieku", in Historia u Piastów, Piastowie w Historii (Z okazji trzechsetlecia śmierci ostatniej z rodu, księżnej Karoliny), ed. Bogusław Czechowicz (Brzeg, 2008), 155–164.
38 Norbert Mika, Dějiny Ratibořska (Krakov, 2012), 53–65.

Mühlberg, Moritz of Saxony acquired a significant part of Saxon territory which had formerly been ruled by his second cousin, Elector John Frederick.[39] However, as part of the "redistribution" of the territory on the borders of the sphere of influence of the Habsburgs, Wettins and Hohenzollerns, the newly-appointed Elector Moritz of Saxony had to make confessions to Habsburg interests in Silesia, and in the year 1549 he transferred the Princedom of Żagań to King Ferdinand. As compensation, he received some Bohemian fiefdoms on Saxon territory.[40] Although the pecuniary value of this property was similar (the "Bohemian fiefdoms" allegedly even generated 500 Rhenish guilders per year more than the regular income from the Princedom of Żagań),[41] this "exchange" was disadvantageous for Moritz of Saxony. Instead of a territorially-unified Silesian princedom (where he was de facto an independent ruler), he acquired a network of small territories in Saxony.

These territorial changes in Silesia were a direct consequence of the Schmalkaldic War, as King Ferdinand managed to take another relatively large part of Silesia, including Opole-Racibórz and Żagań, from the sphere of influence of Imperial princes (the Hohenzollerns and the Wettins) and bring it under the direct rule of the King of Bohemia.[42] The symbolic culmination of the new situation in Silesia became the so-called Prague Treaties, concluded in the year 1549 between Ferdinand I. and the new King of Poland Sigismund Augustus, who assumed reign after the death of his father, Sigismund I. Jagiellon (†1548).

Sigismund Augustus, King of Poland, was much more obliging towards Habsburg interests in Silesia than his late father. One of the reasons for concluding the afore-mentioned treaties was the end of the economic blockade of Silesia by Poland. The economic blockade of the Silesian-Polish border had been repeatedly announced by Sigismund I., King of Poland, since the year 1511, both due to economic reasons (the introduction of poor-qual-

---

39 Hans Baumgartner, Moritz von Sachsen - der Gegenspieler Karls V. (Berlin and Wien, 1943), 426, the Map "Wettinische Lande 1547 u. 1554".

40 The list of all Bohemian fiefs inside the Empire see HNL, Book No. 60 (1547) and ÖNB Wien, sign. Cod. 7549 (1549).

41 Skřivánek, "K některým aspektům lenní politiky", 59–79

42 Werner Bein, Schlesien in der habsburgischen Politik. Ein Beitrag zur Entstehung des Dualismus im Alten Reich. Quellen und Darstellungen zur Schlesische Geschichte, Band 26 (Sigmaringen 1994), 63–65; Vorel, Velké dějiny, VII., 604–605.

ity Silesian coins into Polish monetary circulation) and later as a measure which was to prevent the spreading of the Lutheran Reformation from Silesia to Poland.[43] The long-term blockade of Silesia's commercial link to advantageous Polish markets also represented considerable economic damage for the Habsburgs, which is why this issue was one of the points constantly addressed by contemporary Habsburg-Jagiellonian diplomacy in the 1530s and 1540s.[44]

The results of the Schmalkaldic War significantly changed the negotiating positions in favour of the Habsburgs. After all, as part of the diplomatic pressure on the Polish side, one of the arguments the Habsburgs used was that unless there was unrestricted movement of goods across the Polish-Silesian border (blocked by Poland), Charles V. would make sure that a similar economic embargo was created on the Polish-Imperial border, i.e. on the eastern border of Brandenburg and Pomerania. Generally speaking, this would have been hard to implement in practice unless the Brandenburg Hohenzollerns or the Pomeranian dukes themselves were also interested in such a blockade, but in the late forties (after the Battle of Mühlberg), when the Habsburgs politically controlled the Land Diet, such a decision could have been formally accepted by the Empire as a whole.

However, the year 1549 represented an important milestone in the history of the Bohemian state, and not only because the conclusion of the new Bohemian-Polish alliance treaty. The same year saw two other significant legal acts that had a stabilizing function at the time of their origin: this was the issue of a new edition of the Land Code (the State Constitution of 1549)[45] and the election of the King's eldest son, Archduke Maximilian, as King of Bohemia. In this case, the new Bohemian monarch (who was to assume reign after the death of King Ferdinand) was not selected from a large number of applicants; instead, the Land Diet approved his candidature in the form of a parliamentary election.

---

43 Wiktor Zsymaniak, Organizacja dyplomacji Prus Książęcych na dworze Zygmunta Starego 1525–1548 (Bydgoscz, 1992).

44 Jacek Wijaczka, "Misja biskupa Juliusza von Pflug do Polski w 1541 r. (Przyczynek do dziejów polskiej polityki handlowej w XVI wieku)", in Życie gospodarcze Rzeczypospolitej w XVI-XVIII wieku – Materyały konferencji naukowej, Między zachodem a wschodem, t. IV, ed. Jacek Wijaczka (Toruń, 2007), 48–57.

45 Jaroslav Pánek, "Land Codes of the Bohemian Kingdom in Relation to Constitutional Changes in Central Europe on the Threshold of the Early Modern Age", Historica 9 (2002), 7–39.

The prospect of Archduke Maximilian's future reign as King of Bohemia was attractive for Bohemian society, as at that time the first-born Habsburg was already known for his strong favour for the Lutheran Reformation. At the time of the Schmalkaldic War, some were even of the opinion that the first-born Maximilian could replace his father on the royal throne in Bohemia if the opposition was victorious in the Empire. King Ferdinand was well aware of these possible variants of political development. Thus, he was obliging towards the Bohemian Estates request, most of which wanted Archduke Maximilian to become King of Bohemia. In the given case, it was not just about Maximilian's generally-known personal tendency towards the Reformation: the young Archduke was (unlike King Ferdinand) a monarch of "Bohemian blood" (his mother was a Bohemian princess).

King Ferdinand agreed to the election of his eldest son as King of Bohemia while he was still alive. However, he stipulated that not only was King Maximilian not to directly interfere in monarchal affairs in Bohemia (as long as King Ferdinand was alive) but that, without Ferdinand's explicit consent, he was not even authorized to enter Bohemian territory. With this measure, King Ferdinand wanted to prevent the potential creation of an opposition centre in predominantly Protestant Bohemia, which could theoretically be led by his own son, as elected King of Bohemia, if he created his own Monarchal Court in Prague. After all, the Habsburgs had other plans for Ferdinand's eldest son Maximilian at the time, relating to Spanish domains. Thus, King Ferdinand solved direct rule in Bohemia in a different way: after the year 1547, a governorship administration was established in the country, with the King's second-born son, Archduke Ferdinand, appointed to its helm.

In previous years, the monarchal centre's court environment only affected the Bohemian lands indirectly, as the King of Bohemia did not reside in the country permanently. Neither Ferdinand's pre-election promises nor the entire monarchal family's occasional longer stays (Ferdinand's oldest children were born in Prague) changed anything about this situation. Thus, a body of governors, nominated from the ranks of the domestic lords, regularly represented the physically absent monarch in his ruling duties. However, after his experiences from the years 1546–1547 King Ferdinand did not trust the Bohemian lords, and wanted to make sure that, in his proxy, the wealthiest and most important part of his multi-state coalition (the Kingdom of Bohemia) would be managed in the manner he himself decided. After all, he could not entrust the governorship administration of Bohemia to any of his Spanish or Austrian confidants. Thus, he appointed his second-born son, Archduke Ferdinand, as Governor of Bohemia.[46]

So, Prague got its permanent Monarchal Court during King Ferdinand's lifetime, even though, at first sight, the resulting situation might seem illogical. For fifteen whole years in the mid-16th century (1549–1564) the Kingdom of Bohemia had two kings, neither of whom resided in Bohemia permanently: the older of them did not deem it necessary, while the younger was not allowed to. Nevertheless, a fully functional Monarchal Court operated in Prague even without the personal presence of both titular Kings of Bohemia. On the one hand, this atypical situation reflected a certain custom that became a common norm for the Austrian and Spanish branches of the Habsburgs during the 16th century: the temporary governorship reign by individual members of the family in various countries, belonging to both of the ancestral lines in the Habsburg family. In this way, the ruling monarchs prepared successors to the throne for their future independent rule, while also ensuring loyalty.

In the first years of its existence, the Prague Governor's Court was completely dependent on King Ferdinand's will, and was directly financed from the central Viennese Court budget. It also lacked staff and, beside the titular governor himself, it comprised only a handful of officials whose task was to build adequate technical facilities and hire reliable personnel. It was only in 1549 that the Prague Court was established in its fully-fledged form, and even began to manage its own budget. The most eminent person in the contemporary Prague Court was the King's childhood friend, Spanish noble Ludwig of Tobar, who, as Hofmeister of the Prague Court, supervised the young Archduke and de facto managed the Court's operation.[47] Thus, dur-

---

46 Václav Bůžek, "Ferdinand II. Tyrolský a česká šlechta (K otázce integračních procesů v habsburské monarchii)", Český časopis historický 98 (2000), 261–291.

47 Petr Vorel, "Místodržitelský dvůr arciknížete Ferdinanda Habsburského v Praze roku 1551 ve světle účetní dokumentace", Folia historica Bohemica 21 (2005), 7–66.

ing the first years of his function as Governor of Prague, Archduke Ferdinand was under the direct influence of the King and the Spanish and Austrian advisers and courtiers whom he appointed. It was only after Ludwig of Tobar's death [†1553] that King Ferdinand relaxed his direct control over the Prague Court. In addition to providing technical support for King Ferdinand's plans in Bohemia, the Governor's Court specialized primarily in the social sphere, as a new court centre offering a source of entertainment, mainly to young nobles, in the form of frequent balls, hunting trips (mainly in the chamber dominions of Brandýs and Lysá nad Labem) and tournaments.[48] The most important Renaissance building from the time of the governorship rule, the Hvězda (Star) summer residence beside the game park of the same name, was also built for social purposes (1555).

For the upcoming generation of Bohemian nobles, an unusual and technically quite simple possibility of social advancement had opened when, after many decades, a Monarchal Court was built in Prague Castle once again. The monarch was "only" Archduke Ferdinand; nevertheless, even such a "small" Monarchal Court offered considerable social possibilities. Members of the upcoming generation of Bohemian nobility from the Habsburgs' side were linked to the Prague Governor's Court from a service or social perspective; for them it offered new possibilities of not just court entertainment, organized since the start of the 1550s in Prague and its environs, but also careers as officers in the Habsburg army. Just then an opportunity arose to demonstrate loyalty to the King, as the war with the Imperial opposition in the neighbouring Roman-German Empire re-ignited in the year 1552.

This phase of the religious-political conflict in the Empire did not provoke any organized Estates resistance in the Bohemian lands. It involved only mutually advantageous cooperation. After the confiscations of the year 1547, the King had sufficient resources at his disposal to compensate the Bohemian nobility for participating in the war in the Empire. Thus, he

---

48 Jaroslav Pánek, "Der Adel im Turnierbuch Erzherzog Ferdinands II. von Tirol (Ein Beitrag zur Geschichte des Hoflebens und der Hofkultur in der Zeit seiner Statthalterschaft in Böhmen)", Folia historica Bohemica 16 (1993), 77–96; Václav Bůžek, "Rytířské kratochvíle" na místodržitelském dvoře arciknížete Ferdinanda," In Ad vitam et honorem. Profesoru Jaroslavu Mezníkovi přátelé a žáci k pětasedmdesátým narozeninám, eds. Tomáš Borovský, Libor Jan and Martin Wihoda (Brno, 2003), 613–622; Václav Bůžek, Ferdinand Tyrolský mezi Prahou a Innsbruckem - Šlechta z českých zemí na cestě ke dvorům prvních Habsburků (České Budějovice, 2008).

did not have to use any non-standard legal steps such as the January mandate of 1547, even though the war in the neighbouring Empire (especially Margrave Albert Alcibiades' campaign around Nuremberg) had also seriously damaged the territory of Bohemian fiefdoms. However, King Ferdinand now only used this fact as justification for his military involvement in the Imperial battlefield as King of Bohemia, not as a pretext for forcing the Bohemian nobility to march into German territory.

In the afore-mentioned second phase of the Habsburgs' war with the Imperial opposition, the main commanders of the Bohemian military forces were Bohuslav Felix Hasištejnský of Lobkovice and Henry of Plauen. The Bohemian army which they led (and which King Ferdinand financed) was mainly deployed in military operations against Margrave Albert Alcibiades in the years 1552–1554. At that time, the war in the Empire was waged mainly in Franconia, a vast Imperial region adjacent to the Kingdom of Bohemia. The main centre of this region was the Imperial town of Nuremberg. A peculiarity of this region was a dense network of so-called Bohemian fiefdoms, i.e. both large and small dominions which their sub-holders had accepted as fiefdoms from the King of Bohemia. The town of Nuremberg also found itself in such a position. Thus, King Ferdinand justified the massive participation by the Bohemian army in this war by the need to protect Bohemian interests in Franconia, as the Margrave's troops had caused significant damage in areas that were de jure art of the lands of the Bohemian Crown. The Bohemian army played a particularly important role in the final phase of this war, during the siege of Plassenburg Castle.[49]

These wars in the Empire no longer directly influenced internal political life in Bohemia; nevertheless, the political failure of Emperor Charles V., and the forced compromise talks conducted by King Ferdinand with the Imperial Estates in the years 1552–1555 (until the adoption of the Religious Peace of Augsburg in the year 1555), to a large extent influenced King Ferdinand's negotiations with the Bohemian Estates. King Ferdinand badly needed to maintain peace in the Bohemian lands. That is why he gradually backed away from some originally enforced sanctions, and also relaxed economic life in towns which, after the year 1547, served as important sources

---

49 Weihgand-Karg, Die Plassenburg, 389–419.

of permanent income for the monarchal coffers. Thus, from the mid-16th century, the Bohemian royal towns (as legal persons) found themselves in a state of permanent indebtedness, as all the significant pecuniary assets that the towns had acquired were being drained by royal officials in the form of forced loans. After the year 1547, the Bohemian towns also ceased to fulfil the role of important entities in the world of loan operations, as the public free loan market in Bohemia was paralysed by the Monarchal Chamber's activities, and became a part of the economic "grey zone" (both Jewish and Christian loans, limited by a maximum interest rate).

He was more careful when introducing new economic measures against the nobility, and temporarily even backed away from the effort to consistently apply the monarchal rights to the old liens on Church and Chamber property. It was only his successors to the Bohemian throne that returned to this, several decades later.

The monarchal oppression in Bohemia and Upper Lusatia temporarily averted the monarchal treasury's frightening indebtedness, and warded off the Habsburg government's imminent financial collapse in Central Europe. Through the one-off confiscation of all municipal assets, and the emptying of the private coffers of dozens of imprisoned town council members, the royal treasury obtained a sum of around a million tolars; i.e., significantly more than the King acquired, after lengthy negotiations and complicated technical measures, by collecting taxes for the previous twenty years. Also, significant income was generated for the Monarchal Chamber in the following years by the sale of confiscated aristocratic and urban dominions, as well as from new payment obligations with which the royal towns were burdened.

Thanks to these new sources, after the year 1547 King Ferdinand did not need to enforce any significant change in the main part of the tax system, on whose form the Land Diet still decided. Thus, the development of the main pillar of the Bohemian tax system (land tax) in the second half of the 16th century stagnated in its late medieval form, which created exceptionally favourable conditions for the large aristocratic Estates (after the year 1547, the towns stopped trying to prevent their development), most of whose economic activities escaped the tax system.[50]

---

50 Antonín Gindely, Geschichte der böhmischen Finanzen von 1526 bis 1618 (Wien, 1868); Vorel, "Frühkapitalismus und Steuerwesen", 167–182.

The basis for calculating the determinative part of the aristocratic land tax remained either the number of the servile homesteads in the dominion, or the formal value of the entire dominion. The system of calculating the tax base only marginally took into account the main sources of income, which after the year 1547 increasingly became aristocratic business activities (large-capacity lordly courts, producing corn for export; large breweries which were guaranteed a compulsory purchase of their product in the dominion; sheep pens, wine distilleries, mills etc.). The profitability of these enterprises was guaranteed by the high demand for their products on the international market; thanks to the connection to the Elbe water trade, the Kingdom of Bohemia (just like other lands in this area) also began to experience a "war boom", sparked off by the growth in the prices of agricultural commodities and other products from the last third of the 16th century (both sides in the contemporary military conflict in the Netherlands were able to pay for the goods well, and on time).

However, the specific amounts which were to be collected in the form of taxes, and their purpose, were still subject to approval by the Land Diet, and tax collection was performed by the Estates themselves. Thus, it was an inefficient and lengthy system with tax arrears that were difficult to enforce. To secure higher income, the King began to use a system of forced loans, mainly in relation to the royal towns, which he could not do so easily before the year 1547. The most important example of such a procedure is a transaction from the year 1560. A sum of 400 thousand tolars, which King Ferdinand needed to pay for the expansion of his Chamber dominions in the Elbe region to include Pardubice,[51] had to be collected and provided to the monarch as a non-returnable sum by the Bohemian royal towns.

Of course, this transaction was also related to the Estates Revolt of the year 1547 in a different context. The deep loan crisis of the lords of Pernštejn, formerly the wealthiest Bohemian lordly family, was interpreted in the urban environment and within the Unity of the Brethren as just punishment for betrayal at the time of the revolt. It was a little unfair, as during the political collapse of the Estates Revolt, John of Pernštejn belonged among the Bohemian politicians who had managed to defend the main estate priv-

---

51 Vorel, Páni z Pernštejna, 208–210.

ileges against the King. Only the nobility's privileges, of course – not the towns'. Before the year 1547, John of Pernštejn (†1548), former leading political figure of the Bohemian Neo-Utraquists, was clearly the wealthiest and most influential noble in the entire Bohemian multi-state coalition. His sons entered the services of the Habsburgs, and the two older ones even converted to the Catholic faith shortly after their father's death.

The trio of John of Pernštejn's[52] sons symbolically mirrored the complicated development of Bohemian aristocratic society after the year 1547:

The eldest son Jaroslav (born in 1528) had resided in King Ferdinand's Court since his youth, and believed he belonged among the King's confidants. However, he gradually spent all his property in the monarchal services, and the last remainder of the inheritance that his father had left him (which was the residential dominion of Pardubice) was placed under creditor administration in the year 1558. But the sum of Jaroslav of Pernštejn's debts was higher than the value of his landed property with which the debts were guaranteed. They comprised creditors' pecuniary assets amounting to many hundreds of thousands of tolars, whose repayment was debatable. Therefore, this case significantly undermined the credibility of the entire loan operation system, guaranteed in Bohemia with the great magnates' landed property, and it's comparable to the collapse of one of the large banks in modern times. Without the monarch's direct intervention, such an extensive loan problem was unsolvable. King Ferdinand guaranteed the repayment of Pernštejn's debts (and confiscated the landed property in question), but in reality these debts had to be paid by the Bohemian royal towns. The personal bankruptcy and subsequent death of Jaroslav of Pernštejn under unexplained circumstances in the year 1560 served in the Bohemian non-Catholic opposition environment at the end of Emperor Ferdinand's life (†1564) as a deterrent for young wealthy nobles, showing them the kind of "fame" they could earn in the Habsburg Court (after their anticipated conversion to the Catholic faith).

This interpretation was supported by the fate of Jaroslav's youngest brother, Adalbert of Pernštejn (born in 1532). He was the only one of John of Pernštejn's three sons to retain his "father's faith", and he married a girl from the domes-

---

52 Vorel, Petr, ed. Česká a moravská aristokracie v polovině 16. století - Edice register listů bratří z Pernštejna z let 1550–1551 (Pardubice, 1997); Vorel, Páni z Pernštejna, 184–236.

tic lordly Kostka family of Postupice (actually the daughter of one of the Unity of the Brethren leaders, persecuted in the year 1547). In his youth, he was sent to serve at Archduke Ferdinand's Prague Court, but for reasons unknown he himself renounced this career. He separated himself materially from his older brothers in time, while there was still some inheritance left after his father, settled in Moravia and entered high Estates politics. Unlike both of his older brothers, he not only maintained his property but actually expanded it.

The fates of these two afore-mentioned brothers of Pernštejn developed in completely different directions, and symbolically represented the two camps (royal and estate) which stood against each other in Bohemia at the edge of the armed conflict in the year 1547. Therefore, it's peculiar that of John of Pernštejn's three sons, it was the middle son Vratislav (born in 1530) that achieve the greatest success in the subsequent decades. Since his youth, he had grown up as one of the members of Archduke Maximilian II's "Bohemian company". He even stood at Archduke Maximilian's side at the time of the Schmalkaldic War as a formally high-ranking member of Maximilian's "commanding staff" (in fact he was more like a hostage, whose forced stay in the Habsburg services significantly restricted the opposition activity of his father, John of Pernštejn, in Bohemia). Together with Archduke Maximilian he made many journeys around Europe, including the first part of Maximilian's governorship assignment in Spain, where the young Archduke was sent by his uncle (and future father-in-law) Charles V., so that he could better understand his role in the system of power and renounce his "suspicious" confessional opinions. Later, thanks to his travel and organizational experience, the young Vratislav of Pernštejn led a large expedition by the Bohemian nobility to northern Italy in the years 1551–1552; they were travelling to meet "their" King Maximilian II., who was returning to Central Europe after a stay in Spain with his new Spanish wife. [53]

In the environment of the Habsburg Courts, Vratislav of Pernštejn understood what was expected of him. After conversion to the Catholic faith, and after marriage to a girl from a prominent Spanish family (Maria Manrique de Lara y Mendoza),[54] his undertaking to serve the "Habsburg

53 Jaroslav Pánek, Výprava české šlechty do Itálie v letech 1551 - 1552 (2nd ed. České Budějovice, 2004).

54 Charlotte Fritzová, and Jindřich Růžička, "Španělský sňatek Vratislava z Pernštejna (1555)," Sborník prací východočeských archívů 3 (1975), 63–77.

affair" was also confirmed by the afore-mentioned admission to the Order of the Golden Fleece in the year 1555. However, to a large extent, Vratislav of Pernštejn had to finance this expensive lifestyle himself with the money he had inherited from his father. In the year 1560, at the time of the peak of his elder brother Jaroslav's financial bankruptcy, Vratislav of Pernštejn also had no money, and nothing to pay his debts with. He was saved from bankruptcy by the premature death of his afore-mentioned younger brother Aldabert (†1561), who had left no male descendants behind him ("only" a daughter) so, on the basis of old family treaties,[55] his landed property was inherited by his only living brother Vratislav. Thus, it was only the inheritance from his "heretic" brother (who had attempted to form his own Protestant church, similar to the Unity of the Brethren, in Moravia at the end of the fifties) that enabled the above-mentioned Order of the Golden Fleece member to integrate back into high European aristocracy, linked to the Habsburg-Spanish environment.

However, in his case, an important role was also played by the strong friendly personal bonds with Archduke Maximilian, with whom he had spent many years of his youth travelling. When, after the death of Ferdinand I. in the year 1564, Maximilian II. assumed reign in the Roman-German Empire and in the Kingdom of Bohemia, these "old credits" paid Vratislav of Pernštejn rich dividends. Vratislav of Pernštejn was not only appointed to high Land offices (he became Supreme Chancellor of the Kingdom of Bohemia) and actively entered high European diplomacy in Maximilian's services, but his own family became one of the main mediators for the penetration of contemporary Spanish culture (and naturally also political and confessional interests) among the Bohemian aristocracy. An apt symbol of the Pernštejn family's position in Renaissance Bohemia became the statue of the so-called Infant Jesus of Prague ("Bambino di Praga") which Vratislav's wife, Maria Manrique de Lara, brought from her native Spain to Bohemia with her in the year 1555.[56]

We can use the example of John of Pernštejn's family to clearly document one significant developmental trend: despite all the failures which accompanied Emperor Charles V. in the mid-1550s in his Imperial policy

---

55 Vorel, "Vývoj pozemkové držby", 9–76.
56 Vorel, Páni z Pernštejna, 237–258.

(until the adoption of the Religious Peace of Augsburg in the year 1555, with which Charles V. refused to agree with until his death), these multiple reversals on the Imperial political scene in the years 1546–1555 brought about one significant change in the highly conservative Bohemian environment. In the setting of several of the most prominent Bohemian aristocratic families, strong personal and family links were created to the Spanish environment,[57] which during the first half of the 16th century was still practically unthinkable, not only for confessional reasons, but also for purely technical ones.[58] At that time these were only individual cases but, even back then, the foundation was laid for the gradual penetration of Spanish political and confessional interests into the country, which at the end of the 16th century contemporary "political scientists" logically evaluated as an imaginary "needle on the scales" in the battle for rule in the broader Central European area. Whoever rules in Bohemia can also rule in the Empire; not the other way round. This basic monarchal rule, based on the Luxembourgs' geopolitical interests in the 14th century, was recognized in the late 16th and early 17th century by both branches of the Habsburgs.[59] However, at that stage it still wasn't clear whether this position was an advantage for the Kingdom of Bohemia, or a potential danger.

---

57 Pavel Marek, "Klientelní strategie španělských králů na pražském císařském dvoře konce 16. a počátku 17. století", Český časopis historický 105 (2007), 40–88; Petr Vorel, "Císařská volba a korunovace ve Frankfurtu nad Mohanem roku 1612 a česká účast na těchto událostech." Theatrum historiae 10 (2012), 59–166.

58 Petr Vorel, "Aristokratické svatby v Čechách a na Moravě v 16. století jako prostředek společenské komunikace a stavovské diplomacie," Opera historica 8 (2000), 191–206.

59 Josef Polišenský, Tragic triangle. The Netherlands, Spain and Bohemia 1617–1621 (Prague 1991), 65–84; Vorel, "Císařská volba a korunovace", 135–136.

CONCLUSION

The political crisis in the Roman-German Empire in the years 1546–1547 was used by King Ferdinand I. to implement a purposeful one-off change in the economic situation and political system in the Kingdom of Bohemia. The essence of King Ferdinand's success in his battle against the Estates opposition in Bohemia became the fact that, using diplomatic pressure, he managed to break down aristocratic-urban unity, formed at a time when an acute endangerment of estate rights was sensed, at the start of the year 1547. When the Habsburg armies defeated the Schmalkaldic League in the Empire in April 1547, King Ferdinand did not have sufficient resources to overpower the entire Bohemian Estates with military force. He himself did not want to risk this step, even with the knowledge of possible military assistance from Emperor Charles V.. Thus, in the decisive moment, he offered Bohemian aristocratic leaders (with the exception of the Unity of the Brethren) an alliance against the royal towns, and participation in the future government in the country.

For the nobility this was a tempting offer, as it could solve (and indeed did solve) its long-standing dispute with the royal towns in the economic field. For the monarch, the concession to the aristocratic opposition in the given situation was an advantageous step, as it enabled him to realize one of his long-term political priorities. This was the weakening of the urban estate's importance in the system of power in the country, and the subordination of royal towns to direct monarchal control. That is why anti-municipal sanctions were imposed not only in Bohemia (where the royal towns really did represent the driving force of the revolt) but also in Upper Lusatia, even though the actual participation in the Estates Revolt by the Upper

Lusatian municipal association (the so-called Six Towns) was negligible. However, from the Habsburg Court's perspective, the Upper Lusatian royal towns' clear predominance in the country's political life represented an anomaly which the King wanted to remove, just like in Bohemia.

In this way, the King managed to even out the urban estate's effect as an influential entity in the political life of the entire Lands of the Bohemian Crown multi-state coalition. After all, the dense network of royal towns that was such a great obstacle to the large aristocratic Estates' economic activity in Bohemia was never formed in Moravia or Silesia. That's why the Moravian and Silesian nobility was not forced to look for an ally in the Monarchal Court for its battle against the urban estate. The urban estate's position in these countries was completely different to that in the Kingdom of Bohemia, as these regions were dominated by just a few exceptionally important centres, clearly outstripping other towns in terms of both economy and power. Towns such as Brno and Olomouc (in Moravia) and Wrocław (in Silesia) were able to promote their own interests at Diets and in political life in general, and the sense of belonging to the urban estate did not have as much significance for them as for the dense network of smaller royal towns in Bohemia and Upper Lusatia.

By imposing sanctions on the urban estate in Bohemia, King Ferdinand actually achieved some fundamental changes. The system of power in the country acquired a bipolar form, but it was monarchal-aristocratic rather than aristocratic-urban as was the case during the Jagiellonian period (when monarchal power was significantly weakened). This approach corresponded to the long-term Habsburg monarchal concept, in which the urban estate did not have its own place as a political power. The royal towns in the countries that the Habsburgs directly ruled themselves were, in terms of Habsburg government policy, essentially regarded as a part of monarchal property that was not entitled to its own independent political activity. That is why the brothers Charles V. and Ferdinand I. tried to forcefully suppress the royal towns' formerly-attained autonomy as soon as they seized power, whether in Spain, the Netherlands or in the Austrian hereditary lands, and in its own way also in the Roman-German Empire.[60] The economic and political sanctions from

---

60 Ludolf Pelizaeus, Dynamik der Macht - Städtischer Widerstand und Konfliktbewältigung im Reich Karls V.. Geschichte in der Epoche Karls V., Bd. 9 (Münster, 2007), 143–146; Petr Vorel, "Sankce

the time of the Schmalkaldic War (1546–1547) also significantly affected free Imperial towns which were members of the Schmalkaldic League and which had refused to accept the Habsburg "peace conditions". An extreme case became Konstanz, which paid for its unwillingness to subordinate to Charles V.'s will with the loss of its free Imperial towns estate membership.[61]

In a broader European context, the sanctions against the Bohemian and Upper Lusatian royal towns in the year 1547 were the Habsburgs' last significant success in their effort to subordinate the wealthy and politically influential royal towns to their control. Historically, they represented the last opportunity to utilize the disputes among the individual Estates on a diplomatic level. After the mid-16th century, confessional aspects began to outweigh the estate principle in European politics; i.e. the issue of religious-political affiliation, strengthened by the principle of confessionalization contained within the Religious Peace of Augsburg (1555).[62] This was also one of the reasons why, despite intensive efforts, the Habsburgs did not manage to forcefully control the wealthy towns in the north of the Netherlands in the second half of the 16th century.

However, in Bohemia itself, the restriction of the royal towns' political influence in the year 1547 created a relatively stable balance of power for several decades. Ferdinand of Habsburg's long-term goal in Bohemia certainly wasn't the permanent sharing of monarchal power with the nobility but, as an intermediate step, the agreement with the aristocratic leaders represented a great success for the King. As a pragmatic politician, King Ferdinand knew in the summer of 1547 that, given the current state of affairs, it would be very risky to try to seize power completely, as this approach would quite logically activate the aristocratic-urban alliance. He used the domestic nobility to liquidate the one segment of the Estates opposition that he considered to be the most dangerous (the royal towns).

---

vůči českým královským městům roku 1547 v kontextu habsburské politiky první poloviny 16. století ("Gentský ortel" v politické propagandě stavovského odboje)," Theatrum historiae 16 (2015).

61 Wolfgang Dobras, "Karl V., Ferdinand I. und die Reichsstadt Konstanz" in H. Rabe, ed., Karl V. – Politik und politisches System - Berichte und Studien aus der Arbeit an der politischen Korrespondenz des Kaisers (Konstanz, 1996), 191–221.

62 Robert Friedeburg, "Cuius regio, eius religion: The Ambivalent Meanings of State Building in Protestant Germany 1555–1655", in Diversity and Dissent (National Religious Difference in Cental Europe 1500–1800), ed. Howard Louthan, Gary B. Cohen and Franz A. J. Szabo (New York and Oford, 2011), 73–91.

I believe that the main reason for the long duration of the afore-mentioned power stability during the second half of the 16th century is the fact that the Royal Court did not have any significant ally in the Bohemian lands at the time, with whose help he could greatly weaken the aristocratic opposition's political influence. As a result of the gradual confessionalization of political life in Europe, this missing element in the system of power, which could overturn the stable power structures based on the estate principle, became the Church. This process also occurred in the Bohemian lands, albeit much later than in other parts of Europe.

After the year 1547, King Ferdinand did not have any functional influential Church structure system at his disposal in the Bohemian lands that could become an ally for him in the battle for power with the noble Estates. It did not have to be a priori only the Catholic Church; even radical Lutheran and Calvinist movements were successfully used for the same purpose by monarchs in other countries who were trying to build a strong central government. However, the confessional situation in Bohemia at the time of the Estates' power superiority developed in a way that suited the Estates – i.e. in the form of non-political supra-confessional Christianity. Thus, in the 16th century, we encounter a high level of religious tolerance in practically all countries in which the Estates municipalities preserved a significant share in government. In Central Europe, beside the Bohemian lands (especially the Kingdom of Bohemia and the Margraveship of Moravia) this also includes Poland, the Habsburg part of Hungary, and Transylvania.

The principle of non-political supra-confessional Christianity also enabled Bohemian and Moravian society to absorb other European reformatory movements, that the Catholic-Lutheran Religious Peace of Augsburg (1555) had not even considered. Although individual confessions' orthodox followers and theologists in the Bohemian lands bore grudges against each other and attacked each other in sharp polemics like everywhere else in Europe, religious affiliation did not become the main part of the power struggle in the ruling class of society in the Bohemian lands.

King Ferdinand also respected this situation, as it suited him in the given power constellation. If there had been a confessionally-initiated clash with the Estates at that time, he would have found himself at a disadvantage. The Catholic Church in Bohemia did not have a solid organizational base (Upper Consistory administrators from the ranks of the Prague Canons could only have a negligible power influence); it also had insignificant tangible resources, and was recognized by only a small part of the Estates (the nobility and the towns), who could not be expected to be willing to risk a conflict with members of their own estate because of faith. The restoration of the Catholic Church's influence in the Bohemian lands, and its strong connection with the Monarchal Court policy, was understandably part of King Ferdinand's long-term concept, but no fundamental change was possible in this respect immediately after the Estates Revolt. The first significant successes in building a new Catholic Church structure in Bohemia were achieved by King Ferdinand only at the very end of his reign; to a certain extent this was also thanks to the very active work of the Jesuit order, introduced to Bohemia in the year 1555 and specializing primarily in the field of education.[63]

The symbolic "reconciliation" between Ferdinand of Habsburg and the Bohemian Estates only came about in the year 1558, during his pompous arrival in Prague, which was organized by Archduke Ferdinand, Governor of Bohemia, after Ferdinand's coronation by the Emperor of Rome.[64] Even after the generational change, when young members of Bohemian aristocratic families were established in all the three Habsburgs' courts (i.e. with Emperor Ferdinand at the court in Vienna, at the "travelling" court of King Maximilian II., and at the Prague court of Archduke Ferdinand, Governor of Bohemia), Emperor Ferdinand did not trust the Bohemian Estates, and was constantly aware of the Bohemian environment's latent opposition potential.

Thus, Emperor Ferdinand I. avoided the Kingdom of Bohemia until his death, and only entered Bohemian territory when it was absolutely necessary. This fact was perceived positively by the Bohemian ruling elite (who by then saw the future in King Maximilian, who was to finally be a monarch of "Bohemian blood" after his mother), but it was also welcomed by the Governor of Bohemia, Archduke Ferdinand. Unlike his father, he was very popular in Bohemia. In the safety and comfort of the Prague Court, and within the "Bohemian company", he could enjoy personal and family happiness in his morganatic marriage to Philippine Welser.

---

63 Vorel, Velké dějiny, VII., 264–268.
64 Jiří Pešek, "Slavnost jako téma dějepisného zkoumání," Documenta Pragensia 12 (1995), 7–27.

However, as an experienced politician, Emperor Ferdinand I. looked further into the future, and tried mainly to arrange the most advantageous ruling positions possible for his eldest son, Maximilian II.. He was (thanks to his unusual confessional orientation) acceptable to the Imperial opposition as a future emperor, and in Bohemia his accession to the throne was also anticipated with great hope. The link between the future monarchal position of Maximilian II. and the Bohemian lands was accentuated by Emperor Ferdinand himself in the way he divided the hereditary Habsburg lands among his sons. The importance of the Bohemian lands in the newly-conceived future multi-state coalition increased significantly, as Maximilian II. was to inherit only the Danube part (Upper and Lower Austria, immediately neighbouring the Bohemian lands); the remaining two thirds of the Austrian lands fell upon his younger brothers (Archduke Ferdinand received the Tyrolean part with the seat in Innsbruck, and Archduke Charles received the southern part with the seat in Graz). The afore-mentioned two Danube countries, and the rest of the Kingdom of Hungary that was not yet ruled by the Turks, formed a part of Maximilian II.'s future multi-state coalition that was smaller and significantly economically weaker than the Bohemian lands, and was also constantly threatened by the Ottoman Empire. Thus, quite logically, the centre of the entire multi-state coalition, which was to be directly ruled by the future Emperor, shifted to Prague. Also, it was clear to Ferdinand I. that the main economic resources, which his successor Maximilian II. would have at his disposal, would be available primarily in the Bohemian lands.

Understandably, the future division of the Austrian lands, and the successorship to the Bohemian and Imperial thrones, was generally known even before Ferdinand's death (†1564). That is why even very important political decisions, which King Ferdinand had managed to formally enforce for the Bohemian lands in the final years of his reign (for example the reconfirmation of the validity of the Basel Compacts by Pope Pius IV. in the year 1564), were not implemented in practice, unless they were in the interests of the Bohemian Estates, and the ageing King Ferdinand himself did not even have the power resources to enforce them.

However, the Bohemian Estates obliged him with one of his wishes. Emperor Ferdinand I. wished to be buried in the St. Vitus Cathedral in

Prague Castle, beside his wife Anna Jagiellon, whose premature death during the birth of their youngest daughter in February 1547, at the time of the Estates Revolt, was perceived by everyone in Bohemia as a bad omen from a "higher power". But, at the time, nobody dared to say whom this bad omen was intended for.

Several decades later (in 1584), the second Czech edition of "Karion's World Chronicles", a European best-selling book from Renaissance times, translated into many contemporary languages, was published in Prague. The publisher of this Czech version (and also author of actual chapters from the then "contemporary history" of the 16th century), Prague municipal politician and historian, Daniel Adam of Veleslavín, already knew what followed after Queen Anna's death in the year 1547. Even he did not yet dare publicly criticize King Ferdinand's actions against the Bohemian royal towns; nevertheless, his text attests to the fact that, almost forty years later, the general awareness of these events was still alive in the Bohemian environment. The author only had to insinuate that he was thinking of the changes that took place in Bohemia after the Queen Anna's death, and everyone knew what he meant (it just wasn't appropriate to write it anywhere): "...*after her beatified death, bad things occurred in the Bohemian land; many people remember these events and almost everyone is still suffering as a result...*". However, the overall tone of the author's historical work is predominantly positive as, in his opinion, the Kingdom of Bohemia received a reward for suffered injustices, and became (according to the contemporary view of the history of the human race) the main centre of the "fourth monarchy", i.e. the permanent seat of the Imperial Court during the Rudolphian period (1583).[65]

---

65   Petr Vorel, Dějiny evropského světa 1453–1576: Historický obraz počátku raného novověku v pojetí Daniela Adama z Veleslavína který českému čtenáři předložil v druhém českém vydání Kroniky světa Jana Kariona z roku 1584 (Praha, 2008), 42–43.

LIST OF ABBREVIATIONS

APK = Archív Pražského hradu, Fond Archiv pražské metropolitní kapituly (The Archive of the Prague Castle, Fund Archive of the Metropolitan Chapter by st. Vitus)

BL London = British Library London

ČDKM = Národní archív Praha, Fond České oddělení dvorské momory (National Archive in Prague, Fund Court Chamber's Bohemian division)

fol. = folio

HNL = Národní archív Praha, Hejtmanství německých lén (National Archive in Prague, Fund)

KomS = Národní archív Praha, Fond Komorní soud (National Archive in Prague, Fund Chamber Court)

NK Praha = Národní knihovna (National Library Prague)

No. = Number

ÖNB Wien = Österreichische Nationalbibliothek Wien (Austrian National Library Viena)

Rg = Národní archív Praha, Fond Inventáře a kopiáře – Registra (National Archive in Prague, Fund Inventory Books)

RTA 1545 = Aulinger, Rosemarie, ed. *Der Reichstag zu Worms 1545*. Deutsche Reichtagsakten unter Kaiser Karl V. (Deutsche Reichstagsakten – jüngere Reihe, 16. Band), Teilband I-II. München, 2003.

RTA 1546 = Aulinger, Rosemarie, ed. *Der Reichstag zu Regensburg 1546*. Deutsche Reichtagsakten unter Kaiser Karl V. (Deutsche Reichstagsakten – jüngere Reihe, 17. Band). München, 2005.

RTA 1547/48 = Machoczek, Ursula, ed. *Der Reichstag zu Augsburg 1547/48*. Deutsche Reichtagsakten unter Kaiser Karl V. (Deutsche Reichstagsakten – jüngere Reihe, 18. Band), Teilband I-III. München, 2006.

RTA 1550/51 = Eltz, Erwein, ed. *Der Reichstag zu Augsburg 1550/51*. Deutsche Reichtagsakten unter Kaiser Karl V. (Deutsche Reichstagsakten – jüngere Reihe, 19. Band), Teilband I-II. München, 2005.

RTA 1555 = Aulinger, Rosemarie, Eltz Erwein H. and Machoczek Ursula, eds. *Der Reichstag zu Augsburg 1555*. Deutsche Reichtagsakten unter Kaiser Karl V. (Deutsche Reichstagsakten – jüngere Reihe, 20. Band), Teilband I-IV. München, 2009.

SČ II = *Sněmy české od léta 1526 až po naši dobu* [*Die böhmischen Landtagsverhandlungen und Landtagsbeschlüsse vom Jahre 1526 an bis auf die Neuzeit*], II. (1546–1557), Praha 1880

sign. = Signature

SM = Národní archív Praha, Fond Stará manipulace (National Archive in Prague, Fund Old Treatment)

BIBLIOGRAPHY

Primary sources

Unpublished sources

Archív Pražského hradu (The Archive of the Prague Castle)
Fond Archiv pražské metropolitní kapituly (Fund Archive of the Metropolitan Chapter by st. Vitus)

Národní archív Praha (National Archive in Prague):
Fond Inventáře a kopiáře – Registra [Rg] (Fund Inventory Books)
Fond Komorní soud [KomS] (Fund Chamber Court)
Fond Stará Manipulace [SM] (Fund Old Treatment)
Fond České oddělení dvorské komory [ČDKM] (Fund Court Chamber's Bohemian division)
Fond Hejtmanství německých lén [HNL] (Fund German fiefdoms authority)

Národní knihovna Praha (National Library in Prague)
Sbírka rukopisů a starých tisků (Collection of Manuscripts and Ancient Books)

Knihovna Národního musea Praha (Library of National Museum in Prague)
Sbírka rukopisů a starých tisků (Collection of Manuscripts and Ancient Books)

Österreichische Nationalbibliothek Wien
Collection of Manuscripts and Ancient Books

Printed sources

Abdruck der verwarungs schrift, der Chur und Fürsten, auch Grafen, Herrn, Stette und Stende der Augspurgischen Confession Eynungs verwandten, irer yetzigen hochgenottrangten und verursachten Kriegßrüstung halben, an Keyserliche Mayestet außgangen, und beschehen. b.m., 1546. [Used copy: ÖNB Wien, sign. Alt-302.124–B.]

Abschied der Röm. Keys. Maiest. Und gemeyner Stend, uff dem Reichßtag zu Augspurg uffgericht, Anno Domini M . D. XLVIII. Meyntz: Juon Schörfer, 1548. [Used copy: ÖNB Wien, sign. 30. D. 36.]

Akta všech těch věcí, které sou se mezi nejjasnějším knížetem a pánem, panem Ferdinandem, římským, uherským, českým etc. králem etc., a některými osobami z stavu panského, rytířského a městského království českého léta tohoto etc. XLVII zběhly, Praha 1547.

Artickel wie und auff was zeit und mas Die steur von unsern des Churfürsten zu Sachsen etc. und Burggraven zu Magdeburg. Gemeiner Landschafft und underthanen, von wegen dieser vorstehenden unuesehenlichen und notdrenglichen Defension, So zu erretung Gottes ewigen und allein seligmachenden Worts, Auch des Vaterlandes notwendig gesucht, gefallen, und einbracht werden sollen 1547. Geiten, 1547 [Used copy: ÖNB Wien, sign. 33 M 59.]

Aulinger, Rosemarie, ed. *Der Reichstag zu Regensburg 1546.* Deutsche Reichtagsakten unter Kaiser Karl V. (Deutsche Reichstagsakten – jüngere Reihe, 17. Band). München, 2005.

Aulinger, Rosemarie, ed. *Der Reichstag zu Worms 1545.* Deutsche Reichtagsakten unter Kaiser Karl V. (Deutsche Reichstagsakten – jüngere Reihe, 16. Band), Teilband I-II. München, 2003.

Aulinger, Rosemarie, Eltz Erwein H. and Machoczek Ursula, eds. *Der Reichstag zu Augsburg 1555.* Deutsche Reichtagsakten unter Kaiser Karl V. (Deutsche Reichstagsakten – jüngere Reihe, 20. Band), Teilband I-IV. München, 2009.

Avrea Bvlla Caroli Qvarti Romanorvm Imperatoris & Regis Bohemiae. Moguntiæ: Ivo Schoeffer, 1548. [Used copy: ÖNB Wien, sign. 30. D. 36 – Adl. 6.]

Bednář, František, ed. *Jan Augusta v letech samoty 1548–1564.* Sloupové pamětní, Kniha III. Praha, 1942.

Bollleau de Buillon, Gil, ed. *Commentaire dv seigneur Don Loys d'Auila, contenant la guerre d'Allemaigne, faicte par l'Empereur Charles V. es annes 1547 & 1548.* Paris, 1551. [Used copy: BL London, sign.1194 b. 3.]

Brandenburg, Erich, ed. *Politische Korrespondenz des Herzogs und Kurfürsten Moritz von Sachsen.* Band 1–2. Leipzig, 1900 and 1903.

Bugenhagius, Johannes. *Adhortatio Brevis et plena Pietatis ad vicinos in Bohemia, Silesia & Lusatia, eximia virtute preditos, ne adiuuent hostes Euangelij, qui armis & vi Ecclesias & Schoplas pias in his Regionibus vastare crudelisime decreuerunt, Scripta 1546. Mense Octobri.* Vitenbertg: Georg Rhau, 1546 [Used copy: ÖNB Wien, sign. 20. Da. 1498.]

Der Römischen Kay. Mai. Und gemeyner Stend deß heyligen Reichs angenommene und bewilligte Cammergerichts Ordnung. Meyntz: Juon Schöffer, 1548. [Used copy: ÖNB Wien, sign. 30. D. 36 – Adl. 5.]

Der Römischen Kayserlichen Maiestat Ordnung und Reformation güter Pollicey. Meyntz: Juon Schöffer, 1548. [Used copy: ÖNB Wien, sign. 30. D. 36 – Adl. 7.]

Der Römischen Keiserlichen Maiestat Erklärung, wie es der Religion halben, imm Heyligen Reich, biß zu Auftrag deß gemeynen Concilij gehalten werden soll, uff dem Reichßtag zu Augspurg, den XV. Maii, im M. D. XLVIII. Jar publiciert und eröffnet, unnd von gemeynen Stenden angenommen. Meyntz: Juon Schörfer, 1548. [Used copy: ÖNB Wien, sign. 30. D. 36 – Adl. 2.]

Druffel, August von, ed. *Beiträge zur Reichsgeschichte 1546–1555.* Briefe und Akten zur Geschichte des sechzehenten Jahrhunderts mit besonderer Rücksicht auf bayerns Fürstenhaus, Band I-IV. München 1873–1896.

–––. *Des Viglius van Zwichem Tagebuch des Schmalkaldischen Donaukrieges.* München, 1877.

Eltz, Erwein, ed. *Der Reichstag zu Augsburg 1550/51.* Deutsche Reichtagsakten unter Kaiser Karl V. (Deutsche Reichstagsakten – jüngere Reihe, 19. Band), Teilband I-II. München, 2005.

Fellner, Thomas, and Heinrich Kretschmayr, eds. *Die österreichische Zentralverwalltung* I/2, Aktenstücke 1491–1681. Wien, 1907.

Formula reformationis per Cæsaream Maiestatem Statibus Ecclesiasticis in Comitijs Augustanis ad deliberandum proposita, & ab eisdem, ut paci publicæ consulerent, & per eam Ecclesiarum, ac Cleri sui utilitati commodius prouiderent, probata & recepta. Moguntiæ: Ivo Schoeffer, 1548. [Used copy: ÖNB Wien, sign. 30. D. 36 – Adl. 3.]

Herrmann, Johannes, and Wartenberg Günther, eds. *Politische Korrespondenz des Herzogs und Kurfürsten Moritz von Sachsen.* Dritter Band (1. Januar 1547 – 25. Mai 1548), Berlin, 1978. Vierter Band (26. Mai 1548 – 8. Januar 1551). Berlin, 1992.

Herrmann, Johannes, Wartenberg Günther and Winter Christian, eds. *Politische Korrespondenz des Herzogs und Kurfürsten Moritz von Sachsen.* Fünfter Band (9. Januar 1551 – 1. Mai 1552). Berlin, 1998. Sechster Band (2. Mai 1552 – 11. Juli 1553). Berlin, 2006.

Historia: wie Gonzaga einen Amptman zu Como gestrafft, welcher eines gefangenen Eheweyb beschlaffen, Anno 1547 (Wie der Hertzog von Mantua Gonzaga Stadhalter zu Meyland, gestrafft hat, eine mißhandlung eines Amtmans zu Como, Welchs gleychen Historia auch in S. Augustini Bücher, und in Hertzog Carle von Burgung Geschichten geschrieben ist). Without place of publication, 1548 [Used copy: BL London, sign. 9165. c. 35.]

Hortleder, Friedrich, ed. *Der Römischen Keyser- Vnd Königlichen Maiestete, Auch des Heiligen Römischen Reichs Geistlicher vnnd Weltlicher Stände, Churfürsten, Fürsten, Graffen, Reichs- vnd andeder Stätte, zusampt der heiligen Schrifft, geistlicher und weltlicher Rechte Gelehrten, Handlungen und Außschreiben, Rathschäge, Bedencken, Send- und andere Brieffe, Bericht, Supplicationsschriften, Befehl, Entschuldigungen, Protestationes, Recusationes, Außführungen, Verantwortungen, Ableinungen, Absagungen, Achtserklärungen, Hülfsbrieffe, Verträge, Historische Beschreibungen und andere viel herrliche Schriften und Kunden, mehr: Von Rechtmässigkeit, Anfang, Fort- und endlichen Ausgang deß Teutschen Kriegs, Keyser Karls deß Fünfften, wider die Schmalkaldische Bundsoberste, Chur- und Fürsten, Sachsen und Hessen, und. I. Chur- und Fürstl. G. G. Mitwerwandte, Vom Jahr 1546. biß auf das Jahr 1558.* Frankfurt am Main, 1618. [Used copy: ÖNB Wien, sign. 80. Bb. 25.]

Janáček, Josef, ed. *Sixt z Ottersdorfu - O pokoření stavu městského léta 1547.* Praha, 1950.

Knaake, Jachim K. F., ed. *Beiträge zur Geschichte Kaiser Karl's V. (Briefe Joachim Imhof's an seine Vettern zu Nürnberg aus den Feldzügen 1543, 1544 und 1547).* Stendal, 1864.

Kolár, Jaroslav, ed. *Zrcadlo rozděleného království (Z politických satir předbělohorského století v Čechách).* Praha, 1963.

Krämer, Christel, ed. *Beziehungen zwischen Albrecht von Brandenburg-Ansbach und Friedrich II. von Liegnitz (Ein Fürstenbriefwechsel 1514–1547 - Darstellung und Quellen),* Veröffentlichungen aus den Archiven preussischer Kulturbesitz, Band 8. Köln und Berlin, 1977.

Küch, Friedrich, and Heinemeyer Walter, eds., *Politisches Archiv des Landgrafen Philipp des Großmütigen von Hessen*, Bd. 1–4. Leipzig and Marburg, 1904–1959.

Lacroix, Robert V., and Gross Lothar, eds. *Urkunden und Aktenstücke des Reichsarchivs Wien zur reichsrechtlichen Stellung des Burgundischen Kreises*. Band I. (1454–1548). Wien, 1944.

Lanz, Karl, ed. *Korrespondenz Kaiser Karls V.*, Bd. 1–3. Leipzig, 1844–1846.

———. *Staatspapiere zur Geschichte des Kaisers Karl V.* Stuttgart, 1845.

Lehmann, Rudolf, ed. *Urkundenbuch des Klosters Dobrilugk und seiner Besitzungen*. Dresden and Leipzig, 1941.

Lenz, Max, ed. *Briefwechsel Landgraf Philipp's des Großmüthigen von Hessen mit Bucer*, T. 3. Leipzig, 1891.

z Licka, Brikcí. *Titulové stavu duchovního i světského*. Praha, 1534. [Used copy: NK Praha, sign. 54 B 113.]

Lutz, Heinrich, and Kohler Alfred, eds. *Das Reichtagsprotokoll des kaiserlichen Kommissars Felix Hornung vom Augsburger Reichstag 1555*. Wien, 1971.

Machoczek, Ursula, ed. *Der Reichstag zu Augsburg 1547/48*. Deutsche Reichtagsakten unter kaiser Karl V. (Deutsche Reichstagsakten – jüngere Reihe, 18. Band). Teilband I-III. München, 2006.

Mamerano Lucemburgo, Nicolao. *Catalogvs Omnivm Generalivm, Tribvnorvm, Dvcum, Primorumq[ue], totius Exercitus Caroli V. Imp. Aug. & Ferdinandi Regis Roman. Super Rebelleis & inobedienteis Germ. quosdam Principes ac Ciuitates conscripti, Anno 1546*. Colonia, 1550. [Used copy: BL London, sign. 1194. b. 2./1.]

———. *D. Caroli V. Roma. Imp. Avg. inter ex inferiore Germania ab Anno 1545. Vsq[ue] ad Comitia apud Augustam Rheticam indicta Anni 1547. quo vsq[ue] singulis diebus & ad quor militaria rexerit*. Augsburg 1548 [Used copy: BL London, sign. 1194. b. 2./3.]

Mandát Krále jeho Milosti do všech Krajův Království Českého z Litoměřic v Pátek po slavném Hodu Seslání Ducha Svaté[h]o vyšlý Léta MDXLVII. Litoměřice, 1547. [Used copy: ÖNB, sign. 169025–B-Alt.]

Oesterreich, Gerhard, and Holzer E., eds. "Übersicht über die Reichsstände I.: Die Reichsstände nach der Matrikel von 1521 mit vergleichenden Angaben nach der Matrikel von 1755." In *Gebhart Bruno - Handbuch der deutschen Geschichte*, Bd. 2, edited by Herbert Grundmann, 769–784. Stuttgart, 1970.

Osiander, Lucas. *Widerlegung Der Bekandtnus Caspar Schweckfelds, welche Anno 1547. gedruckt worden*. Tübingen, 1591. [Used copy: BL London, sign. 3906. h. 22.]

Pešák, Václav, ed., *Berní rejstříky z roku 1544 a 1620*. Praha, 1953.

Römischer Kaiserlischer Maiestat Achterclärung gegen der Alten Statt Magdenburg M. D. XLVII. Augsburg, 1547. [Used copy: ÖNB Wien, sign. 75. D. 107.]

Römischer Kayserlicher Maiestat und deß heyligen Reychs Landfriden auff dem Reychstag zu Augspurg declariert, erneüweret. Auffgericht, unnd beschlossen, Anno Domini M. D. XLVIII. Meyntz: Juon Schöffer, 1548. [Used copy: ÖNB Wien, sign. 30. D. 36 – Adl. 4.]

Roth, Friedrich, ed. "Paul Hektor Mairs 2. Chronik von 1547–1565." In *Die Chroniken der deutschen Städte vom 14. bis ins 16. Jahrhundert, Band 33: Die Chroniken des schwäbischen Städte – Augsburg (8. Band), 245–471. 2nd ed. Göttingen, 1966.

Sacræ Cæsareæ Maiestatis Daclaratio, quomodo in negocio Religionis per Imperium usq[ue] ad definitionem Concilij generalis uiuendum sit, in Comitijs Augustanis XV. May, Anno M. D. XLVIII. Proposita & pblicata & ab omnibus Imperij ordinibus recepta. Moguntiae: Ivo Schoeffer, 1548. [Used copy: ÖNB Wien, sign. 30. D. 36 – Adl. 1.]

Sibemwurger, Dionysius. *Practica Teutsch Auff das 1547 Jare.* Salzburg, 1546. [Used copy: BL London, sign. 1608/643.]

Sněmy české od léta 1526 až po naši dobu, sv. II (1546–1547). Praha, 1880.

Šůd ze Semanína, Mikuláš. ---. *Formy a notule listův všelijakých a Titulář stavův duchovního a světského,* Praha 1556 [Used copy: NK Praha, sign. 54 D 120]

Šůd ze Semanína, Mikuláš. ---. *Novina a příhoda,* Praha 1550 [Used copy: NK Praha, sign. 54 G 2845]

Šůd ze Semanína, Mikuláš. *Formulář listův všelijakých.* Praha, 1547. [Used copy: NK Praha, sign. 54 E 123.]

The commentaries of Don Lewes de Auela, and Suniga, great Master of Aranter, which treateth of the great wars in Germany made by Charles the fifth, maximo Emperoure of Rome, king of Spain, against John Frederike Duke of Saxon, and Philip the Lantgraue of Hesson, London, 1555. [Used copy: reproduction of the original in the Henry E. Huntington Library and Art Gallery]

Teige, Josef, ed. *Sixt z Ottersdorfu - Knihy památné o nepokojných letech 1546–1547.* I-II. Praha, 1919.

Urtheil So Keiserliche Maiestadt, über den gewesen Churfürsten von Sachsen decernirt, und gesprochen hatt, M.D. XLVII. [Used copy: ÖNB Wien, sign. 75. D. 107.]

Verthrag und Fruntliche aufgerichte Ordnung, Aus gewissen Kraysenn, der Stennde, dises Konigreychs Behem, Prag, Erichtag nach Sannd Valentin M. D. xxxxvii. (Praha), 1547. [Used copy: ÖNB Wien, sign. 20. T. 206.]

Vertrag zwischen Kaiserlicher Maie. und dem gewesenen Churfürsten von Sachsen, M.D. XLVII. [Used copy: ÖNB Wien, sign. 75. D. 107.]

Verzeigungs der gefangenen, so mitt Hertzog Johans Friderichen von Sachsen dem Eltern, und gewesenen Churfürsten, in seiner niderlag gefangen worden sein, M.D. XLVII. [Used copy: ÖNB Wien, sign. 75. D. 107.]

Verzeichuß der Artickel, so die Römisch Kayser: Mayestat, Hertzog Johan[n] Friderich von Sachsen, auch Landtgraff Philipsen von Hessen fürgehalten, vnd sie beide bemelte Fürsten die selbe Artickel geschworn, Sampt dem Fueßfal vnd begnaduge bemeltes Landtgrauen von Hessen, Geschehen zu Hall inn Sachsen am xviiii. tag Junÿ. Anno Salutis M. D. XLVII. 1547. [Used copy: ÖNB Wien, sign. 37. E. 135.]

Von Marggraf Albrecht von Brandenburg Whrhafftige Zeitung, Der sich unbedacht seiner Ehren und Pflicht, Under Erdichtem Schein, mutwilliglich und freuenlich. Wider den Churfürsten zu Sachsen und Burggraffen zu Magdeburg, zuuerdrückung Warer Christlichen Religion, als eyn Feind, eingelassen, durch Gottes gnedige schickung, sampe dem Lantgrauen von Leuchtenburg, mit allem irem Kriegsvolck, zu Roß und fuß, um bund bei Rochlitz erlegt, und gefangen worden seind. 1547. [Used copy: ÖNB Wien, Sign. 308.825. B. Alt – Adl. 5.]

Vorel, Petr, ed. Česká a moravská aristokracie v polovině 16. století (Edice register listů bratří z Pernštejna z let 1550–1551). Pardubice, 1997.

Vybíral, Zdeněk, ed. *Paměti Pavla Korky z Korkyně (Zápisky křesťanského rytíře z počátku novověku)*, Prameny k českým dějinám 16. – 18. století – Documemta res gestat Bohemicas saeculorum XV. – XVIII. Illustrantia, Řada B, sv. IV.. České Budějovice, 2014.

Warhafftige Zeyttun, von eroberung Placentz vn[nd] Parma, Und wie Petrus Farnesius, des yetzigen Bapts Son, dis vergangen 1547. Jar vmbkom[m]en ist (Etliche Namhafftige Geschicht, so sich in Italia zugetragen, dis vorgangen Jar, M. D. xLvij.). 1548. [Used copy: BL London, sign. 9165. c. 35.]

Wie Hertzog Erich von Braunschweig, in die flucht geschlagen, durch Grauen von Mansfeld, Grauen von Altenburg, und Thomshirn, und widerumb durch den Christoff Bußberger, mit seinem gerügten volck, das feld behaltem, wie folget, M.D. XLVII. 1547. [Used copy: ÖNB Wien, sign. 75. D. 107.]

Wrede, Adolf, ed. "Reichsmatrikel von 1521." In *Deutsche Reichstagsakten unter Kaiser Karl V.*, 2. Bd. Göttingen, 1962.

Zeumer, Karl, ed. *Quellensammlung zur Geschichte der deutschen Reichsverfassung in Mittelalter und Neuzeit, II. Teil – Von Maximilian I. bis 1806.* 2nd ed. Tübingen, 1913.

Secondary sources

Adamová, Karolina. "Apelační soud v Českém království v letech 1548 – 1651." In *Pocta akademiku Václavu Vaněčkovi k 70. narozeninám*, 101 – 112. Praha, 1975.

Albert, Franz. "Die Türkensteuer der Jahre 1542/43." *Glatzer Haimatblätter* 16 (1930).

Álvarez, Manuel Fernández. *Carlos V, el César el Hombre*. 18th ed. Madrid, 2006.

Avila y Zuniga de, Luis. *Geschichte des Schmalkandischen Krieges - Mit Zusätzen und Erläuterungen*. Berlin, 1853.

Angermaier, Heinz. *Die Reichsreform 1410–1555 (Die Staatsprobleatik n Deutschland zwischen Mittelalter und Gegenwart)*. München, 1984.

Aulinger, Rosemarie. "Die Verhandlungen der Kurfürsten Albrecht von Mainz und Ludwig von der Pfalz mit Karl V. 1532 in Mainz ("Missing-link" zwischen dem Reichstag 1530 und dem Nürnberger Anstand 1532)." In *Im Schatten der Confessio Augustana*, 185–210. Münster, 1997.

Badea, Andrea, "Es trieb ihn längst zum Krieg in der Unruhe seines Geistes." Markgraf Albrecht von Brandenburg-Kulmbach und der Fürstenaufstand." In *Kaiser und Kurfürst – Aspekte des Fürstenaufstandes 1552*. Geschichte in der Epoche Karls V., Band 11, edited by Martina Fuchs and Robert Rebitsch, 99–118. Münster, 2010.

Bahlcke Joachim, "Einen gar considerablen Platz in denen merkwürdigen Geschichten Teutschlandes und des Königreiches Böhmen" (Die Stellung der Oberlausitz im politischen Systém der Böhmischen Krone)". In *Welt – Macht – Geist (Das Haus Habsburg und die Oberlausitz 1526 – 1635)*, edited by Joachim Bahlcke and Volker Dudeck, 73–88. Görlitz and Zittau, 2002.

–––. "Schlesien im politischen System der böhmischen Krone". *Zeitschrift für Ostmittel-europaforschung* 44 (1995): 27–55.

Bahlcke, Joachim, Bömelburg, Hans-Jürgen and Kersken, Norbert, eds. *Ständefreiheit und Staatsgestaltung in Ostmitteleuropa (Übernationale Gemeinsamkeiten in der politischen Kultur vom 16.-18. Jahrhundert)*. Leipzig, 1996.

Bartsch, Heinrich. *Geschichte Schlesiens (Land unterm schwarzen Adler mit dem Silbermond – Seine Geschichte, sein Werden, Erblühen und Vergehen)*. Würzburg, 1985.

Baumgartner, Hans. *Moritz von Sachsen - der Gegenspieler Karls V.* Berlin and Wien, 1943.

Begert, Alexander. *Böhmen, die böhmische Kur und das Reich vom Hochmittelalter bis zum Ende des Alten Reiches (Studien zur Kurwürde und zur staatsrechtlichen Stellung Böhmens)*. Historische Studien Nr. 475. Husum, 2003.

Bein, Werner. *Schlesien in der habsburgischen Politik. Ein Beitrag zur Entstehung des Dualismus im Alten Reich.* Quellen und Darstellungen zur Schlesische Geschichte, Band 26. Sigmaringen 1994.

Beneš, Zdeněk. "Akta aneb Knihy památné čili historie Sixta z Ottersdorfu (Studie o genezi jednoho historického textu)." *Český časopis historický* 90 (1992): 188–203.

–––. *Historický text a historická skutečnost (Studie o principech českého humanistického dějepisectví)*. Praha, 1993.

Bennassar, Bartolomé and Vincent, Bernard. *Spanien 16. und 17. Jahrhndert*. Stuttgart, 1999.

Bizer, Ernst. "Reformationsgeschichte 1532 bis 1555". In *Reformationsgeschichte Deutschlands bis 1555, Die Kirche in ihrer Geschichte (Ein Handbuch)*, Band 3, Lieferung K, edited by Franz Lau and Ernst Bizer, 67–170. Göttingen, 1964.

Blaschke, Karlheinz. "Der Oberlausitzer Sechstädtebund als bürgerlicher Träger früher Staatlichkeit." In *650 Jahre Oberlausitzer Sechsstädtebund 1346–1996*, Mitteilungen des Zittauer Geschichts- und Museumsvereins Bd. 35, 17–27. Bad Muskau, 1997.

–––. "Lausitzen." In *Die Territorien des Reichs im Zeitalter der Reformation und Konfessionalisierung (Land und Konfesion 1500 - 1650)*, Bd. 6, edited by Anton Schindling and Walter Ziegler, 93–113. Münster, 1997.

Blicke, Peter. *Die Reformation im Reich.* 3rd ed. Stuttgart, 2000.

Blockmans, Wim. "Der Kampf und die Vorherrschaft in Europa." In *Kaiser Karl V. (1500–1558) – Macht und Ohnmacht Europas (Eine Ausstellung des Kunsthistorischen Museums Wien)*, edited by Wilfried Seipel, 17–26. Wien, 2000.

Blume, Gundmar. *Goslar und der Schmalkaldische Bund 1527/31–1547.* Goslar, 1969.

Bobková, Lenka. "Poměr korunních zemí k českému království ve světle ustanovení Karla IV.". *Právně-historické studie* 34 (1997): 17–36.

–––. "Pönfall neboli Šestiměstí v protihabsburském odboji roku 1547." In *Stavovský odboj roku 1547 – První krize habsburské monarchie (Sborník příspěvků z vědecké konference konané v Pardubicích 29.- 30. 9. 1997)*, edited by Petr Vorel, 41–64. Pardubice and Praha, 1999.

–––. "Vedlejší země České koruny v politice Lucemburků a jejich následovníků (1310–1526)." In *Korunní země v dějinách českého státu I. – Integrační a partikulární rysy českého státu v pozdním středověku (Sborník příspěvků přednesených na kolokviu pořádaném dne 4. června 2002 na FF UK)*, edited by Lenka Bobková, 9–31. Praha, 2003.

– – –. *"Zemská zřízení a zemské stavy v Horní a Dolní Lužici v 16. století."* In Vladislavské zřízení zemské a počátky ústavního zřízení v českých zemích (1500–1619), edited by Karel Malý and Jaroslav Pánek, 165–179. Praha, 2001.

Bobková, Lenka, and Hanousková Jana. "Die böhmischen Lehen in Mitteldeutschland und die Erneuerung der Böhmischen Krone durch Georg von Podiebrad im Lichte der Vorträge von Eger." In *Eger 1459 – Fürstentreffen zwischen Sachsen, Böhmen und ihrer Nachbarn: Dynastische Politik, fürstliche Repräsentation und kulturelle Verflechtung / Cheb 1459 – Setkání panovníků Saska, Čech a jejich sousedů: Dynastická politika, panovnická reprezentace a kulturní vazby*. Saxonia. Schriften des Vereins für sächsische Landesgeschichte e. V., Bd. 13, edited by André Thieme and Uwe Tresp, 241–262. Wettin-Löbejün, 2011.

Bonora, Elena. *Aspettando l' imperatore – Principi italiani tra il papa e Carlo V*. Torino, 2014.

Bonwetsch, Gerhard. *Geschichte des Passauischen Vertrags von 1552*. Göttingen, 1907.

Bornkamm, Heinrich. *Das Jahrhundert der Reformation – Gestalten und Kräfte*. 2nd ed. Göttingen, 1966.

Boubín, Jaroslav. *Česká "národní" monarchie*. Opera Instituti Historici Pragae, Monographia A-5. Praha, 1992.

Brady, Thomas A. Jr. *German Histories in the Age of Reformations, 1400–1650*. Cambridge, 2009.

– – –. "Phases and Strategies of the Schmalkaldic League: A Perspektive after 450 Years." *Archiv für Reformationsgeschichte* 74 (1983): 162–181.

– – –. *Protestant Politics: Jacob Sturm (1489–1553) and the German Reformation*. New Yersey, 1995.

Brandi, Karl. *Beiträge zur Reichsgeschichte 1546–1551*. München, 1896.

– – –. *Kaiser Karl V. – Werden und Schicksal einer Persönlichkeit und eines Weltreiches*. München, 1937.

– – –. *Kaiser Karl V. – Werden und Schicksal einer Persönlichkeit und eines Weltreiches. Zweiter Band – Quellen und Erörterungen*. München, 1941.

Braudel, Fernand. *Civilisation and Capitalism, 15th-18th Centuries*, Bd. 2, London, 1982.

Braun, Bettina. *Die Eidgenossen, das Reich und das politische System Karls V*. Schriften zur Verfassungsgeschichte, Band 53. Berlin, 1997.

Brauneder, Wilhelm, and Höbelt, Lothar, eds. *Sacrum Imperium – Das Reich und Österreich 996–1806*. Wien, München and Berlin, 1996.

Brecht, Martin. "Martin Luther und Karl V." In *Aspectos históricos y culturales bajo Carlos V – Aspekte der Geschichte und Kultur unter Karl V.*, Studia Hispanica 9, edited by Christoph Strosetzki, 78–96. Madrid, 2000.

Brendle, Franz. *Dynastie, Reich und Reformation (Die württembergischen Herzöge Ulrich und Christoph, die Habsburger und Frakreich)*. Veröffentlichungen der Kommission für geschichtliche Landeskunde in Baden-Württemberg, Reihe B – Forschungen, 141. Band. Stuttgart, 1998.

– – –. "Um Erhalt und Ausbreitung des Evangeliums: Die Reformationskriege der deutschen Protestanten." In *Religionskriege im Alten Reich und in Alteuropa*, edited by Franz Brendle and Anton Schindling, 71–92. Münster, 2006.

Bryce, James. *The Holy Roman Empire*. New York, 3rd ed. 1966.

Bucholz, Franz Bernhard. *Geschichte der Regierung Ferdinand des Ersten*, I. - IX. Wien, 1831–1838.

Burckhardt, Paul. "Basel zur Zeit des Schmalkaldischen Krieges." *Basler Zetschrift für Geschichte und Altertumskunde* 38 (1939): 5–103.

Burkhardt, Carl August Hugo. "Die Wurzerner Fehde." *Archiv für die Sächsische Geschichte* 4 (1865): 57–81.

Bůžek, Václav. "Rytířské kratochvíle' na místodržitelském dvoře arciknížete Ferdinanda." In *Ad vitam et honorem. Profesoru Jaroslavu Mezníkovi přátelé a žáci k pětasedmdesátým narozeninám*, edited by Tomáš Borovský, Libor Jan and Martin Wihoda, 613–622. Brno, 2003.

– – –. "Ferdinand II. Tyrolský a česká šlechta (K otázce integračních procesů v habsburské monarchii)." *Český časopis historický* 98 (2000): 261–291.

– – –. *Ferdinand Tyrolský mezi Prahou a Innsbruckem (Šlechta z českých zemí na cestě ke dvorům prvních Habsburků)*. České Budějovice, 2008.

– – –. *Úvěrové podnikání nižší šlechty v předbělohorských Čechách*. Praha, 1989.

Carande, Ramón. "Das westindische Gold und die Kreditpolitik Karls V." *Spanische Forschungen der Görresgesellschaft (Erste Reihe) - Gesammelte Aufsätze zur Kulturgeschichte Spaniens* 10 (1955): 1–22.

Carsten, Francis Ludwig. *Princes and Parliaments in Germany from the Fifteenth to the Eighteent Century*. Oxford, 1959.

Clifford, Roggers, ed. *The Military Revolution Debate: Readings on Military Transformation of Early Modern Europe*. Boulder and Colorado, 1995.

Collischon, Paul. *Frankfurt a. M. im Schmalkaldische Kriege*. Strassburg, 1890.

Conrad, Hermann. *Deutsche Rechtsgeschichte*, Bd. 2 - Neuzeit bis 1806. Karlsruhe, 1966.

Cowell, Henry John. *Strasbourg Protestant Refugees in England 1547–1553*. London, 1932.

David, Zdeněk V. *Finding the Middle Way – The Utraquists' Liberal Challenge to Rome and Luther*. Washington, 2003.

– – –. "Perennial Hus: Views from the Protestant Reformation to the Enlightenment." *Comenius – Journal of Euro-American Civilization* 2 (2015), No. 2.

Diestelkamp, Bernhard. *Recht und Gericht im Heiligen Römischen Reich (Ius Commune - Sonderhefte, Studien zur Europäische Geschichte, Bd. 122)*. Frankfurt a. M., 1999.

– – –. "Reichskammergericht und Reichshofrat im Spannungsfeld zwischen Reichsständischer Libertät und habsburgischem Kaisertum (Ferdinand I. bis Leopold I.)." In *Reichsständische Libertät und habsburgisches Kaisertum* (Veröffentlichungen des Instituts für Europäische Geschichte Mainz, Abteilung Universalgeschichte, Beiheft 48), edited by Heinz Durchhardt and Matthias Schnettger, 185–194. Mainz, 1999.

Dillon, Kenneth J. *King and Estates in the Bohemian Lands 1526–1564*, Studies presented to the International Commission for the History of Representative and Parliamentary Institutions LVII. Bruxelles, 1976.

Dixon, C. Scott, "Martin Luther and the German Nation: The Reformation and the Roots of Nationalism." In *Confession and Nation in the Era of Reformations (Central Europe in comparative Perspective)*, edited by Eva Doležalová and Jaroslav Pánek, 123–138. Prague 2011.

Dobras, Wolfgang. "Karl V., Ferdinand I. und die Reichsstadt Konstanz." In *Karl V. – Politik und politisches System - Berichte und Studien aus der Arbeit an der politischen Korrespondenz des Kaisers,* edited by Horst Rabe, 191–221. Konstanz, 1996.

Doležalová, Eva. "National and religious aspects of the Czech reform movement in the 14th and 15th centuries and of the Hussite revolution in the mirror of Western historiography." In *Confession and Nation in the Era of Reformations (Central Europe in comparative Perspective)*, edited by Eva Doležalová and Jaroslav Pánek, 63–75. Prague 2011.

Dotzauer, Winfried. *Die deutschen Reichskreise in der Verfassung des Alten Reiches und ihr Eigenleben (1500–1806)*. Darmstadt, 1989.

Druffel, August von. "Sendung des Cardinals Sfondrato an den Hof Karls V. 1547–1548 - Erster Teil." *Abhandlungen des historischen Classe der königlich bayerischen Akademie der Wissenschaften* 20 (1893): 291–362.

Duffy, Michael, ed. *The military revolution and the State 1500–1800*. Exeter, 1980.

Durchhardt, Heinz. *Deutsche Verfassungsgeschichte 1495–1806*. Stuttgart, 1991.

Durchhardt, Heinz, and Schnettger, Matthias, eds. *Reichsständische Libertät und habsburgisches Kaisertum* (Veröffentlichungen des Instituts für Europäische Geschichte Mainz, Abteilung Universalgeschichte, Beiheft 48). Mainz, 1999.

Eberhard, Winfried. "Die deutsche Reformation in Böhmen 1520–1620." In *Deutsche in böhmischen Ländern*, Studien zum Deutschtum im Osten 25/1, edited by Hans Rothe, 103–123. Köln, Weimar and Wien, 1992.

– – –., "Der Weg zur Koexistenz (Kaiser Sigmund und das Ende der hussitischen Revolution)." *Bohemia* 33 (1992): 1–43.

– – –., "Entstehungsbedingungen für öffentliche Toleranz am Beispiel des Kuttenberger Religionsfriedens von 1485". *Communio Viatorum* 29 (1986): 129–154.

– – –. "Konfesionelle Polarisierung, Integration und Koexistenz im Böhmen von 15. bis zum 17. Jahrhundert." In *Religion und Politik im frühneuzeitlichen Böhmen (Der Matestätsbrief Kaiser Rudolfs II. von 1609)*, Forschungen zur Geschichte und Kultur des östlichen Mitteleuropa, Band 46, edited by Jaroslava Hausenblasová, Jiří Mikulec and Martina Thomsen, 25–45. Stuttgart, 2014.

– – –. *Konfessionsbildung und Stände in Böhmen 1478–1530,* Veröffentlichungen des Collegium Carolinum, Band 38. München and Wien, 1981.

– – –. "Landesfreiheiten und Freiheit der Krone in den böhmischen Ländern 1547 und 1619 (Zur Innovationsfähigkeit ständischer politischen Denken)." *Zeitschrift für Ostmitteleuropa-Forschung* 57 (2008): 62–80.

– – –. *Monarchie und Widerstand (Zur ständischen Oppositionsbildung im Herrschaftssys-*

tem Ferdinands I. in Böhmen), Veröffentlichungen des Collegium Carolinum, Band 54. München, 1985.

Edelmayer, Friedrich, Lanzinner, Maximilian, and Rauscher Peter, eds. *Finanzen und Herrschaft (Zu den materiellen Grundlagen fürstlicher Politik in den habsburgischen Ländern und im Heiligen Römischer Reich im 16. Jahrhundert),* Veröffentlichungen des Instituts für österreichische Geschichtsforschung, Band 38. München and Wien 2003.

Ehrenberger, Richard. *Das Zeitalter der Fugger (Geldkapital und Creditverkehr im 16. Jahrhudert),* I-II. Jena, 1912.

Egelhaas, Gottlob. *Deutsche Geschichte im sechzehnten Jahrhundert bis zum Augsburger Religionsfrieden (Zeitalter der Reformation) Zweiter Band 1526–1555.* Stuttgart, 1892.

Eickels, Christine. *Schlesien in böhmischen Ständestaat.* Köln, Weimar and Wien, 1994.

Ekman, Ernst. "Albrecht of Prussia and the Count's War 1533–1536." *Archiv für Reformationsgeschichte* 51 (1960): 19–36

Eltz, Erwein. "Zwei Gutachten des Kurfürstenrates über die Wormser Matrikel und den Gemeinen Pfennig (Ein Beitrag zur Reichssteuerproblematik von Reichstag in Speyer 1544)", in *Aus der Arbeit an den Reichstagen unter Kaiser Karl V. (Sieben Beiträge zu Fragen der Forschung und edition),* Schriften des Historischen Kommision der bayerischen Akademie der Wissenschaften, Band 26, edd. Heinrich Lutz and Alfred Kohler, 273–300. Göttingen, 1986.

Evans, Robert J. W. *Das Werden der Habsburgermonarchie 1550–1700 (Gesellschaft, Kultur, Institutionen).* Wien and Köln, 1989.

–––. "Language and Politics: Bohemia in International Context 1409–1627". In *Confession and Nation in the Era of Reformations (Central Europe in comparative Perspective),* edited by Eva Doležalová and Jaroslav Pánek, 155–182. Prague 2011.

Evans, Robert J. W., Wilson Peter H. *The Holy Roman Empire 1495–1806. A European Perspective.* Leiden, 2012.

Fabian, Ekkehard. *Die Entstehung des Schmalkaldischen Bundes und seiner Verfassung 1524/29 - 1531/35.* Tübingen, 1962.

–––. *Die schmalkaldischen Bundesabschiede 1533 – 1536 (Mit Ausschreiben der Bundestage und anderen archivalischen Beilagen).* Schriften zur Kirchen- und Rechtsgeschichte (Darstellungen und Quellen), 8. Heft. Tübingen, 1958.

Fischer, Gerhard. *Die persönliche Stellung und politische lage König Ferdinands I. vor und während der Passauer Verhandlungen des Jahres 1552.* Königsberg, 1891.

Frauenholz, Eugen von. *Das Heerwesen der Schweizer Eidgenossenschaft in der Zeit des freien Söldnertums,* Entwicklungsgeschichte des deutschen Heerwesens, Zweiter Band, I. Teil. München, 1936.

–––. *Das Heerwesen des Reiches in der Landsknechtszeit,* Entwicklungsgeschichte des deutschen Heerwesens, Zweiter Band, II. Teil. München, 1937.

–––. *Lazarus von Schwendi – Der erste deutsche Verkünder der allgemeinen Wehrpflicht.* Hamburg, 1939.

Friedeburg, Robert. "Cuius regio, eius religion: The Ambivalent Meanings of State Building in Protestant Germany 1555–1655." In *Diversity and Dissent (National Religious*

Difference in Cental Europe 1500–1800), edited by Howard Louthan, Gary B. Cohen and Franz A. J. Szabo, 73–91. New York and Oford, 2011.

Fritzová, Charlotte, and Růžička, Jindřich. "Španělský sňatek Vratislava z Pernštejna (1555)." *Sborník prací východočeských archívů* 3 (1975), 63–77.

Fueter, Eduard. *Geschichte des europäischen Staatensystems von 1492–1559,* Handbuch der Mitteralterlichen und Neueren Geschichte, Abteilung II: Politische Geschichte. München and Berlin, 1919.

Fukala Radek. *Slezsko – Neznámá země Koruny české. Knížecí a stavovské Slezsko do roku 1740.* Hradec Králové, 2007.

Funk, Albert. *Kleine Geschichte des Föderalismus (Vom Fürstenbund zur Bundesrepublik).* Paderborn, München, Wien and Zürich, 2010.

Gindely, Antonín. *Geschichte der böhmischen Finanzen von 1526 bis 1618.* Wien 1868.

Glete, Jan. *War and the State in Early Modern Europe (Spain, the Dutch Republic and Sweden as Fiscal-Military States 1500–1660).* London and New York, 2002.

Gmiterek, Henryk. *Bracia czescy a kalwini w Rzeczypospolitej. Połowa XVI – połowa XVII wieku (Studium porównawcze).* Lublin, 1987.

Greengras, Mark. *Christendom Destroyed (Europe 1517–1648).* London, 2014.

Grünhagen, Colmar. "Schlesien unter der Herrschaft König Ferdinands 1527–1546." *Zeitschrift des Vereines für Geschichte uld Altertums Schlesiens* 19 (1885): 63–139.

Grzybowski, Stanisław. "Dzieje Polski i Litwy (1506–1648)." In *Wielka Historia Polski,* Tom II, Częźć II, 321–715. Kraków and Warszawa, 2003.

Haas, Irene. *Reformation - Konfesion - Tradition: Frankfurt am Main im Schmalkandischen Bund 1536–1547.* Frankfurt am Main, 1991.

Haimerl, Franz. *Die deutsche Lehenhauptmannschaft (Lehenschranne) in Böhmen – Ein Beitrag zur Geschichte des Lehenwesens in Böhmen mit urkundlichen Beilagen.* Praha, 1848.

Häpke, Rudolf. *Die Regierung Karls V. und der europäische Norden.* Lübeck, 1914.

Hartung, Fritz. *Deutsche Verfassungsgeschichte von fünfzehnten Jahrhundert bis zur Gegenwart.* 6th ed. Stuttgart, 1956.

–––. *Karl V. und die deutschen Reichsstände von 1546–1555.* Darmstadt, 1971.

Hasenclever, Adolf. *Die Kurpfälzische Politik in den Zeiten des schmalkaldischen Krieges (Januar 1546 bis Januar 1547).* Heidelberg, 1905.

Haugh-Moritz, Gabriele, "Der Schmalkaldische Krieg (1546/47) - ein kaiserlicher Religionskrieg?", in *Religionskriege im Alten Reich und in Alteuropa,* edited by Franz Brendle and Anton Schindling, 93–106. Münster, 2006.

Hauser, Henri, and Augustin Renaudet. *L'età del Rinascimento e della Riforma.* Torino, 1957.

Hecker, Oswald Artur. *Karls V. Plan zur Gründung eines Reichsbundes - Ursprung und erste Versuche bis zum Ausgange des Ulmer Tages (1547).* Leipziger historische Abhandlungen, Heft 1. Leipzig, 1906.

Heer, Friedrich. *The Holy Roman Empire.* 4th ed. London, 2003.

Heiliges Römisches Reich Deutscher Nation 962 bis 1806. II. 1495–1806. Berlin, 2006.

Heinemeyer, Walter. *"Das Zeitalter der Reformation."* In *Das Werden Hessens,* edited by Walter Heinemeyer, 225–266. Marburg, 1986.

Heister, Carl von. *Die Gefagennehmung und die Gefangenschaft Philipps des Grossmüthigen Landgrafen von Hessen (1547 bis 1552)*. Marburg and Leipzig, 1868.

Held, Wieland. *1547 – Die Schlacht bei Mühlberg / Elbe (Entscheidung auf dem Wege zum albertinischen Kurfürstentum Sachsen)*. Beucha, 1997.

Hellinga, Gerben Graddesz. *Karel V – Bondgenoten en tegenstanders*. Zutphen, 2010.

Herrman, Johannes. *Moritz von Sachsen (1521–1553) - Landes-, Reichs- und Friedenfürst*. Beucha, 2003.

Herzog, Emil. "Geschichte des Klosters Grünhain." *Archiv für die sächsische Geschichte* 7 (1869): 60–96.

Heřman, Josef. "Zemské berní rejstříky z let 1523 a 1529." *Československý časopis historický* 10 (1962): 248–257.

Heydenreuter, Reinhard. "Der Steuerbetrug und seine Bestrafung in den deutschen Territorien der frühen Neuzeit." In *Staatsfinanzen – Staatsverschuldung – Staatsbankrotte in der europäischen Staaten- und Rechtsgeschichte*, edited by Lingelbach Gernhard, 167–183. Köln, Weimar and Wien, 2000.

Hillebrand, Hans J. *The World of the Reformation*. New York, 1973.

Hrejsa, Ferdinand. *Dějiny křesťanství v Československu V. - Za krále Ferdinanda I. 1526–1564*, Spisy Husovy československé evangelické fakulty bohoslovecké, řada A, Sv. IX. Praha, 1948.

Houley, Norman. *The Later Crusades from Lyons to Alcazar 1274–1580*. Oxford, 1995.

Hoyer, Siegfried. "Jan Hus und der Hussitismus in den Flugschriften des ersten Jahrzehnts der Reformation." In *Flugschrift als Massenmedium der Reformationszeit*. Spätmittelalter und Frühe Neuzeit – Tübinger Beiträge zur Geschichtsforschung, Band 13, edited by Hans-Joachim Köhler, 291–307. Stuttgart, 1981.

Hrubý, František. "Luterství a novoutrakvismus v českých zemích v 16. a 17. století." *Český časopis historický* 45 (1939): 31–44.

Huelsse, Friedrich. *Die Stadt Magdeburg im Kampfe für den Protestantismus während der Jahre 1547–1551*, Verein für Reformationsgeschichte (Schriften für das deutsche Volk), Heft 17. Halle, 1892.

Janáček, Josef. *České dějiny – Doba předbělohorská 1526–1547*, kniha I, díl I. Praha, 1971; díl II. Praha, 1984.

– – –. "Die Fugger und Joachimstal." *Historica* 6 (1963): 109–144

– – –. "Zrušení cechů roku 1547." *Československý časopis historický* 7 (1959): 231–242

Jež, Radim. "Jan z Pernštejna ve sporu o Opolsko-Ratibořsko ve třicátých a čtyřicátých letech 16. století." *Východočeský sborník historický* 14 (2007): 69–85

Just, Jiří. "Acta Unitatis Fratrum." *Folia Historica Bohemica* 29 (2014): 451–462.

– – –. "Internace Jana Augusty na Křivoklátu jako příklad konfesijního násilí a problém její interpretace." *Folia Historica Bohemica* 30 (2015): 33–46.

– – –. "Luteráni v našich zemích do Bílé hory." In *Luteráni v českých zemích v proměnách staletí*, eds. Jiří Just, Zdeněk R. Nešpor, Ondřej Matějka et all., 23–120. Praha, 2009.

Kadlec, Jaroslav. *Přehled českých církevních dějin* 2. Řím, 1987.

Kellenbenz, Hermann. "Die Römisch-Deutsche Reich im Rahmen der wirtschafts- und finanzpolitischen Erwägungen Karls V. im Spannungsfeld imperialer und dynastischer Interessen." In *Das römisch-deutsche Reich im politischen System Karls V.*, Schriften des Historischen Kollegs – Kolloquien 1, edited by Heinrich Lutz, 35–54. München and Wien, 1982.

–––. "Hugo Angelo – Bürger von Augsburg und kaiserlicher Agent." In *Gesellschaftsgschichte – Festschrift für Karl Bosl zum 80. Geburtstag*, Band II, edited by Ferdinand Seibt, 115–130. München 1988.

Kersken, Norbert. "*Die Oberlausitz von der Gründung des Sechsstädtebundes bis zum Übergang an das Kurfürstentum Sachsen (1346–1635).*" In Geschichte der Oberlausitz (Herrschaft, Gesellschaft und Kultur vom Mittelalter bis zum Ende des 20. Jahrhunderts), edited by Joachim Bahlcke, 99–142. Leipzig, 2003.

Kieckhefer, Richard. *Repression of Heresy in Medieval Germany*. Philadelphia, 1979.

Kieslich, Günther. *Das "Historische Volkslied" als publizistische Erscheinung (Untersuchungen zur Wesenbestimmung und Typologie der gereimten Publizistik zur Zeit des Regensburger Reichstages und des Krieges der Schmalkaldener gegen Herzog Heinrich den Jüngeren von Braunschweig 1540–1542)*. Studien zur Publizistik, Band 1. Münster, 1958.

Kirsch, Hermann Joseph. *Die Fugger und der Schmalkaldische Krieg*. München and Leipzig, 1915.

Kohler, Alfred. *Antihabsburgische Politik in der Epoche Karls V. - Die Reichsständische Opposition gegen die Wahl Ferdinands I. zum Römischer König und gegen die Anerkennung seines Königstums (1524–1534)*, Schriftenreihe der Historischen Komission bei der Bayerische Akademie der Wisssenschaften, Schrift 19. Göttingen, 1982.

–––. *Das Reich im Kampf um die Hegemonie in Europa 1521–1648*. München, 1990.

–––. "Die innerdeutsche und die außerdeutsche Opposition gegen das politische System Karls V." In *Das römisch-deutsche Reich im politischen System Karls V.*, Schriften des Historischen Kollegs – Kolloquien 1, edited by Heinrich Lutz, 107–127. München and Wien, 1982.

–––. *Ferdinand I. (1503–1564) – Fürst, König und Kaiser*. München, 2003.

–––. *Karl V. 1500–1558*. München, 2000.

Köhler, Walter. "Die Doppelehe Landgaf Philipps von Hessen." *Historische Zeitschrift* 94 (1905): 385–411.

Körber, Kurt. *Kirchengüterfrage und schmalkaldischer Bund (Ein Beitrag zur deutschen Reformationgeschichte)*. Schriften des Vereins für Reformationsgeschichte, Jg. 30, Stück 3–4, Nr. 111/12. Leipzig, 1913.

Kořán, Josef, Rezek Antonín, Svátek Josef, and Prášek Justin Václav. *Dějiny Čech a Moravy nové doby, I. 1526–1609*. Praha, 1939.

Köstler, Andreas. "Eine Konstruktion Lausitzer Geschichte in der wilhelminischen Klosterkirche Dobrilugk." In *Die Nieder- und Oberlausitz – Konturen einer Integrationslandschaft, Band I: Mittelaler* (Studien zur branderbungischen und vergleichenden Geschichten, Band 11), edited by Heinz-Dieter Heimann, Klaus Neitmann and Uwe Tresp, 390–407. Berlin, 2013.

Kotulla, Michael. *Deutsche Verfassungsgeschichte – Vom Alten Reich bis Weimar (1495–1934)*. Berlin – Heidelberg 2008

Krämer. Christel. *Beziehungen zwischen Albrecht von Brandenburg-Ansbach und Friedrich II. von Liegnitz (Ein Fürstenbriefwechsel 1514–1547 – Darstellungen und Quellen)*, Veröfentlichungen aus den Archiven Preussischer Kulturbesitz, Band 8. Köln and Berlin, 1977.

Kraus, Andreas, ed., *Handbuch der bayerischen Geschichte*. I. Band., 2nd ed. München, 1988.

Krämer, Christel. *Beziehungen zwischen Albrecht von Brandenburg-Ansbach und Friedrich II. von Liegnitz (Ein Fürstenbriefwechsel 1514–1547 – Darstellungen und Quellen)*. Veröfentlichungen aus den Archiven Preussischer Kulturbesitz, Band 8. Köln and Berlin, 1977.

Krofta, Kamil. "Bohemia in the Fifteenth Century." In *Decline of Empire and Papacy*, Cambridge medieval History, Volume VII, eds. C. W. Previté-Orton and Z. N. Brooke, 65–155, Cambridge, 1936.

Krüger, Kersten. *Finanzstaat Hessen 1500–1567*. Marburg 1980.

Lau, Franz, and Bizer Ernst. *A History of the Reformation in Germany to 1555*. London, 1969.

Laubach, Ernst. *Ferdinand I. als Kaiser. Politik und Herrscherauffassung des Nachfolgers Karls V.* Münster, 2001.

–––. "Karl V., Ferdinand I. und die Nachfolge im Reich." *Mitteilungen des österreichisches Staatsarchivs* 29 (1976): 1–51.

Lehmann, Rudolf. *Die älteste Geschichte des Klosters Dobrilug in der Lausitz*. Kirchhain, 1917.

–––. *Geschichte der Niederlausitz*. Berlin, 1963.

Lenz, Max. *Die Schlacht bei Mühlberg (Mit neuen Quellen)*. Gotha, 1879.

Lockyer, Roger. *Habsburg & Bourbon Europe 1470–1720*. New York, 1982.

Lommer, Franz Xaver. *Die böhmischen Lehen in der Oberpfalz*. Bd. I. Amberg, 1907.

Lucke, Helmut. *Bremen im Schmalkandischen Bund 1540–1547*. Schriften der Wittheit zu Bremen, Reihe F: Veröffentlichungen aus dem Staatsarchiv der Freien Hansenstadt Bremen, Heft 23. Bremen, 1955.

Luttenberger, Albrecht Pius. *Glaubenseinheit und Reichsfriede: Konzeptionen und Wege konfesionsneutraler Reichspolitik 1530–1552 (Kurpfalz, Jülich, Kurbrandenburg)*. Göttingen, 1982.

–––. "*Karl V., Frankreich und der deutsche Reichstag.*" In *Das römisch-deutsche Reich im politischen System Karls V.*, Schriften des Historischen Kollegs – Kolloquien 1, edited by Heinrich Lutz, 189–221. München and Wien, 1982.

–––. *Kurfürsten, Kaiser und Reich (Politische Führung und Friedensicherung unter Ferdinand I. und Maximilian II.)*, Veröffentlichungen des Instituts für Europäische Geschichte Mainz, Abteilung Universalgeschichte, Band 149. Mainz, 1994.

–––. "*Reichspolitik und Reichstag unter Karl V.: Formen zentraler politischen Handels.*" In *Aus der Arbeit an den Reichstagen unter Kaiser Karl V. (Sieben Beiträge zu Fragen der Forschung und edition)*, Schriften des Historischen Kommission dei der bayerischen Akademie der Wissenschaften, Band 26, edited by Heinrich Lutz and Alfred Kohler, 18–68. Göttingen, 1986.

–––. *Glaubenseinheit und Reichsfriede [Konzepzionen und Wege konfessionsneutraler Reichspolitik 1530–1555 (Kurpfalz, Jülich, Kurbrandenburg)]*. Göttingen, 1982.

Lutz, Heinrich. "Augsburg und seine politiche Umwelt 1490–1555." In *Geschichte der Stadr Augsburg (2000 Jahre von der Römerzeit bis zur Gegenwart)*, 413–433. Stuttgart, 1984.

–––. *Das Ringen um deutsche Einheit und kirchliche Erneuerung (Von Maximilian I. bis zum Westfälischen Frieden) 1490 bis 1648*. Propyläen Geschichte Deutschlands 4. Frankfurt am Main, Berlin and Wien 1983.

–––. *Christianitas afflicta - Europa, das Reich und die päpstliche Politik im Niedergang der Hegemonie Karls V. (1552–1556)*. Göttingen, 1964.

–––. "Kaiser Karl V., Frankreich und das Reich." In *Frankreich und das Reich im 16. und 17. Jahrhundert*, edited by Heinrich Lutz, Friedrich Hermann Schubert and Hermann Weber, 7–19. Göttingen, 1968.

–––. *Reformation und Gegenreformation*. 3rd ed. München, 1991.

Lutz, Heinrich, ed., *Das römisch-deutsche Reich im politischen System Karls V.* München and Wien, 1982.

MacHardy, Karin J. *War, Religion and Court Patronage in Habsburg Austria - The Social and Cultural Dimensions of Political Interaction, 1521–1622*. New York, 2003.

Machilek, Franz. "Schlesien." In *Die Territorien des Reichs im Zeitalter der Reformation und Konfessionalisierung (Land und Konfesion 1500 - 1650), Bd. 2*, edited by Anton Schindling and Walter Ziegler, 102–139. Münster, 1993.

Majewski, Dennis. "Die territorile Politik der Zisterzienserabtei Dobrilugk (Die Herrschaft des Lausitzklosters in Zeit und Raum)." In *Die Nieder- und Oberlausitz – Konturen einer Integrationslandschaft, Band I: Mittelaler* (Studien zur branderbungischen und vergleichenden Geschichten, Band 11), edited by Heinz-Dieter Heimann, Klaus Neitmann and Uwe Tresp, 177–188. Berlin, 2013.

Marek Pavel, "Klientelní strategie španělských králů na pražském císařském dvoře konce 16. a počátku 17. století." *Český časopis historický* 105 (2007): 40–88.

Marquard, Bernd. *Das Römisch-Deutsche Reich als segmentäres Verfassungssystem (1348–1806/48) – Versuch zu einer neuen Verfassungstheorie auf der Grundlage der lokalen Herrschaften*. Zürcher Studien zur Rechtsgeschichte 39. Zürich, 1999.

Maur, Eduard. "Vznik a územní proměny majetkového komplexu českých panovníků ve středních Čechách v 16. a 17. století." *Středočeský sborník historický* 11 (1976): 53–63.

Maurenbrecher, Wilhelm. *Karl V. und die deutschen Protestanten 1545–1555 (nebst einem Anhang von Aktenstücken aus dem spanischen Staatsarchiv von Simancas)*. Frankfurt am Main, 1865.

Menzel, Thomas. *Der Fürst als Feldherr - Militärische Handeln und Selbstdarstellung zwischen 1470 und 1550. Dargestellt an ausgewählten Beispielen)*. Berlin, 2003.

Mertens, Bernd. *Im Kampf gegen die Monopole (Reichstags-verhandlungen und monopolprozesse im frühen 16. Jahrhundert)*, Tübinger rechtwissenschaftliche Abhandlungen, Bd. 81. Tübingen, 1996.

Meyer, Christian. "Die Feldhauptmannschaft Joachims II. im Türkenkriege von 1542." *Zeitschrift für Preußische Geschichte und Landeskunde* 16 (1879): 480–538.

Mika, Norbert. *Dějiny Ratibořska*. Krakov 2012.

Mikulski, Krzystof and Wijaczka Jacek. *Historia powszechna – Wiek XVI-XVIII*. Warszawa, 2012.

Müller, Johannes. "Über einen auf dem Augsburger Reichstag 1548 aufgekommenen Reichssteuermodus." *Bayerische Zeitschrift für Realschulwesen* 18 (1897): 278–285.

———. "Veränderungen im Reichsmatrikelwesen um die Mitte des sechzehnten Jahrhunderts." *Zeitschrift des Historischen Vereins für Schwaben und Neuburg* 23 (1896): 115–176.

Müller, Josef Theodor. *Dějiny Jednoty bratrské*. I., Praha, 1923.

Münkler, Herfried. "Nation als politische Idee im frühneuzeitlichen Europa." In *Nation und Literatur im Europa der Frühen Neuzeit (Akten des I. Internationalen Osnabrücker Kongresses zur Kulturgeschichte der frühen Neuzeit)*, edited by Garber Klaus, 56–86. Tübingen, 1989.

Naujoks, Eberhard. *Kaiser Karl V. und die Zunftverfassung: ausgewählte Aktenstücke zu den Verfassungsänderungen in den oberdeutschen Reichsstädten (1547–1556)*. Stuttgart, 1985.

Mašek, Petr. *Význam Bartoloměje Netolického pro český knihtisk 16. století*. Příspěvky ke knihopisu 4. Praha, 1987.

Nemeškal, Lubomír. *Jáchymovská mincovna v první polovině 16. století*. Praha, 1964.

———. *Snahy o mincovní unifikaci v 16. století*. Praha, 2001.

Nemeškal, Lubomír, and Vorel Petr. *Dějiny jáchymovské mincovny a katalog ražeb I. 1519/1520–1619*. Pardubice, 2010.

Neuhaus, Helmut. *Das Reich in der Frühen Neuzeit*. München 1997.

———. "Die Entwicklung im Reich bis zum Ende des Dreißigjährigen Krieges." In *Ploetz – Große illustrierte Weltgeschichte in 8 Bänden*, Band 4 (Das Werden des modernen Europa), 69–85. Freiburg and Würzburg 1984.

———. "Die Römische Königswahl vivente imperatore in der Neuzeit (Zum Problem der Kontinuität in einer frühneuzeitlichen Wahlmonarchie)." In *Neue Studien zur frühneuzeitlichen Reichsgeschichte*, Zeitschrift für historische Forschung (Vierteljahreschrift zur Erforschung des Spätmittelalters und der frühen Neuzeit), Beiheft 19, edited by Johannes Kunisch, 1–54. Berlin, 1997.

———. *Reichsständische Repräsentationsformen im 16. Jahrhundert (Reichstag – Reichskreistag – Reichsdeputattionstag)*. Schriften zur Verfassungsgeschichte, Band 33. Berlin, 1982.

———. "Von Karl V. zu Ferdinand V. - Herrschaftsübergang im Heiligen Römischen Reich 1555–1558." In *Recht und Reich im Zeitalter der Reformation (Festschrift für Horst Rabe)*, edited by Roll Christine and others, 417–440. Frankfurt am Main, Berlin, Bern, New York, Paris and Wien, 1996.

———. "Von Reichstag(en) zu Reichstag (Reichsständische Beratungsformen von der Mitte des 16. bis zur Mitte des 17. Jahrhunderts." In *Reichsständische Libertät und habsburgisches Kaisertum*. Veröffentlichungen des Instituts für Europäische Geschichte Mainz, Abteilung Universalgeschichte, Beiheft 48, edited by Heinz Durchhardt und Matthias Schnettger, 135–149. Mainz, 1999.

Neumann, Theodor. *Beiträge zur Geschichte des Schmalkaldischen Krieges, der Böhmischen Empörung von 1547, sovie des Pönfalles der Oberlausitzischen Sechsstädte in demselben Jahre*. Görlitz, 1848.

North, Michael. *"Finances and power in the German state system."* In The Rise of Fiscal States: A Global History 1500–1914, edited by B. Yun-Casalilla, P. K. O´Brien and F. C. Comín, 145–163. Cambridge 2012.

Novotný, David. *Královští rychtáři ve východočeských zeměpanských městech v době předbělohorské*. Olomouc 2012.

Odložilík, Otakar. *The Hussite King – Bohemia in European Affairs 1440–1471*. New Brunswick, 1965.

Oestreich, Gerhard. "Zur Heeresverfassung der deutschen Territorien von 1500 bis 1800 (Ein Versuch vergleichender Betrachtung)." In *Forschungen zu Staat und Verfassung (Festgabe für Fritz Hartung)*, edited by Richard Dietrich and Gerhard Oestrich, 419–439. Berlin, 1958.

Pánek, Jaroslav. "Bohemia and the Empire: Acceptance and Rejection." In *The Holy Roman Empire 1495–1806. A European Perspective*, edited by Robert J. W. Evans and Peter H. Wilson, 121–141. Leiden, 2012.

–––. "Böhmen, Mähren und Österreich in der Frühen Neuzeit: Forschungsprobleme ihres Zusammenlebens." In *Kontakte und Konflikte - Böhmen, Mähren und Österreich: Aspekte eines Jahrtausends gemeinsamer Geschichte (Referate des Symposiums "Verbindungen und Trennendes an der Grenze III" vom 24. - bis 27. Oktober 1992 in Zwettl)*, edited by Thomas Winkelbauer, 125–136. Horn and Waidhofen a. d. Thaya, 1993.

–––. "Břemeno politiky. Raně novověká Svatá říše římská v proměnách moderní české historiografie." In *Dějiny ve věku nejistot (Sborník k příležitosti 70. narozenin Dušana Třeštíka)*, edited by Jan Klápště, Eva Plešková, and Josef Žemlička, 187–200. Praha, 2003.

–––. "Český stát a stavovská společnost na prahu novověku ve světle zemských zřízení." In *Vladislavské zřízení zemské a počátky ústavního zřízení v českých zemích (1500–1619) – Sborník příspěvků z mezi-národní konferenmce konané ve dnech 7. - 8. prosince 2000 v Praze*, edited by Karel Malý and Jaroslav Pánek, 13–84. Praha, 2001.

–––. "Český a moravský zemský sněm v politickém systému České koruny doby předbělohorské." In *Sejm czeski od czasów najdawniejszych do 1913 roku*, edited by Marian J. Ptak, 31–47. Opole, 2000.

–––. "Das Politische System des böhmischen Staates im ersten Jahrhundert des habsburgischen Herrschaft (1526-1620)." *Mitteilungen des Instituts für österreichische Geschichtsforschung* 98 (1989): 53 – 82

–––. "Das Ständewesen und die Gesellschaft in den Böhmischen Ländern in der Zeit vor der Schlacht auf dem Weißen Berg (1526 - 1620)." *Historica* 25 (1985): 73 – 120.

–––. "Der Adel im Turnierbuch Erzherzog Ferdinands II. von Tirol (Ein Beitrag zur Geschichte des Hoflebens und der Hofkultur in der Zeit seiner Statthalterschaft in Böhmen)." *Folia Historica Bohemica* 16 (1993): 77 – 96.

–––. "Der böhmische Staat und das Reich in der Frühen Neuzeit." In *Alternativen zur Reichsverfassung in der Frühen Neuzeit?* Schriften des Historischen Kollegs Kolloquien 23, edited by Volker Press, 169–178. München, 1995.

–––. "Der tschechische Blick auf die Reichsgeschichte und die spezifische Stellung des böhmischen Staates." *Zeitschrift für Ostmitteleuropa-Forschung* 53 (2004): 373–390.

–––. "Kaiser, König und Ständerevolte (Die böhmischen Stände und ihre Stellung zur Reichspolitik Karls V. und Ferdinands I. im Zeitalter der Schmalkandischen Krieges)." In *Karl V. 1500–1558 (Neue Perspektiven seiner Herrschaft in Europa und Übersee),* edited by Alfred Kohler, B. Haider and Ch. Ottnar, 303–406. Wien, 2002.

–––. "Land Codes of the Bohemian Kingdom in Relation to Constitutional Changes in Central Europe on the Threshold of the Early Modern Age." *Historica* 9 (2002): 7–39.

–––. "Města v politickém systému předbělohorského českého státu." In *Česká města v 16.-18.století (Sborník příspěvků z konference v Pardubicích 14. a 15. listopadu 1990),* edited by Jaroslav Pánek, 15–39. Praha, 1991.

–––. "Nation and Confession in the Czech Lands in the pre-White Mountain Period." In *Confession and Nation in the Era of Reformations (Central Europe in comparative Perspective),* edited by Eva Doležalová and Jaroslav Pánek, 139–154. Prague, 2011.

–––. "Podíl předbělohorského českého státu na obraně střední Evropy proti osmanské expanzi." *Český časopis historický* 36 (1988): 856 – 873; 37 (1989): 71 – 85.

–––. "První krize habsburské monarchie." In *Stavovský odboj roku 1547 – První krize habsburské monarchie (Sborník příspěvků z vědecké konference konané v Pardubicích 29.- 30. 9. 1997),* edited by Petr Vorel, 11–27. Pardubice – Praha, 1999.

–––. "Regierungsstrategie und Regierungsformen Ferdinands I. in den böhmischen Ländern." In *Kaiser Ferdinand I. – Ein mitteleuropäischen Herrscher,* edited by Martina Fuchs, Teréz Oborni, and Gábor Ujváry, 323–338. Münster, 2005.

–––. *Stavovská opozice a její zápas s Habsburky 1547–1577.* Praha, 1982.

–––. *Výprava české šlechty do Itálie v letech 1551 – 1552.* 2nd ed. České Budějovice, 2004.

–––. "Zápas o vedení české stavovské obce v polovině 16. století (Knížata z Plavna a Vilém z Rožmberka)." *Československý časopis historický* 31 (1983): 855–884.

–––., "Zemská zřízení v kontextu ústavních proměn ve střední Evropě v 16. a na počátku 17. století – Die Landesordnungen im Kontext der Verfassungsrechtlichem Veränderungen in Mitteleuropaim 16. und zu Beginn des 17. Jahrhunderts – Ustawy krajowe w kontekście zmian konstucyjnych w Europie Środkowej w XVI i na początku XVII wieku." In *Vladislavské zřízení zemské a počátky ústavního zřízení v českých zemích (1500–1619), Sborník příspěvků z mezinárodní konference konané ve dnech 7.–8. prosince 2000 v Praze,* edited by Karel Malý and Jaroslav Pánek, 403–441. Praha, 2001.

Parker, Geoffrey. *The military revolution: Military innovation and the rise of the west, 1500–1800.* Cambridge, 1996.

–––. "Die politische Welt Karls V." In *Karl V. 1500–1558 und seine Zeit,* edited by Hugo Soly, 113–226. Köln, 2003.

Parma, Anna. "La Corte Lontana – Poteri e strategie nel Marchesato Farnesiano di Novara.", In *Familiglia" del Principe a famiglia aristocratica*, edited by Cesare Mozzarelli, 487–505. Roma, 1988.

Parrott, David. *The Bussiness of War - Military Enterprise and Military Revolution in Early Modern Europe*. Cambridge, 2012.

Pastor, Ludvig von. *Geschichte Papst Pauls III. (1534–1549)*. Geschichte der Päpste seit dem Ausgang des Mittelalters, Bd. V. 13ᵗʰ ed. Freiburg, 1956.

–––. *Geschichte Päpste im Zeitalter der katholischen Reformation und Restauration – Julius III., Marcellus II. und Paul IV. (1550–1559). Geschichte der Päpste seit dem Ausgang des Mittelalters*, Bd. VI. 13ᵗʰ ed. Freiburg, 1957.

Pelant Jan, "České zemské sněmy v létech 1471–1500". *Sborník archívních prací* 31 (1981): 340–414.

Pelizaeus, Ludolf. *Dynamik der Macht - Städtischer Widerstand und Konfliktbewältigung im Reich Karls V.*. Geschichte in der Epoche Karls V., Bd. 9. Münster, 2007.

Pešák, Václav. *Dějiny královské české komory od roku 1527 - Část I. Začátky organisace české komory za Ferdinanda I.* Sborník Archivu Ministerstva vnitra Republiky československé, svazek III. Praha, 1930.

Pešek, Jiří. "Political Culture of the Burghers in Bohemia and Central Europe during the Pre-White Mountain Period." In *Political Culture in Central Europe (10ᵗʰ – 20ᵗʰ Century)*, edited by Halina Manikowska and Jaroslav Pánek, 203–214. Prague, 2005.

–––. "Reformační konfesionalizace v Německu 16. – 17. století (Publikace a diskuse 80. a 90. let)". *Český časopis historický* 96 (1998): 602–610.

–––. "Slavnost jako téma dějepisného zkoumání." *Documenta Pragensia* 12 (1995): 7–27.

Pešek, Jiří, and Vorel Petr, eds. *Neue tschechische Interpretationen der Fragen des tschechisch-deutschen Zusammenlebens (47. Deutscher Historikertag / Dresden 2008 - Die Vortragende der tschechischen Gastsection)*. Magdeburg, 2011.

Petráň, Josef. "Rok 1547 v českých dějinách." In *Stavovský odboj roku 1547 – První krize habsburské monarchie (Sborník příspěvků z vědecké konference konané v Pardubicích 29.- 30. 9. 1997)*, edited by Petr Vorel, 5–10. Pardubice and Praha, 1999.

–––. "Stavovské království a jeho kultura v Čechách 1471–1526." In *Josef Petráň - České dějiny ve znamení kultury (Výbor studií)*, ed. Jaroslav Pánek and Petr Vorel, 60–122, Pardubice, 2010.

Petri, Franz. "Nordwestdeutschland im Wechselspiel der Politik Karls V. und Philipps des Großmütigen von Hessen." *Zeitschrift des Vereins für hessische Geschichte und Landeskunde* 71 (1960): 37–60.

Petry, Walter. *Irrwege Europas 1519–1648*. Göttingen, 1967.

Philip, Benedict. "Religion and Politics in Europe, 1500–1700." In *Religion und Gewalt – Konflikte, Rituale, Deutungen (1500–1800)*, Veröffentlichungen des Max-Planck-Instituts für Geschichte, Band 215, ed. Kaspar von Greyerz and Kim Siebenhüner, 156–173. Göttingen, 2006.

Polišenský, Josef. *Tragic triangle. The Netherlands, Spain and Bohemia 1617–1621*. Prague, 1991.

Press, Volker. "Adel in den österreichisch – böhmischen Erblanden und im Reich zwischen dem 15. und dem 17. Jahrhundert." In *Adel im Wandel (Politik – Kultur – Konfession 1500–1700) - Niederösterrichische Landesausstellung*, 19–32. Rosenburg, 1990.

–––. "Die Bundespläne Kaiser Karls V. und die Reichsverfassung." In *Das römisch-deutsche Reich im politischen System Karls V.*, Schriften des Historischen Kollegs – Kolloquien 1, edited by Heinrich Lutz, 55–106. München and Wien, 1982.

Rabe, Horst. *Reich und Glaubensspaltung (Deutschland 1500–1600)*, Neue Deutsche Geschichte, Band 4. München, 1989.

–––. *Reichsbund und Interim - Die Verfassungs- und Religionspolitik Karls V. und der Reichstag von Augsburg 1547/1548*. Köln and Wien, 1971.

Rabe, Horst, ed.. *Karl V. – Politik und politisches System (Berichte und Studien aus der Arbeit an der politischen Korrespondenz des Kaisers)*. Konstanz, 1996.

Rak, Jiří. "Vývoj utrakvistické správní organizace v době předbělohorské." *Sborník archívních prací* 31 (1981): 182–184.

Ranke, Leopold von. *Deutsche Geschichte im Zeitalter der Reformation*. I-II. Essen, (1996).

Rassow, Peter. *Die Kaiser-Idee Karls V., dargestellt an der Politik der Jahre 1528–1540*. Berlin, 1932.

Rauscher, Peter. "Kaiser und Reich – Die Reichstürkenhilfen von Ferdinand I. bis zum Beginn des "Langen Türkenkriegs" (1548–1593)." In *Finanzen und Herrschaft (Materielle Grundlagen fürstlicher Politik in den habsburgischen Ländern und im Heiligen Römischen Reich im 16. Jahrhundert)*, edited by Friedrich Edelmayer, Maximilian Lanzinner and Peter Rauscher, 45–83. München, 2003.

–––. *Zwischen Ständen und Gläubigern - Die Kaiserlichen Finanzen unter Ferdinand I. und Maximilian II. (1556–1576)*. Veröffentlichungen des Instituts für Österrichische Geschichtsforschung, Band 41. Wien and München 2004.

Rebitsch Robert, "Der Kaiser auf der Flucht. Die militärische Niederlage Karls V. gegen die deutsche Fürstenopposition im Jahre 1552", in *Kaiser und Kurfürst – Aspekte des Fürstenaufstandes 1552*. Geschichte in der Epoche Karls V., Band 11, edited by Martina Fuchs and Robert Rebitsch, 119–138. Münster, 2010.

Reich, Jürgen. "Schmalkalden und der Schmalkaldische Bund." In *Grenzgänge (Festgabe für Hans Geißer)*, edited by Horst Licker, 111–119. Zürich, 2003.

Rezek, Antonín. "Statky zkonfiskované r. 1547 a jejich rozprodávání." *Památky archeologické a místopisné* 10 (1874–1877): 451–482.

Rockwell, William Walker. *Die Doppelehe Landgaf Philipps von Hessen*. Marburg, 1904.

Roll, Christine, and others, eds. *Recht und Reich im Zeitalter der Reformation (Festschrift für Horst Rabe)*. Frankfurt am Main, Berlin, Bern, New York, Paris and Wien, 1996.

Rössler, Hellmuth. "Geschichte des europäischen Staatensystems von Maximilian I. bis zum Ende des Dreißigjährigen Krieges." In *Historia Mundi – Ein Handbuch der Weltgeschichte in zehn Bänden, VII. Band (Übergang zur Moderne)*, 161–227. Bern, 1957.

Salomies, Martti. *Die Pläne Kaiser Karls V. für eine Reichsreform mit Hilfe eines allgemeinen Bundes*. Helsinki, 1953.

Seibt, Ferdinand. "Die Krone auf dem Hradschin. Karl IV. bündelt die Macht in Prag." In

Die Hauptstädte der Deutschen - Von der Kaiserpfalz in Aachen zum Regierungssitz Berlin, edited by Ewe Schultz, 67–75. München, 1993.

– – –. "Karl V. und die Konfession." In *Aspectos históricos y culturales bajo Carlos V – Aspekte der Geschichte und Kultur unter Karl V.*, Studia Hispanica 9, edited by Christoph Strosetzki, 146–158. Madrid, 2000.

Semotanová, Eva, Cajthaml Jiří and others, eds. *Akademický atlas českých dějin*. Praha, 2014.

Schilling, Heinz. *Aufbruch und Krise (Deutschland 1517–1648)*. Berlin, 1998.

Schindling, Anton, and Ziegler Walter, eds. *Die Territorien des Reichs im Zeitalter der Reformation und Konfessionalisierung (Land und Konfesion 1500 - 1650)*, Bd. 1 - 7 (Katholisches Leben und Kirchenreform im Zeitalter der Glaubensspaltung - Vereinsschriften der Gesellschaft zur Herausgabe des Corpus Catholicorum, Heft Nr. 49 - 53, 56 - 57). 2nd ed. Münster, 1992–1997.

Schirmer ,Uwe. "Die Finanzen der Kurfürsten und Herzöge von Sachsen zwischen 1485 und 1547." In *Landesgeschichte als Herausforderung und Programm (Karlheinz Blaschke zum 70. Geburtstag)*, Quellen und Forschungen zur sächsischen Geschichte 15, edited by Uwe John and Josef Matzerath, 259–283. Stuttgart, 1997.

Schmid, Peter. "Reichssteuer, Reichsfinanzen und Reichsgewalt in der ersten Hälfte des 16. Jahrhunderts." In *Säkulare Aspekte der Reformationszeit*, edited by Heinz Angermeier, 153–199. München and Wien, 1983.

Schmidt, Berthold. *Burggraf Heinrich IV. zu Meißen, Oberstkanzler der Krone Böhmen, und seine Regierung im Vogtland*. Gera, 1888.

Schmidt, Georg. *Der Städtetag in der Reichsverfassung (Eine Untersuchung zur korporativen Politik der Freien- und Reichsstädte in der ersten hälfte des 16. Jahrhunderts)*. Veröffentlichungen des Instituts für Europäische Geschichte Mainz, Abteilung Universalgeschichte, Band 113 – Beiträge zur Sozial- und Verfassungsgeschichte des Alten Reiches Nr. 5. Stuttgart, 1984.

– – –. "Deutschland am Beginn der Neuzeit: Reichs-Staat und Kulturnation?" In *Recht und Reich im Zeitalter der Reformation (Festschrift für Horst Rabe)*, edited by Roll Christine and others, 1–30. Frankfurt am Main, Berlin, Bern, New York, Paris and Wien, 1996.

– – –. *Geschichte des Alten Reiches (Staat und Nation in der Frühen Neuzeit 1495–1806)*. München, 1999.

– – –. "Reich und Nation (Krieg und Nationsbildung in Deutschland)." In *Krieg und Kultur (Die Rezeption von Krieg und Frieden in der Niederländischen Republik und im Deutschen Reich 1568–1648)*, edited by Horst Lademacher and Simon Groenveld, 57–76. Münster, New York, München and Berlin, 1998.

Schmidt, Hans-Achim. "Landsknechtwesen und Kriegsführung in Niedersachsen 1533–1545." *Niedersächsisches Jahrbuch – Neue Folge der "Zeitschrift des Historischen Vereins für Niedersachsen"* 6 (1929): 167–223.

Schmidt, Heinrich Richard. *Konfessionalisierung im 16. Jahrhundert*. München, 1992.

Schmidt, Peter. *Der Gemeine Pfennig von 1495 (Vorgeschichte und Entstehung, verfassungsgeschichte, politische und finanzielle Bedeutung)*. Göttingen, 1989.

– – –. "Reichssteuern, Reichsfinanzen und Reichsgewalt in der ersten Hälfte des 16. Jahrhunderts." In *Säkulare Aspekte der Reformationszeit*, edited by Hanz Angermeier and Reinhard Seyboth, 153–198. München, 1983.

Schnabel, Franz. *Deutschlands geschichtliche Quellen und Darstellungen in der Neuzeit. Erster Teil: Das Zeitalter der Reformation 1500–1550*. Darmstadt, 1972.

Schorn-Schütze, Luise, ed. *Das Interim 1548/50 – Herrschaftskrise und Glaubenskonflikt*, Schriften des Vereins für Reformationsgeschichte, Band 203. Heidelberg, 2005.

Schottenloher, Karl. *Bibliographie zur deutschen Geschichte im Zeitalter der Glaubensspaltung 1517–1585*. IV. Band. 2nd ed. Stuttgart, 1957.

Schröcker, Alfred. *Die deutsche Nation (Beobachtungen zur politischen Propaganda des ausgehenden 15. Jahrhunderts)*. Lübeck, 1974.

Schulten, Wolfgang. *Deutsche Münzen aus der Zeit Karls V. (Typenkatalog der Gepräge zwischen dem Beginn Talerprägung (1484) und der dritten Reichsmünzordnung (1559)*. Frankfurt am Main, 1974.

Schulze, Hagen. "Deutschland in der Neuzeit." In *Mittelalterliche nationes – neuzeitliche Nationen (Probleme der Nationenbildung in Europa)*, edited by Almut Bues and Rex Rexheuser, 103–120. Wiesbaden, 1995.

Schulze Winfried, "Das Problem der Toleranz in Heiligen Römischen Reich nach dem Augsburger Religionsfrieden." *Studia Germano-Polonica* 1 (1992): 167–182.

–––. "Der deutsche Reichstag des 16. Jh. zwischen traditioneller Konsensbildung und Paritätisierung der Reichspolitik." In *Im Spannungsfeld von Recht und Ritual*, 447–464. Köln, 1997.

–––. "Majority Decision in the Imperial Diets of the Sixteenth and Seventeenth Centuries." In *Politics and Society in the Holy Roman Empire, 1500–1806*. The Journal of Modern History, Volume 58 – Supplement, December 1986, 46–63. Chicago, 1986.

Schweinzer, Silvia. "Die Vorgeschichte des Reichstags von Speyer 1542 im Spiegel der politischen Korrespondenz Kaiser Karls V." In *Aus der Arbeit an den Reichstagen unter Kaiser Karl V. (Sieben Beiträge zu Fragen der Forschung und edition)*, Schriften des Historischen Kommision dei der bayerischen Akademie der Wissenschaften, Band 26, edited by Lutz Heinrich – Kohler Alfred, 228–272. Göttingen, 1986.

Sieber, Johannes. *Zur Geschichte des Reichsmatrikelwesens im ausgehenden Mittelalter (1422–1521)*. Leipziger historische Abhandlungen, Heft XXIV. Leipzig, 1910.

Simms, Brendan. *Kampf um Vorherrschaft. Eine deutsche Geschichte Europas 1453 bis Heute*. München, 2014.

Skřivánek, Milan. "K některým aspektům lenní politiky za prvních Habsburků." *Sborník prací východočeských archívů* 1 (1970): 59–79.

Steglich, Wolfgang. "Die Reichstürkenhilfe in der Zeit Karls V." *Militärgeschichtliche Mitteilungen* 11 (1972): 7–55. Stierstorfer, Kurt. *Die Belagerung Hofs 1553*. Hof, 2003.

Stratenwerth, Heide und Rabe Horst. "Politische Kommunikation und Diplomatie." In *Kaiser Karl V. (1500–1558) – Macht und Ohnmacht Europas, Eine Ausstellung des Kunsthistorischen Museums Wien*, edited by Wilfried Seipel, 27–34. Wien, 2000.

Streisand, Joachim, ed. *Deutsche Geschichte*. Band 1 – Von der Anfängen bis 1789. 3rd ed. Berlin, 1974.

Strosetzki, Christoph, ed. *Aspectos históricos y culturales bajo Carlos V – Aspekte der Geschichte und Kultur unter Karl V.,* Studia Hispanica 9. Madrid, 2000.

Šmahel, František. *Die Hussitische Revolution.* I-III. Hannover, 2002.

– – –. *"Pax externa et interna - Vom Heiligen Krieg zur erzwungenen Toleranz im hussitischen Böhmen (1419–1485)."* In *Toleranz im Mittelalter.* Vorträge und Forschungen des Konstanzer Arbeitskreises für mittelalterliche Geschichte 45, edited by A. Patschkowsky and H. Zimmermann, 221–273. Konstanz, 1998.

Thieme, André, and Uwe Tresp, eds. *Eger 1459 – Fürstentreffen zwischen Sachsen, Böhmen und ihrer Nachbarn: Dynastische Politik, fürstliche Repräsentation und kulturelle Verflechtung / Cheb 1459 – Setkání panovníků Saska, Čech a jejich sousedů: Dynastická politika, panovnická reprezentace a kulturní vazby.* Saxonia. Schriften des Vereins für sächsische Landesgeschichte e. V., Bd. 13. Wettin-Löbejün, 2011.

Tjernagel, Neelak Serawlook. *Henry VIII and the Lutherans. A Study in Anglo-Lutheran Relations from 1521 to 1547.* Saint Louis: Concordia Publishing House, 1965.

Thomä, Siegfried. *Der Schmalkaldische Krieg 1546/47 im Vogtland – Adorf unter der Geißel der Hussauer.* Aalen, 1992.

Tieftrunk, Josef. *Odpor stavův českých proti Ferdinandovi I. l. 1547.* Praha, 1872.

Tomek, Václav Vladivoj. *Dějepis města Prahy,* XI. Praha, 1897.

Tracy, James D. *Emperor Charles V, Impresario of War – Campaign Strategy, International Finance, and Domestic Politics.* Cambridge, 2010.

Traut, Hermann. *Kurfürst Joachim II. von Brandenburg und der Türkenfeldzug vom Jahre 1542.* Gummersbach, 1892.

Turba, Gustav. *Verhaftung und Gefangenschaft des Landgrafen Philipp von Hessen 1547–1550.* Archiv für österreichische Geschichte Bd. 83. Wien, 1896.

Veselý, Jiří. "Obnova zahraničních lén České koruny za Jiříka z Poděbrad." *Právněhistorické studie* 8 (1962): 261–279.

– – –. "O soudech hejtmanství německých lén." *Právněhistorické studie* 16 (1971): 113–124.

Válka, Josef. "Konflikt české zemské obce s králem 1546–1547 (Ferdinand I. a počátky absolutismu II)." *Časopis Matice moravské* 125 (2006): 33–51.

– – –. "Morava a porážky českých stavovských povstání." In *Stavovský odboj roku 1547 – První krize habsburské monarchie (Sborník příspěvků z vědecké konference konané v Pardubicích 29.- 30. 9. 1997),* edited by Petr Vorel, 29–40. Pardubice and Praha, 1999.

– – –. "Politika a nadkonfesijní křesťanství Viléma a Jana z Pernštejna." In *Pernštejnové v českých dějinách (Sborník příspěvků z vědecké konference, konané v Pardubicích 8. - 9. 9. 1993),* edited by Petr Vorel, 173–186. Pardubice, 1995.

– – –. "Trest a obnova pořádku - Normalizace (Ferdinand I. a počátky absolutismu III)." *Časopis Matice moravské* 125 (2006): 343–365.

Voigt, Georg. "Die Geschichtschreibung über den schmalkaldischen Krieg." *Abhandlungen der philologisch-historischen Classe der Königl. Sächsischen Gesellschaft der Wissenschaften* VI., 569–758. Leipzig, 1874.

– – –. *Moritz von Sachsen 1541–1547.* Leipzig, 1876.

Voit, Petr. *Český knihtisk mezi pozdní gotikou a renesancí, I. severinsko-kosořská dynastie 1488–1557*. Praha, 2013.

–––. "K dějinám cenzury v předbělohorské době (Některé problémy období 1547 - 1567)." *Folia Historica Bohemica* 11 (1987): 305 – 320.

Vorel, Petr. "Aristokratické svatby v Čechách a na Moravě v 16. století jako prostředek společenské komunikace a stavovské diplomacie." *Opera historica* 8 (2000): 191–206.

–––. "Aristokratische Residenzstädte im regionalen Kontext (Die böhmischen Länder während der Frühen Neuzeit)." In *Städtelandschaft – Réseau Urbain – Urban Network (Städte im regionalen Kontext in Spätmittelalter und Frühen Neuzeit)*, Städteforschung – Veröffentlichungen des Instituts für vergleichende Städtegeschichte in Münster, Reihe A: Darstellungen, Band 62, edited by Holger Th. Gräf and Karin Keller, 155–169. Köln, Weimar and Wien, 2004.

–––. "Císařská volba a korunovace ve Frankfurtu nad Mohanem roku 1612 a česká účast na těchto událostech." *Theatrum historiae* 10 (2012): 59–166.

–––. "Česká účast-neúčast na volbě římského krále Maxmiliána I. ve Frankfurtu nad Mohanem roku 1486." In *Středověký kaleidoskop pro muže s hůlkou (Věnováno Františku Šmahelovi k životnímu jubileu)*, edited by Eva Doležalová and Petr Sommer, 678–693. Praha, 2014.

–––. "Český velmocenský komplex pozdního středověku." In *Velmocenské ambice v dějinách (Tři studie)*, edited by Jaroslav Pánek, Jiří Pešek and Petr Vorel. Praha, 2015.

–––. *Dějiny evropského světa 1453–1576: Historický obraz počátku raného novověku v pojetí Daniela Adama z Veleslavína který českému čtenáři předložil v druhém českém vydání Kroniky světa Jana Kariona z roku 1584*. Praha, 2008.

–––. "Die Außenbeziehungen der böhmischen Stände um die Mitte des 16. Jahrhundert und das Problem der Konfessionalisierung." In *Konfessionalisierung in Ostmitteleuropa. Wirkung des religiösen Wandels im 16. und 17. Jahrhundert in Staat, Gesellschaft und Kultur*, edited by Joachim Bahlcke and Arno Strohmeyer, 169–178. Stuttgart, 1999.

–––. "Die Länder der böhmischen Krone und das Heilige Römische Reich in der Frühen Neuzeit." In *Neue tschechische Interpretationen der Fragen des tschechisch-deutschen Zusammenlebens (47. Deutscher Historikertag / Dresden 2008 - Die Vortragende der tschechischen Gastsection)*, edited by Jiří Pešek and Petr Vorel, 21–32. Magdeburg, 2011.

–––. "Důsledky tzv. Šmalkaldské války z let 1546–1547 pro vývoj měnové integrace Evropy." *Theatrum historiae* 3 (2008): 47–64.

–––. *From the Silver Czech Tolar to a Worldwide Dollar (The Birth of the Dollar and its Journey of Monetary Circulation in Europe and the World from the 16th to the 20th Century)*. New York: Columbia University Press, 2013.

–––. "Frühkapitalismus und Steuerwesen in Böhmen (1526–1648)." *Anzeiger der philosophisch - historischen Klasse, Österreichische Akademie der Wissenschaften* 137 (2002): 167–182.

–––. "Hrabství kladské a finanční politika krále Ferdinanda I. ve druhé třetině 16. století." *Východočeský sborník historický* 12 (2005): 3–14.

– – –. "Landesfinanzen und Währung in Böhmen (Finanz- und Münzpolitik im Spannungsfeld von Ständen und Königtum während der Regierung Ferdinands I. und Maximilians II.)." In *Finanzen und Herrschaft (Zu den materiellen Grundlagen fürstlicher Politik in den habsburgischen Ländern und im Heiligen Römischer Reich im 16. Jahrhundert)*, Veröffentlichungen des Instituts für österreichische Geschichtsforschung, Band 38, edited by Friedrich Edelmayer, Maximilian Lanzinner and Peter Rauscher], 186–214. München and Wien, 2003.

– – –. "Majetko-právní důsledky panovnických sankcí roku 1547 pro pozemkový majetek rodu Tluksů Vrábských z Vrábí." *Folia Historica Bohemica* 29 (2014): 201–255.

– – –. "Měnová politika Ferdinanda I. v Čechách a ukončení ražby pražských grošů." Český časopis historický 100 (2002): 265–292.

– – –. "Mezi Augsburgem a Komárnem (Cestování Jaroslava z Pernštejna v Podunají v polovině 16. století)." In *Cesty a cestování v životě společnosti (Sborník příspěvků z konference konané 6.-8.září 1994 v Ústí nad Labem)*, Acta Universitatis Purkyniae, Philosophica et historica, Studia historica II, edited by Lenka Bobková and Michala Neudertová, 191–197, Ústí nad Labem, 1995.

– – –. "Místodržitelský dvůr arciknížete Ferdinanda Habsburského v Praze roku 1551 ve světle účetní dokumentace." *Folia historica Bohemica* 21 (2005): 7–66.

– – –. *Monetary Circulation in Central Europe at the Beginning of the Early Modern Age – Attempts to Establish a Shared Currency as an Aspect of the Political Culture of the 16th Century (1524–1573)*. Univerzita Pardubice – Filozofická fakulta, Monographica VI. Pardubice, 2006.

– – –. *Páni z Pernštejna (Vzestup a pád rodu zubří hlavy v dějinách Čech a Moravy)*. 2nd ed. Praha, 2012.

– – –. "Pernstein." In *Höfe und Residenzen im Spätmittelalterlichen Reich – Grafen und Herren*. Residenzforschung (Herausgegeben von der Residenzen-Kommision der Akademie der Wissenschaften zu Göttingen), Band 15. IV, Teilband 2, edited by Werner Paravicini, 1098–1103. Ostfildern, 2012.

– – –. "Pernštejnská diplomacie v době stavovského povstání roku 1547 (edice listů Jaroslava z Pernštejna z února a ž června 1547)." *Východočeský sborník historický* 3 (1993): 231–272.

– – –. "Pernštejnská svatba v Prostějově roku 1550." Časopis Matice moravské 114, (1995): 139–162.

– – –. "Petr Hamza ze Zábědovic a regentská správa pernštejnských dominií v Čechách v letech 1550–1552." *Scientific papers of the University of Pardubice*, Series C, Institute of Languages and Humanities 2 (1996): 115–142.

– – –. "Politická komunikace české stavovské opozice roku 1547 (Regionální aspekt a role "Přátelského snešení" ve stavovském odboji)." *Theatrum historiae* 15 (2014): 51–96.

– – –. "Problemy rodzinne i finansowe Piastów Cieszyńskich w połowie XVI wieku." In *Historia u Piastów, Piastowie w Historii (Z okazji trzechsetlecia śmierci ostatniej z rodu, księżnej Karoliny)*, edited by Bogusław Czechowicz, 155–164. Brzeg, 2008.

– – –. "Přátelské snešení stavův českých" z března 1547 a jeho signatáři." In *Stavovský odboj roku 1547 – První krize habsburské monarchie (Sborník příspěvků z vědecké konference konané v Pardubicích 29.- 30. 9. 1997)*, edited by Petr Vorel, 81–124. Pardubice and Praha, 1999.

–––. "Říšské sněmy a jejich vliv na vývoj zemí Koruny české v letech 1526–1618. Pardubice 2005.

–––. "Sankce vůči českým královským městům roku 1547 v kontextu habsburské politiky první poloviny 16. století („Gentský ortel" v politické propagandě stavovského odboje)." *Theatrum historiae* 16 (2015).

–––. "Směnné kursy jako nástroj mocenské politiky v Římsko-německé říši počátkem čtyřicátých let 16. století." *Český časopis historický* 112 (2014): 379 – 401.

–––. "Sňatkový projekt Pernštejnů se saskými Wettiny z roku 1529." *Východočeský sborník historický* 24 (2013): 81–98.

–––. "Státoprávní vyčlenění českých zemí ze Svaté říše římské (Důsledky říšské reformy Maxmiliána I.)." *Český časopis historický* 111 (2013): 743–804.

–––. *Stříbro v evropském peněžním oběhu 16. - 17. století 1472–1717.* Praha, 2009.

–––. "The political context of the origin and the exportation of thaler-coins from Jáchymov (Joachimsthal) in the first half of the sixteenth century." In *Proceedings of the XIVth International Numismatic Congress Glasgow 2009*, II, edited by Nicholas Holmes, 1778–1782. Glasgow, 2011.

–––. "The Importance of the Bohemian Reformation for the Political Culture of Central Europe from the 15th to the 17th century." *Comenius – Journal of Euro-American Civilization* 2 (2015), No. 2

–––. "Úvěr, peníze a finanční transakce české a moravské aristokracie při cestách do zahraničí v polovině 16. století." *Český časopis historický* 96 (1998): 754–778.

–––. *Velké dějiny zemí Koruny české, svazek VII. 1526–1618.* Praha, 2005.

–––. "Vývoj pozemkové držby pánů z Pernštejna v 15.-17.století." In *Pernštejnové v českých dějinách (Sborník příspěvků z konference konané 8. - 9. 9. 1993 v Pardubicích)*, edited by Petr Vorel, 9–76. Pardubice, 1995.

–––. "Zánik aristokratického dvora pánů z Pernštejna v Pardubicích v roce 1550." In *Poddanská města v systému patrimoniální správy (Sborník příspěvků z konference v Ústí nad Orlicí 12. - 13. září 1995)*, 70–77. Ústí nad Orlicí, 1996.

Wagner, Johannes Volker. *Graf Wilhelm von Fürstenberg 1491–1549 und die politisch-geistigen Mächte seiner Zeit.* Pariser historische Studien IV. Stuttgart, 1966.

Wartenberg, Günther. "Die Politik des Kurfürsten Moritz von Sachsen gegenüber Frankreich zwischen 1548 und 1550." In Deutschland und Frankreich in der frühen Neuzeit, edited by Heinz Duchhardt and Eberhard Schmidt, 71–102. München, 1987.

–––. "Philipp Melanchton und die sächsisch-albertinische Interimspolitik." *Lutherjahrbuch* 55 (1988): 60–80.

Weber, Hermann. "Zur Heiratspolitik Karls V." In *Das römisch-deutsche Reich im politischen System Karls V.*, Schriften des Historischen Kollegs – Kolloquien 1, edited by Heinrich Lutz, 129–160. München and Wien, 1982.

Weber, Matthias. *Das Verhältnis Schlesiens zum Alten Reich in der Frühen Neuzeit.* Köln und Weimar, 1992.

–––. "Zur Bedeutung der Reichsacht in der Frühen Neuzeit." In *Neue Studien zur früh-neuzeitlichen Reichsgeschichte, Zeitschrift für historische Forschung (Vierteljah-reschrift zur Erforschung des Spätmittelalters und der frühen Neuzeit*, Beiheft 19, edited by Johannes Kunisch, 55–90. Berlin, 1997.

Weihgand-Karg, Sabine. *Die Plassenburg – Residenzfunktion und Hofleben bis 1604.* Weißenstadt. Weißenstadt, (1985).

Wentrup, Friedrich. "Die Belagerung Wittenbergs im Jahre 1547." In *Programm des Gymnasi-ums zu Wittenberg*, Ostern 1861, edited by Hermann Schmidt, 1–24. Wittenberg, 1861.

Whaley, Joachim. *Germany and the Holy Roman Empire, Volume I: Maximilian I to the Peace of Westphalia 1493–1648.* Oxford, 2013.

Wijaczka, Jacek. "Misja biskupa Juliusza von Pflug do Polski w 1541 r. (Przyczynek do dziejów polskiej polityki handlowej w XVI wieku)." In *Życie gospodarcze Rzeczypospo-litej w XVI-XVIII wieku – Materyały konferencji naukowej, Między zachodem a wscho-dem*, t. IV, edited by Jacek Wijaczka, 48–57. Toruń, 2007.

–––. *Stosunki dyplomatyczne Polski s Rzeszą niemecką v czasach panowania cesarza Karola V (1519–1556)*, Prace Instytutu Historii Wyższej Szkoly Pedagogicznej w Kielcach, Nr 7. Kielce, 1998.

Wille Jakob, *Philipp der Grossmuthige von Hessen und die Restitution Ulrichs von Wirtem-berg*. Tübingen, 1882.

Jacek Wijaczka, *Stosunki dyplomatyczne Polski z Rzeszą niemecką w czasach panowania cesarza Karola V (1519–1556)*, Prace Instytutu Historii Wyższej Szkoly Pedagogicznej w Kielcach, Nr 7, Kielce, 1998

Wild, Erich. *Das Vogtland im Schmalkaldischen Kriege.* Plauen, 1939.

Winkelbauer, Thomas. *Österreichische Geschichte 1522–1699 (Ständefreiheit und Fürsten-macht - Länder und Untertanen des Hauses Habsburg im konfessionellen Zeitalter)*, Bd.1. - 2. Wien, 2003.

Winter, Christian. "Kurfirst Moritz von Sachsen als Haupt der reichsständischen Oppo-sition genen Kaiser Karl V.". In *Kaiser und Kurfürst – Aspekte des Fürstenaufstandes 1552.* Geschichte in der Epoche Karls V., Band 11, edited by Martina Fuchs and Rob-ert Rebitsch, 51–70. Münster, 2010.

–––. "Prag 1546. Die sächsisch-böhmische Erbeinung zwischen Herzog Moritz und König Ferdinand." In *Eger 1459 – Fürstentreffen zwischen Sachsen, Böhmen und ihrer Nachbarn: Dynastische Politik, fürstliche Repräsentation und kulturelle Verflechtung / Cheb 1459 – Set-kání panovníků Saska, Čech a jejich sousedů: Dynastická politika, panovnická reprezentace a kulturní vazby.* Saxonia. Schriften des Vereins für sächsische Landesgeschichte e. V., Bd. 13, edited by André Thieme and Uwe Tresp, 354–380. Wettin-Löbejün, 2011.

Witter, Julius. *Die Beziehungen und der Verkehr des Kurfürsten Moritz von Sachsen mit dem Römischer Könige Ferdinand sei dem Abschlusse der Wittenberger Kapitulation bis zum Passauer Vertrage.* Neustadt a. d. Haardt, 1886.

Wójcik, Zbigniew. *Historia powszechna – Wiek XVI–XVII.* Warszawa, 2008.

Wotschke, Theodor, "Die Truppenwerbung für die schmalkandischen Verbündeten im Posener Lande 1546." *Historische Monatsblätter für die Provinz Posen* 14 (1913): 65–73.

Zelenka, Aleš. *Der Wappenfries aus dem Wappensaal zu Lauf - Zum 600. Todestag Karls IV. 1378/1978 dargestellt in maßstabgerechten Zeichnungen und kommentiert.* Passau, 1978.

Zsymaniak, Wiktor. *Organizacja dyplomacji Prus Książęcych na dworze Zygmunta Starego 1525–1548.* Bydgoscz, 1992.

INDEX OF NAMES

INDEX OF PLACE NAMES

INDEX

1. Schmalcaldic League, Brunswick-Wolfenbüttel, John Frederick of Saxony and Philipp of Hesse. Thaler 1546 (photo by the Author; coin from private collection).

2. Holy Roman Empire, Charles V., Free Imperial City of Donauwörth.
Thaler 1544 (photo by the Author; coin from
Collection of East Bohemia Museum in Pardubice).

3. Holy Roman Empire, Moritz of Saxony as the Elector. Thaler 1547
minted in Annaberg (photo by the Author; coin from private collection).

4. Holy Roman Empire, County of Tirol, Ferdinand I. Undated Imperial Güldener = 72-kreuzer from 1558 minted in compliance with the Second Imperial Minting Order of 1551 in Hall in Tirol (photo by the Author; coin from Collection of East Bohemia Museum in Pardubice).

5. Holy Roman Empire, Margraveship Brandenburg in Franconia, Georg of Brandensburg-Ansbach and Albert Alcibiades of Brandenburg-Kulmbach. Thaler 1544 minted in Schwabach (photo by the Author; coin from Collection of East Bohemia Museum in Pardubice).

6. Kingdom of Bohemia, Ferdinand I. Taler 1529 minted in Jáchymov
(photo by the Author; coin from Collection of East Bohemia
Museum in Pardubice).

7. Kingdom of Bohemia, County of Kłodzko (Glatz), John of Pernštejn. Thaler 1542 (photo by the Author; coin from Collection of East Bohemia Museum in Pardubice).

8. Castle of Pardubice, main residency of John of Pernštejn in 1547.
Nowadays quarters of the East Bohemia Museum
(photo by the East Bohemia Museum in Pardubice).